CATHOLICISM AND ANTI-CATHOLICISM
IN EARLY MODERN ENGLISH TEXTS

EARLY MODERN LITERATURE IN HISTORY

General Editor: Cedric C. Brown
Professor of English and Head of Department, University of Reading

Within the period 1520–1740 this series discusses many kinds of writing, both within and outside the established canon. The volumes may employ different theoretical perspectives, but they share an historical awareness and an interest in seeing their texts in lively negotiation with their own and successive cultures.

Titles include:

Anna R. Beer
SIR WALTER RALEGH AND HIS READERS IN THE SEVENTEENTH CENTURY: Speaking to the People

Cedric C. Brown and Arthur F. Marotti (*editors*)
TEXTS AND CULTURAL CHANGE IN EARLY MODERN ENGLAND

John Dolan
POETIC OCCASION FROM MILTON TO WORDSWORTH

Pauline Kiernan
STAGING SHAKESPEARE AT THE NEW GLOBE

Ronald Knowles (*editor*)
SHAKESPEARE AND CARNIVAL: After Bakhtin

James Loxley
ROYALISM AND POETRY IN THE ENGLISH CIVIL WARS: The Drawn Sword

Arthur F. Marotti (*editor*)
CATHOLICISM AND ANTI-CATHOLICISM IN EARLY MODERN ENGLISH TEXTS

Mark Thornton Burnett
MASTERS AND SERVANTS IN ENGLISH RENAISSANCE DRAMA AND CULTURE: Authority and Obedience

The series Early Modern Literature in History is published in association with the Renaissance Texts Research Centre at the University of Reading.

Catholicism and Anti-Catholicism in Early Modern English Texts

Edited by

Arthur F. Marotti

PR
428
.C3
C38
1999

 First published in Great Britain 1999 by
MACMILLAN PRESS LTD
Houndmills, Basingstoke, Hampshire RG21 6XS and London
Companies and representatives throughout the world

A catalogue record for this book is available from the British Library.

ISBN 0–333–73218–9

 First published in the United States of America 1999 by
ST. MARTIN'S PRESS, INC.,
Scholarly and Reference Division,
175 Fifth Avenue, New York, N.Y. 10010

ISBN 0–312–21871–0

Library of Congress Cataloging-in-Publication Data
Catholicism and anti-Catholicism in early modern English texts /
edited by Arthur F. Marotti.
p.   cm. — (Early modern literature in history)
Includes bibliographical references (p.   ) and index.
ISBN 0–312–21871–0 (cloth)
1. English literature—Early modern, 1500–1700—History and
criticism.   2. Christian literature, English—Catholic authors–
–History and criticism.   3. English literature—Protestant authors–
–History and criticism.   4. English literature—Catholic authors–
–History and criticism.   5. Christianity and literature—England–
–History—17th century.   6. Christianity and literature—England–
–History—16th century.   7. Anti-Catholicism—England—History.
8. Catholic Church—England—History.   9. Anti-Catholicism in
literature.   10. Catholic Church—In literature.   I. Marotti,
Arthur F., 1940– . II. Series.
PR428.C3C38   1999
820.9'38282—dc21
                                                98–45552
                                                       CIP

This book is printed on paper suitable for recycling and made from fully managed and
sustained forest sources.

10   9   8   7   6   5   4   3   2
08   07   06   05   04   03   02   01

Printed and bound in Great Britain by Antony Rowe Ltd, Chippenham, Wiltshire

With love for my son Bill, whose academic interests
embrace two hemispheres

Contents

List of Figures

Notes on the Contributors

Ronald Corthell, Professor of English at Kent State University, is the author of *Ideology and Desire in Renaissance Poetry: the Subject of Donne* (1997) and of many articles and book chapters on English Renaissance poetry and prose. He also is the editor of *Prose Studies: History, Theory, Criticism*.

Frances E. Dolan, Associate Professor of English, Miami University of Ohio, is the author of *Dangerous Familiars: Representations of Domestic Crime in England, 1550–1700* (1994) and of many articles on early modern English literature and culture. Her recently completed book, *Whores of Babylon: Catholicism, Gender, and Seventeeth-Century Print Culture*, will be published by Cornell University Press.

Simon Healy is a Research Fellow at The History of Parliament Trust.

John N. King, Professor of English, Ohio State University, is the author and editor of several books, including *English Reformation Literature: the Tudor Origins of the Protestant Tradition* (1982), *Tudor Royal Iconography: Literature and Art in an Age of Religious Crisis* (1989) and *Spenser's Poetry and the Reformation Tradition* (1990). He is currently working on a book that will complete a three-volume study of the English Protestant literary tradition, *Milton and the Reformation Tradition*.

Arthur F. Marotti, Professor of English, Wayne State University, is the author and editor of several books, including *John Donne, Coterie Poet* (1986) and *Manuscript, Print, and the English Renaissance Lyric* (1995). He is currently working on a book-length study of *Catholic and Anti-Catholic Discourses in Early Modern England*.

Anthony Milton, who teaches in the Department of History at the University of Sheffield, is the author of *Catholic and Reformed: The Roman and Protestant Churches in English Protestant Thought 1600–1640* (1995). He is the co-editor, with Peter Lake and Ann Hughes, of a new University of Manchester Press series, *Politics, Culture, and Society in Early Modern Britain*.

Michael Questier, formerly post-doctoral fellow in history of the British Academy, currently at the Westminster Diocesan Archive, is the author of *Conversion, Politics and Religion in England, 1580–1625* (1996) and of articles on early modern English Catholicism.

Alison Shell, who teaches English at the University of Durham, is the author of articles on Catholicism in early modern England and is finishing a book developed out of her Oxford University thesis, 'English Catholicism and Drama, 1578–1688', *Written in Scarlet: Studies in the Literary Culture of English Catholicism, 1558–1680*.

John Watkins, Associate Professor of English at The University of Minnesota, is the author of *The Spector of Dido: Spenser and the Virgilian Epic* (1995) and is finishing a new book, *'In Queene Elizabeth's Day': The Legend of Elizabeth I, 1603–1714*.

Julian Yates, Assistant Professor of English at The University of Delaware, completed a dissertation at UCLA entitled 'Towards a Geography of Recusancy: Parasites, Seminaries, Prisons and Priest Holes'. His paper 'The Limits of Space: Priest-Holes and the Technology of Concealment in Early Modern England', is forthcoming in a collection of essays edited by Arthur L. Little and Lowell Gallagher, *Configuring Bodies in Early Modern England*.

Preface

Partly in response to recent new-historicist and cultural-materialist literary scholarship and revisionist as well as Marxist historical scholarship, scholars specializing in the literature and history of early modern England have begun to re-emphasize the importance of religion in early modern culture. Rather than relegating religious and theological issues to the history of ideas, or treating them and ecclesiastical history as separate from the larger cultural formation of which they were part, they have approached religious developments, negotiations and conflicts in early modern England with a new sensitivity to the many sociocultural issues at stake: they have examined afresh in their complex historical contexts the relatively neglected history and literature of early modern English Catholicism, as well as the interplay of both Catholic and anti-Catholic discourses throughout the period.

In the sixteenth and seventeenth centuries, English nationalism was gradually being defined in relation to a (constantly contested) Protestant identity, so international Catholicism, especially in its militant Counter-Reformation forms, was cast as the hated and dangerous antagonist. In a period punctuated by various (real or fabricated) crises and threats, such as the Spanish Armada (1588), the Gunpowder Plot (1605), the late Jacobean negotiations for a Spanish spouse for Prince Charles and Titus Oates' 'Popish Plot' (of the late 1670s), a nationalistic Protestant myth of providential 'deliverance' was fabricated to explain England's escape from various Catholic menaces, but, in less dramatic circumstances a language of anti-Catholicism was developed and used to consolidate English national characteristics, as well as to conduct domestic and international polemical and political arguments.

The languages of Catholicism and anti-Catholicism were involved in a number of major historical developments and changes. These include: Protestantism's reinforcing of (the new) print culture's diminishment of the importance of visual communication – most marked in the waves of iconoclasm from the mid-sixteenth to the mid-seventeenth century; the related shift from 'iconic' to 'representational' modes of communication; the desacralizing of the sacred and the secular, political appropriation of religious imagery and ceremonialism; the internecine Protestant struggles over Church governance and doctrine; the Protestant masculinization of Christianity and misogynistic assault on a feminized Catholicism, whose modes of 'carnal' thinking were related to women's supposed susceptibility to conversion by Catholic missionaries and their husbands' 'seduction' by their wives into the religion of the 'Whore of Babylon'; the ideological and political battles conducted over the constitutional relationship of Parliament and the monarchy and of the government and the rights of citizens. Complex conflicts among conservative Protestants, aggressively reformist Protestants and Catholics, as well as fights between hardline and accommodationist Catholics, were expressed in political action as well as in the voluminous polemical literature of the period. They were indices of large-scale as well as small, incremental cultural changes that helped shape the modern world – including the reformulation of the relationship of national political centers and the power of localities and the contest between monarchical and republican (sometimes democratic) ideologies.

This collection of nine essays focuses on polemical, historical and literary texts that dramatize the conflicts between Catholic and anti-Catholic discourses in early modern England. It highlights the politically malleable and situational character of anti-Catholic codes and language both in the context of larger Catholic–Protestant national and international conflict and within the fiercely contested terrain of the English Protestant Church. In addition to foregrounding some major authors and canonical texts, the essays examine non-canonical literary texts as well as extra-literary documents that embody the kinds of ideological fantasies and languages that connect the political and religious discourses of early modern English culture with their literary manifestations.

The authors of these essays are largely writing against the grain of the historiographical and literary-historical traditions that have tended either to marginalize, demonize or obscure the writings, as well as the religious and cultural beliefs, of English Catholics. They are influenced by the recent revisionary work of such historians as Peter Lake, Christopher Haigh, Eamon Duffy and Anthony Milton (the last a contributor to this anthology).[1] In approaching religious discourse and conflict in early modern England, they avoid not only confessional apologetics, but also the Marxist characterization of religion as merely the mystification of economic and political relations and the Protestant biases of a Whig historiography (and its literary-historical derivative) that celebrates a political progress from Protestant reform to modern political liberalism. They invite literary scholars and historians to pay attention to important neglected aspects of early modern English culture, specifically to examine the ideological (anti-Catholic) biases of an era in which English Protestant national identity was being shaped in the context of religio-political opposition to international Catholicism. Given the long history of anti-Catholicism in Anglo-American culture, it is useful to re-examine its roots in the early modern period.

The chronological range of the studies runs from the early Elizabethan period through the Restoration era. The topics covered include the gap between official anti-Catholic legislation and the practical conduct of both intellectual life and of social relations, the complexities of both conversion and apostasy, the demonization of Jesuits, the use of anti-Catholic rhetoric within Protestant sectarian conflict and the gendering of religious representation. Texts discussed include religious autobiography, dramas (designed either for the stage or for private reading), prose satire, religious polemics, polemical fictions, and philosophical and narrative verse. Writers examined include not only such canonical authors as John Donne, Thomas Dekker, Thomas Campion and John Milton, but also such neglected or relatively unknown writers as Richard Carpenter, John Mush, John Good and Elizabeth Cellier.

The essays are arranged in (roughly) chronological order, from the Elizabethan era, through the early Stuart period, concluding with a piece concerned with the era of the 'Popish Plot' of the late 1670s and its aftermath. Some of the studies highlight individual figures, such as Robert Persons (Corthell), Richard Carpenter (Shell), John Good (Questier and Healy), John Milton (King) and Elizabeth Cellier (Dolan). Others deal with such special topics as the cultural impact of priest holes (Yates), the representation of the deceased Queen Elizabeth in religious debate (Watkins), the cultural 'othering' of recusant women and Jesuits (Marotti), and the contrast between sharp divisions of polemical and ideological anti-Catholicism and the cross-confessional interactions of practical intellectual, social and political life (Milton). Although there are clear differences in the interpretive methods of the historians and the literary scholars, the latter have obviously profited from the kinds of historical analyses done by the former, and the former have obviously absorbed the techniques of textual analyses practiced in the field of literary studies. All of the contributors have a sophisticated sense of written texts' interrelationships with ideologies, cultural discourses and specific historical moments and developments.

Some early modern literary scholars, like those represented in this collection, have become especially interested in both the suppressed history of English Catholicism and in the sociocultural and religious uses of Catholic and anti-Catholic discourses as flexible and context-sensitive languages of sociopolitical negotiation that are embodied in some of the most important texts of the period.[2] Historians, on the other hand, have become more sensitized to the subtle ways language functioned in the texts and documents they examine in their studies. Although literary scholars dominate this particular collection of essays, three historians are included – both for the different historical perspectives and methods they exemplify and because it is hoped that their presence might help foster more cross-disciplinary cooperation on this particular topic and on other related subjects. This collection is designed to demonstrate the complexity of the relationship of Catholic and anti-Catholic discourses as well as to open up a wide variety of approaches and lines of inquiry that other historians and literary scholars might pursue further.

NOTES

1. See, for example, Peter Lake, 'Anti-Popery: the Structure of a Prejudice', in Richard Cust and Ann Hughes, eds., *Conflict in Early Stuart England: Studies in Religion and Politics 1603–1642* (London: Longman, 1989), 72–106; Christopher Haigh, *English Reformations: Religion, Politics, and Society under the Tudors* (Oxford: Clarendon Press, 1993), 'The Continuity of Catholicism in the English Reformation', *Past and Present* 93 (1981): 37–69, and 'From Monopoly to Minority: Catholicism in Early Modern England', *Trans. of the Royal Hist. Soc.*, 5th ser., 31 (1981): 129–47; Eamon Duffy, *The Stripping of the Altars: Traditional Religion in England, 1400–1580* (New Haven and London: Yale University Press, 1992); and Anthony Milton, *Catholic and Reformed: The Roman and Protestant Churches in English Protestant Thought 1600–1640* (Cambridge: Cambridge University Press, 1995). See also John Bossy, *The English Catholic Community 1570–1850* (New York: Oxford University Press, 1976); Alexandra Walsham, *Church Papists: Catholicism, Conformity and Confessional Polemic in Early Modern England* (Woodbridge, Suffolk and Rochester, NY: The Boydell Press [for the Royal Historical Society], 1993; and Michael Questier,

Conversion, Politics, and Religion in England, 1580–1625 (Cambridge: Cambridge University Press, 1996).

2.   See, for example, F. W. Brownlow, *Shakespeare, Harsnett and the Devils of Denham* (Newark, London, and Toronto: University of Delaware Press, 1993); Huston Diehl, *Staging Reform, Reforming the Stage: Protestantism and Popular Theater in Early Modern England* (Ithaca and London: Cornell University Press, 1997); Lowell Gallagher, *Medusa's Gaze: Casuistry and Conscience in the Renaissance* (Stanford: Stanford University Press, 1991); and John King, *Spenser's Poetry and the Reformation Tradition* (Princeton: Princeton University Press, 1990).

Acknowledgements

I would like to thank, first, the contributors to this collection for their enthusiasm for the project and for their helpful cooperation with the editor. Next, I would like to thank two particular archivists who facilitated my own research, Rev. Thomas McCoog, S.J. of the English Jesuit Archive, London, and Rev. Ian Dickie of the Westminster Diocesan Archive, London. I am grateful also to Wayne State University for a Gershenson Faculty Fellowship and for a Humanities Center Fellowship, which supported my research and the work on this volume. The libraries and archives that have given permission to use illustrations for particular essays are acknowledged in the captions, but I would like to express my own gratitude to them.

1

Alienating Catholics in Early Modern England: Recusant Women, Jesuits and Ideological Fantasies

Arthur F. Marotti

> ... Protestants, who had started Elizabeth's reign as a minority ... [were] able to produce an image of England as inherently Protestant because Protestantism's opposite, popery, was inherently foreign.
>
> Peter Lake[1]

In the sixteenth century, once the monarch had been designated as the head of the English Church, religious conformity and political loyalty were inextricably bound.[2] Recusant Protestants, such as Anabaptists, and recusant Catholics were, therefore, political threats to the government: in refusing to conform outwardly to the state-mandated religious services, the former, with their democratic ideology, called the top-down system of political authority into question,[3] and the latter, by their allegiance to an international Catholic Church answering to the authority of the Bishop of Rome, either signalled a divided religio-political allegiance or, at an extreme, a traitorous commitment to foreign powers ready to invade the country. Of course, priests and laymen who were religious exiles awaiting or working for the restoration of Catholicism in England were most easily identified as a political menace, especially when they returned to the country as missionaries to strengthen the resolve of recusant Catholics, move 'church papists'[4] to active recusancy and convert Protestants.

During the Elizabethan era, a series of laws, statutes and royal proclamations were designed to punish lay Catholics for a wide range of activities – from simple non-attendance at Protestant services, to hearing mass and harboring priests, to sending their sons and daughters to foreign Catholic schools, seminaries and convents.[5] While there had been a small measure of toleration for the aging population of Marian priests surviving from the mid-century, the laws targeted at secular and Jesuit missionaries arriving in England from the Continent after 1574[6] were especially severe: the 1585 statute identified them as 'traitors' and pronounced them, and the laypeople who assisted them, guilty of a capital crime.

The harsh anti-recusancy laws were designed not only to prevent the spread of Catholicism, but also, mainly, to force external (patriotic) conformity to the ceremonies of a national Protestant Church. They and the required loyalty oaths[7] were intended to terrorize Catholics into conformity: even those sentenced to death were often given the opportunity to save themselves by attending a Protestant service, hearing a Protestant sermon or even praying with Protestants. Hard-line priests and lay Catholics faced imprisonment and, possibly, exile or execution as well, if they stood by their belief in papal supremacy (including the right to depose monarchs), refused to enter a Protestant church or engage in any religious practices with Protestant Christians, or would not acknowledge the moral and legal authority of the state to demand oaths of allegiance from them or to judge them in matters of religion and religio-political activity. In part, they were caught in the middle of an international conflict not of their making, one that put their consciences or their lives in peril; in part, they found themselves in legal and judicial circumstances in which the final outcome rested on their own choice.

The laws and the social practices in late sixteenth-century England worked both to erode the Catholicism of those who decided to become church papists and to alienate the recusant laity and the priests who ministered to them as disloyal, un-English. From a Jacobean perspective, Godfrey Goodman looked back on late Elizabethan attitudes towards Catholics and observed: 'The common people did hate them above measure; for they must have ever an object to their hate. Heretofore the Welsh, the Scots, or the Spaniard, and the French upon occasion; but now in these later times only the papists.'[8] Here I focus on two particular Catholic figures of religio-political resistance alienated by their actions and by the state legal and political machinery from their status as loyal English citizens: the recusant Catholic woman and the Jesuit missionary priest. Both figures have a long history in the political mythology of English nationalism, constituting the most powerful danger when they are found in a combination that marks not only sociopolitical alienation, but also essential religious differences between Protestantism and Catholicism.

I

The recusant Catholic woman was an important character in the religious and cultural drama of early modern England for a number of reasons.[9] First, married either to a conforming church papist or to a Protestant spouse, she was a figure of resistance to state authority, a sign of the persistence of the 'old religion' within the new Protestant nation. The fact that the first four Stuart monarchs had Catholic queens placed this threat in the very heart of the state. The Catholic convert, Anne of Denmark, the French princess Henrietta Maria, Catherine of Braganza and Mary of Modena, all were objects of anti-Catholic rhetoric and paranoia. The rabidly anti-Catholic Puritan Thomas Scott, for example, writing against the possible Spanish Match of Charles with the Spanish Infanta, defended his right as a subject to question the wisdom of a monarch's (or heir-apparent's) having a Catholic spouse:

> ... it is Objected, I have meddled with the mariage of the Prince, which concernes not the subject. Concernes it not the subject to pray, that the wife of his Soveraigne may be of the same Religion with her Lord? If I may pray thus, wish thus may not I endevor to have it thus? & shew the inconveniences (that I may not say mischiefs) which are likely to fall, if it be not thus? Princes are maried to the commonwealth; & the wife hath power of the husbands body, as he the husband of hers. The Common-wealth then hath power of the Prince in this point. Their Wives ought to be as Mothers to every Subject. And were not he a Foole, that would not desire a Naturall Mother, rather then a Step-Mother? Queenes ought to be nurcing Mothers to the Church: Who then would seeke a dry-Nurse, that might have another.[10]

When Milton referred to King Solomon's vulnerability to female temptation in *Paradise Lost*, he called him 'that uxorious king whose heart, though large, / beguiled by fair idolatresses, fell to idols foul'.[11]

The imagined danger such Catholic women posed to monarchs lay
behind a Parliamentary Act of 1689 that made it illegal for an
English monarch not only to be a Catholic, but also to be married to
a Catholic spouse.

The recusant woman was, like Catholicism itself (the religion of
the 'Whore of Babylon'),[12] the target of Protestant misogyny: a mas-
culinized, reform Christianity, which attacked not only the cult of
the Virgin, but also devotion to female (as well as male) saints,[13]
associated women's 'carnality' with some of the alleged corruptions
of Catholicism, contrasting the devotional and sacramental practices
of the Roman Church (with their reliance on the physical mediation
of the spiritual) with the supposedly more spiritual orientaton of
Protestant text- and language-based religion. Protestant iconoclasm
and misogyny shared a basic set of assumptions about the senses,
about the place of the body in religious practice, and about the
seductive dangers of the feminine. Woman and Catholicism were
both feared as intrinsically idolatrous, superstitious and carnal, if not
also physically disgusting. Duessa in Edmund Spenser's *The Faerie
Queene* is alternately attractive and repulsive – the Catholic Church
embodied in the images of the dangerously beautiful wanton, the
Whore of Babylon, and the bestialized, filthy woman.[14] Mary, Queen
of Scots, was feared and hated by English Protestants as a 'wicked
Popish woman'.[15] Sir Philip Sidney referred to Catherine de Medici,
the mother of the Duke of Alençon (the French suitor of Queen
Elizabeth), as 'the Jezebel of our age'.[16] On the one hand, women
were seen as particularly vulnerable to being 'seduced' into
Catholicism: in one of his literary 'Characters', Samuel Butler says
that the 'Popish Priest' '[i]s one that takes the same Course, that the
Devil did in Paradise, he begins with the Woman …. Christ made
St. Peter a Fisher of Men; but he believes it better to be a Fisher of
Women, and so becomes a Woman's Apostle.'[17] On the other hand,
Catholic women were seen as seductresses leading Protestant men
to their spiritual destruction – like Spenser's Duessa or Dalila of
Milton's *Samson Agonistes*. At worst, Catholicism and Catholic
women were associated with witchcraft, black magic and the diabol-
ical arts.[18] Frances Howard, convicted of arranging the poisoning of
Sir Thomas Overbury, was an object of abuse partly because of the
Catholicism of her family.[19] When Shakespeare portrayed Joan of
Arc in the first part of *Henry VI*, following his sources, he cast her as
a wanton woman, 'Joan La Pucelle', and as a witch, whose powers
were due to her diabolical familiars.[20]

The recusant Catholic woman was 'unruly' in her disobedience to the state's authority, and, possibly, to her husband's as well. In refusing to attend Protestant services, she asserted her personal, individual religious autonomy – an act that led some Protestant husbands to take rather harsh punitive measures, especially in times when the men had to pay high recusancy fines for their wives' refusal to comply with the law.[21] In the case of Catholic marriages where the man went through the motions of obeying the law by attending church services and his wife refused, the church-papist husbands put themselves morally and spiritually in a position inferior to their wives – a situation that inverted the hierarchical arrangement expected in the patriarchal order.[22]

The first woman to be executed under the Elizabethan anti-recusancy laws was a prosperous butcher's wife from York, Margaret Clitherow, who was pressed to death in 1586.[23] This 'Proto-martyr of her Sext [*sic*] in the Kingdome of England'[24] was converted to Catholicism after her marriage to a Protestant man (who tolerated her religious practices) and was known for over a decade as a recusant Catholic to the authorities, who imprisoned her several times. She not only assisted imprisoned Catholics but also harbored priests, arranged for Catholic instruction for her children and provided Mass for her family and friends. She was arrested as part of the Northern campaign of persecution conducted by the Earl of Huntington, in the aftermath of the passing of the 1585 Anti-Recusancy Act. Her biography was written (and circulated in manuscript within the Catholic community) by the man who was her last personal confessor and spiritual guide, the secular priest John Mush.[25] He used some of the conventions of heroically romantic hagiography[26] to portray this female martyr as the exemplary recusant Catholic woman.

John Mush presents a Catholic narrative of how the wife of a Protestant husband cheerfully performs her marital duties to spouse and children, but, as a zealous convert to Catholicism, follows a devotional and ascetic regime as rigorous as that of a member of a strict religious order.[27] She uses the man who served as her last confessor and adviser[28] to deepen her religious commitment and to empower herself as a social agent, unwilling in matters of religion to bend to the demands of any superior earthly authority – whether that of her husband or of the state. Refusing to be terrorized into betraying her religious commitment, she heroically stands up to judicial coercion and forces the authorities to

execute her so she can experience the martyrdom she wholeheart-
edly desires.[29] After her death, her confessor writes an inspiring
account of her life.

In Mush's culturally symptomatic text, the biographer and his
subject have a complicated relationship. He is at once her fatherly
guide, her religious lover and, finally, her spiritual son. Mush states
that, as a religiously exemplary Catholic woman, she 'did utterly
forsake her own judgment and will in all her actions, to submit
herself to the judgment, will, and direction of her ghostly father'
(Morris, 3: 378). When Margaret asks her spiritual counsellor
whether it is right for her to 'receive priests and serve God as I have
done, notwithstanding these new laws, without my husband's
consent' (Morris, 3: 381), he tells her it is best for her husband not to
know and 'in this, your necessary duty to God, you are not any
whit inferior to him' (Morris, 3: 382) In the spiritual matters that
meant most to her, Margaret Clitherow was beyond her Protestant
husband's authority. Mush portrays her emotional life as centred in
the priests she sheltered and who gave her spiritual direction
(Morris, 3: 389).

In a particularly emotional section of the biography, where Mush
apostrophizes the city of York for its corruption and its persecution
of this saintly woman, he notes how she used some deception to
escape her domestic confines and have the freedom for a whole
day's meeting with her confessor:

> Sometimes ... she used to go on pilgrimage, but not in any pro-
> hibited manner; as, when she was invited with her neighbours to
> some marriage or banquet in the country, she would devise
> twenty means to serve God that day more than any other at
> home; for she would take horse with the rest, and after that she
> had ridden a mile out of the city, one should be there ready pro-
> vided to go in her stead, and all that day she would remain in
> some place nigh hand, where she might quietly serve God, and
> learn of her ghostly Father some part of her Christian duty as her
> heart most desired, and at night return home again with the rest
> as though she had been feasting all the day long.
>
> This she used even from the beginning of her conversion, at
> which time also she procured some neighbours to feign the travail
> of some woman, that she might under that colour have access and
> abide with her ghostly Father the longer to be instructed in the
> necessary points of Catholic religion. (Morris, 3: 396–7)

In one sense, this wife of a Protestant husband (whose patriarchal role includes presiding over the religious affairs of his household), an independent-minded woman who changes her religion (and, therefore, the nature of the marital bond they share), is committing a kind of spiritual adultery in meeting her priest in a secluded place away from home. There is something of the character of a romantic adventure to this activity and of the relationship Margaret Clitherow has with the priests in whom she confides, thus some pretext for the slandering of her reputation by her politically opportunistic stepfather and for the nasty accusation of one of her judges: 'It is not for religion that thou harbourest priests, but for whoredom' (Morris, 3: 414).[30] Using the testimony of a terrorized twelve-year-old boy, the judge claims that 'she had sinned with priests, and that the priests and she would have delicate cheer, when she would set her husband with bread and butter and red herring'; to which she answered '"God forgive you for these forged tales; and if the boy said so, I warrant you he will say as much more for a pound of figs"' (Morris, 3: 427).[31] The Protestant minister Edmund Bunny (using a common anti-Catholic trope) accuses her of being 'seduced by these Romish Jesuits and priests' (Morris, 3: 424). Mush insists, however, that she was a model wife and describes her husband's emotional response to her condemnation: '"Alas! will they kill my wife? Let them take all I have and save her, for she is the best wife in all England, and the best Catholic also"' (Morris, 3: 418). This understanding and devoted spouse, over the years, willingly paid the recusancy fines and answered to the authorities in her defense.[32]

In defending her recusancy in the face of an intimidating judicial tribunal, this proper woman refuses to capitulate to the demands of either the malicious persecutors or the more merciful authorities who would like to see her spared execution. She refuses to plead and thus forces the judges to sentence her to death, though they obviously do not want that outcome. She is alternately a woman with the supposed infirmities of her sex and an heroic saint whose virtue and constancy make her superior not only to her Protestant adversaries, but also to her husband and to her spiritual guide. She answers her accusers, as Mush puts it paradoxically, 'boldly and with great modesty' (Morris, 3: 416). The cruellest of her judges calls her a 'naughty, wilful woman' (Morris, 3: 417). Mush portays her as a saintly female warrior who has conquered her male persecutors on behalf of the Catholicism they have betrayed (Morris, 3: 435).

Mush is quite conscious of the fact that he is writing about a martyr who is also a 'comely, beautiful young woman'.[33] He makes much of the way his religious/romantic heroine is clothed, or unclothed, for her execution. Although the court sentences her to die 'naked' (Morris, 3: 431), she has prepared a kind of smock to wear for her 'marriage' (Morris, 3: 430) to Christ, 'a linen habit like to an alb, which she had made with her own hands three days before to suffer martyrdom in' (Morris, 3: 429). She carries this garment as she walks to her execution 'barefoot and barelegged, her gown loose about her' (Morris, 3: 429). When reminded that she is to be unclothed for her execution, '[t]he martyr with the other women requested [the sheriff] … that for the honour of woman-hood they would not see her naked; but that would not be granted' (Morris, 3: 431). Nevertheless, when the women remove her clothes, they put on the 'long habit of linen … over her as far as it would reach, all the rest of her body being naked' (Morris, 3: 431) and she is allowed to die partly clothed with her hands bound in such a way 'so that her body and her arms made a perfect cross' (Morris, 3: 432).

In the imprecatory peroration at the end of the biography, Mush addresses her:

> … O sacred martyr …. Remember me … whom thou hast left miserable behind thee, in times past thine unworthy Father, and now thy most unworthy servant, made ever joyful by thy virtu-ous life, and comfortable by lamenting thy death, lamenting thy absence, and yet rejoicing in thy glory …. Be not wanting, there-fore, my glorious mother, in the perfection of thy charity … to obtain mercy and procure the plenties of such graces for me, thy miserable son, as thou knowest to be most needful to me, and ac-ceptable in the sight of our Lord, which hath thus glorified thee; that I may honour Him by imitation of thy happy life, and by any death, which He will give me, to be partaker with thee and all holy saints of His kingdom, to whom be all glory and honour, now and for ever. Amen. (Morris, 3: 440)

At once an address to a deceased beloved (like Dante's Beatrice or Petrarch's Laura) and a prayerful petition for intercession from a saint, this final rhetorical flourish uses the language of Marian devo-tion to craft an utterance for the reader to internalize, so that the biography can work its religious-didactic purpose.[34] No longer father or holy lover, Mush has become son to this 'glorious mother'.

Many other recusant women sacrificed or suffered for their faith in early modern England, a number of them famous for harboring secular priests and Jesuits during the fiercest times of persecution. The list includes Anna Line,[35] Jane Wiseman,[36] Anne Vaux,[37] the Countess of Arundel (whose husband St. Philip Howard, Earl of Arundel, died in the Tower),[38] Magdalen Lady Montague,[39] Mary Ward,[40] Gertrude More[41] and Elizabeth Cary.[42] More receptive than male Catholics to fervent baroque devotion, either as converts to or adherents of the old religion, recusant women were alienated from their native country and its dominant religious practices – especially when, in the Caroline period, they were associated with the court of a foreign Catholic queen, Henrietta Maria.[43]

II

For John Mush, Margaret Clitherow was a perfect example of Catholic martyrdom, because her motives and activities could easily be separated from charges of political subversion. Her commitment was to a life of devotion and charity, rather than to religio-political activism. The Jesuit martyrs whose deaths preceded and followed her execution, however, were entangled with larger matters of national and international import. Militantly defending the papal supremacy, including the right to depose monarchs and to sanction foreign invasion to change a state's religion, the Jesuits were at odds with more nationalistic and accommodationist lay and clerical Catholics who hoped that a less confrontational strategy might lessen the persecution and eventually lead to toleration.[44] At the turn of the century, as one of the leaders of the Appellants (those secular priests who appealed against the Pope's decision to appoint the Jesuit-sponsored secular priest George Blackwell as 'Archpriest' or supreme religious authority for England), John Mush partic- ipated in a government-supported anti-Jesuit campaign that drew a sharp line between English Catholic loyalism and the Jesuits' sup- posedly treasonous, Spanish-oriented subversiveness. Like the other Appellants, Mush defended his own patriotism and loyalty by characterizing the Jesuits as dangerous aliens, thus hoping to redirect the government's attack on recusant Catholics towards the most militant of the missionaries that began to enter England in the latter part of Queen Elizabeth's reign.[45]

Certainly, such a distinction made sense in terms of the actual loyalism of the mass of English Catholics during the Armada crisis versus the politically treasonous stance of the pro-invasion forces represented both by Cardinal Allen, by Robert Persons, S.J. and by most of the English Jesuits. After all, Persons, for example, whom one writer excoriates as 'an Hispanized Camelion ... no true Englishman',[46] was associated with the Guises and the militant Catholic League and, in the six years leading up to the Armada and in the decade following it, had urged the 'empresa' that entailed the invasion of England by papally sanctioned foreign Catholic forces (supposedly to be aided by native English Catholics). He also later presented in print the case for the Spanish Infanta as Queen Elizabeth's rightful successor.[47] Such a political program could be disavowed by English lay and clerical Catholics in the name of an allegedly 'natural' patriotism it violated. One of the most rabidly anti-Jesuit Appellants, William Watson, accused the Jesuits of trying to 'alien the mindes of most loyall subjects, and draw them to consent to ... unnaturall invasion, rebellion, conspiracie, riot, or what else ... '.[48] Treasonous Jesuits have 'laboured', in the words of another writer, 'nothing more then to betray that sweete aportion, this sweete plot, our Country to Spaine, a meere forraine and Morisco nation'.[49] In his conspiracy theory approach to contemporary politics in the early 1620s, Thomas Scott makes a connection between the papacy, which supports the Spanish king's desire for universal monarchy, and the Jesuits, as members of 'the Spanish faction, though they be Polonians, English, French & residing in those countries & Courts'.[50] Even those who are 'the Penitents ... and all with whom they deale and converse in their spirituall traffique must needs be so too' (A4v). The taint of Spanishness thus spreads to everyone dealing with Jesuits.

The growing polemical association of Jesuits with the theory and practice of political assassination made it possible for their Catholic and Protestant antagonists to criticize them as enemies not only of national sovereignty (a consequence of their belief in papal supremacy) but also of monarchy and monarchical political theory. Juan de Mariana's justification of tyrranicide was, by politically paranoid reasoning, made into the proof that the Jesuits were the instigators of such political murders as that of William of Orange and Henry III and Henry IV of France. Jesuits were 'bloody' – even made responsible, in some accounts, for the notorious St Bartholomew's Day Massacre of 1572.[51] After the English government succeeded in associating the Jesuits with the Gunpowder Plot of 1605 by convicting Henry Garnet, the Jesuit superior (on insufficient evidence) of complicity in the sordid affair,[52] the outlines were complete of an anti-Jesuit mythology that, like the anti-Hispanic 'Black Legend',[53] took deep root in British culture. Some of this anti-Jesuit rhetoric was borrowed from French anti-Jesuit writing, which was a Gallican, 'Politique', anti-Spanish strain in Catholic internecine disputes;[54] also anti-Jesuit feeling was increased by the attempted Spanish Match for James's son Charles, by the relative tolerance of priests and Jesuits in late Jacobean and Caroline England, by the establishment of an official English Jesuit Province in 1623,[55] and by Jesuit association with the Irish Rebellion of 1641. In the wake of the Gunpowder Plot, James's chief minister, Robert Cecil, expressed some willingness to be lenient to secular priests, but he was unbending in his attitude towards the Jesuits, whom he called 'that generation of vipers'.[56]

In a Restoration pamphlet addressed to Charles II, *An Account of the Jesuites Life and Doctrine* (1661), a Catholic author (identified only as 'M.G.' [perhaps Martin Grene]) offers a defense of the Jesuit Order against the charges traditionally levelled against them. This text makes it clear why the Jesuit priest was a prime target for anti-Catholic rhetoric in early modern England. Looking back to the previous two decades of Civil War and political unrest, M.G. claims that Jesuits were the easiest scapegoat for England's troubles:

> Many will needs conceive, or pretend they conceive, that the Papists were occasion of all our disorders, and the Jesuits the Boutefeu's [firebrands] in the ruine of both King and Country .... 'tis the stile of our times to lay all to the Papists, and no Man concludes with applause, but he that Perorat's against the Jesuits. (A3)

Objecting to the vicious portrayal of Jesuits in the pamphlets, libels and sermons of the time, the author defines the Jesuit stereotype:

> Every Jesuit ... hath a Pope in his belly, a Macchiavel in his head, Mercuries wings on his feet, and the Mysterious feather of Lucian's cocks tail in his hand. The Pope in his belly makes him still big with malice, still giving birth to new mischief. Macciavel in his head Orders all so dextrously as to make him out reach all

the World. Mercurie's wings on his feet carry him from place to place, from Country to Country, and make him every where in a trice. The Cocks feather in his hand opens all closets and Cofers, and Secrets, and discovers to the Jesuit, the Want and Wealth of every one, that he may know where to places his labours with thrift. (A3^v–A4)

Jesuits are the superpapists, the diabolical schemers, liars who justify their deceit with the doctrine of equivocation and mental reservation, the international vagrants threatening the modern nation-state, the political subversives with access to the wealthy and powerful. They also are Protean disguisers, appearing 'Now a Cobler, now a Preacher, now a Tinker, now a Courtier, now a Peasan [peasant or country fellow]; now a States-man, and what not', 'the only contrivers of all the mischiefs in the World' (A4). They are the perfect object of paranoid imagining:

> The Jesuits are to our Fabulous heads, what the Evil-Genius's or Pestiferous Gods were to old times, when fictions made Deities. They are Presbyterians, and Episcopal Protestants, and Levellers, and Quakers, and what you will, provided it be … a name of disgrace. They have overthrown learning, destroyed Philosophy, undone Morals, ravaged Divinity, poysoned States, corrupted manners, betrayed Kingdomes, subverted the Church, confounded the Gospel, and as with the dregs of Pandor's box poured out more mischief on the World then all the Devils in Hell could ever have wished. (A5)

Addressing himself to 'rational Protestants' (64) who are open to argument, M.G. enumerates and answers seven objections to the Jesuits' lives and four objections to their doctrine, as well as one other 'objection' directed at neither. The list is revealing:

1. '[T]hey are crafty' (79).
2. 'Jesuites are rich' (82).
3. 'Jesuites are ambitious' (85).
4. 'Jesuites are nice and lead a lazie and delicate life' (88).
5. 'Jesuites are dangerous men, because they meddle in intrigues of State, and thrust themselves into Court affairs' (89).
6. 'The Jesuites cannot be trusted, because they reveal all secrets, even confessions, to their superiours' (91).

7. 'Jesuites make a vow to the Pope, and therefore must be supposed not to be so loyal as others, being already tyed to a for-
reign prince, and therefore but half Subjects' (96–7).

The last objection might be broadened to define the conflicted position of all Catholics in early modern England: their faith puts them
potentially in a situation of divided religio-political loyalty that, in
an earlier period, needed to be tested judicially by 'bloody questions'[57] or civilly by requiring oaths of allegiance. They are, at best,
'half Subjects'. The other objections more specifically constitute the
Jesuit as a composite object of scorn.

The objections to Jesuit teaching allege:

1. '[T]he Jesuites teach the Doctrine of Equivocation and mental
reservation, and therefore … can not be trusted' (100);
2. '[T]he Jesuites teach that horrid maxime, *Fides non est servanda
haereticus*, Faith is not to be kept to Hereticks' (104);
3. '[T]hey maintain the Popes authority in prejudice to
Sovereignty, teaching that the Pope hath power to depose
Kings' (105); and
4. '[T]hey teach the killing of Kings, though under the name of
Tyrants' (113).

The association of Jesuits with the doctrine of 'equivocation', with
its sanctioning of withholding or distorting the truth by means of
'mental reservation', goes back to Robert Southwell's and Henry
Garnet's trials, especially the latter's since it followed that landmark
Catholic outrage, the Gunpowder Plot of 1605.[58] Although the
broad use of equivocation and mental reservation was later condemned by Pope Innocent XI in 1679, M.G. argues that the Jesuits'
teaching on this subject was 'common Doctrine of all Schools, and
Universities, none excepted' (103). The second supposed 'doctrine'
(not keeping faith in dealings with 'heretics') is denied outright.
Regarding the third, M.G. points out that two successive Jesuit
Generals issued prohibitions on teaching or discussing the doctrine
of papal supremacy (110–12). The fourth doctrine, a theory of tyrannicide with which radical Protestants were also associated, is traced
back to the teachings of Mariana, whose writings the Jesuit General
Claudio Aquaviva censured in 1606, four years before the Sorbonne
condemned them, well before the assassination of Henry IV by
Ravillac, who was supposed to have been inspired by them.[59] M.G.

emphatically denies the Jesuit connections of both Ravillac and the failed (Jesuit-educated) assassin Catell with Mariana's work.[60] Long before Titus Oates's 'Popish Plot' of the late 1670s and the exclusion crisis centered on Charles II's Catholic brother James, this Catholic writer takes stock of anti-Jesuit propaganda (and of 'anti-popery' in general) at a moment just after the exiled Stuart court has returned from France, where both King and Queen were supposedly exposed to dangerous Jesuit influence.

Despite their small numbers and despite the government's capture and execution or deportation of them throughout the Elizabethan era, English Jesuits and Jesuit missionaries steadily increased in numbers between 1580 and the time of the Civil War. As Hugh Aveling points out,

> In 1593 there were forty-nine English Jesuits, of whom thirty were priests, and only nine in England. By 1610 there were fifty-three Jesuits in England and possibly 120 in the Society .... By 1620 there were 211 in the Province and 106 missioners in England. By 1641 overall numbers had risen to nearly 400, and missioners to about 180.[61]

While the English Catholic community gradually grew through the seventeenth century, despite the continuing persecution, the number of Jesuits dramatically increased and Protestant anti-Jesuit paranoia burgeoned.[62]

Jesuits (and many other Catholics, especially missionaries) were alienated by their Continental exile, by their sympathy with Spain in the conflict in the Low Countries between Spanish power and Dutch Protestant rebels, by their international, rather than national, perspective as missionaries with a global orientation reaching both to the Far East and the New World. The anti-Catholic association of Catholicism with paganism, especially the paganism of the East – which is well illustrated in the work of both Spenser and Milton – took the specific form of connecting the Jesuits with both Islam and the Turks. Jesuit militancy and their direct service to the Pope led to their being thought of as the Pope's Janissaries. In a Europe in which religious warfare continued to flare up in the post-Reformation period, Biblical metaphors of spiritual battle were connected with actual sectarian violence (such as the St Bartholomew's Day Massacre), with anti-colonial and other kinds of rebellion (for example, in Ireland and the Low Countries), and with the kind of international religious conflict that led to the Thirty Years' War (1618–48). If English Catholic laymen were regarded as potentially traitorous and secular priests as actually traitorous, the Jesuits were, in effect, arch-traitors, so thoroughly alienated from their native country as to work tirelessly on behalf of its enemies, particularly Spain. Robert Persons was, in effect, the prime example of the arch-traitor: he not only attacked the English Protestant establishment in a series of polemical writings, but also briefly conspired with the Guises in formulating plans to invade England and to assassinate Queen Elizabeth, tried to use his relationship with Philip II and Spain to bring 'the great enterprise' to fruition, and then, after the failure of the Armada, later argued for the legitimacy of the claim of the Spanish Infanta as successor to Elizabeth. Jesuits were commonly regarded as 'Hispaniolated' or 'Hispanzed', and Englishmen influenced by them or under their spiritual control were called 'Jesuited' – with the implication that they were unEnglished or alienated from their nationality.[63]

III

One of the points that John O'Malley makes in his superb study of *The First Jesuits* is that, with their emphasis on auricular confession and spiritual guidance of the laity, Jesuits were especially sought out by women. At various points, they had to be concerned with the possible scandal that might arise from private home visits to female Catholics and, O'Malley states, the interposition of a grill between confessor and penitent was developed as a partial solution to this problem.[64] In a Paul's Cross sermon of 15 February 1618, Robert Sibthorpe referred to 'Romanists who creep into great houses to lead captive "simple women laden with sinnes"', alluding to priests', particularly Jesuit priests', power as confessors to the elite.[65] One anti-Jesuit pamphlet contains supposed instructions to members of the order on 'How to procure the friendship of rich Widows' (in order to obtain money from them):

> For this purpose must be called out some of the Fathers of the livelyest fresh complexions, and of a middle age. These must frequent Their houses, and if they find a kindness towards our Society, impart to Them its great worth. If they come to our Churches, we must put a Confessour to them, that shall

perswade them to continue in their Widowhood, representing to
them the great pleasure, delight, and advantage that will accrue
to them by remaining in that state …. The first thing that their
Confessours are to do, is to get into their Counsels, and to let
them understand how necessary it is for the good of their souls to
give themselves wholly up into their hands …. presently they
must be put upon entring into some religious Order, not in a
Cloister, but after the manner of Paulina. Thus when they are
caught in the Vow of chastity, all danger of their Marrying again
is over.[66]

The following chapter is entitled 'How to keep Widows to our
selves, so far as concerns the disposing of their Estates' (38 ff.).

A short, popular pamphlet, published in 1642, associated the
Jesuit's use of the confession not only with his hunger for other
people's 'secrets' but also with his sexual exploitation of women:

… the Serpent is a Bungler to him: Confession is his engine by
which he Skrews himselfe into acquaintance with all Affairs, all
Dispositions; which he makes the best conducing to his ends, that
is, the worst use of. But for this point of Craft, he is owing to the
Serpent, to grow inward with the Woman when he dares not immediately adventure on the Man; whose Secrets whilest he in-
deavours to discover in Confession, if she be Obediently yielding
(a matter which he earnestly presseth her unto, as a thing simply
necessary for her salvation) then he proves most Indulgent unto
her in Penance, which himselfe Acts upon her; and he is therefore the most Impious Lecher of the world, because he prostitutes
not only her Body, but her Conscience to his Lust; the ancient
manner of confessing was, the Penitents kneeled at the
Confessors Side, but he humbleth the women to his Bosome, and
thus he becomes a Father, by his Supernumerary Vow of Mission
and getting children.[67]

In 1612, the letter writer John Chamberlain reported on a sermon
preached by one of Prince Henry's chaplains who supposedly said

that the Prince told him not a moneth before he died that religion
lay a bleeding, and no marvayle (saide he) when divers [Privy]
counsaillors heare masse in the morning, and then go to a court
sermon and so to the counsaile, and then tell theyre wives what

passes, and they carie yt to theyre Jesuites and confessors, with other like stuffe...[68]

In the straitened circumstances of the English persecution, various English Jesuits were forced to rely on the harboring and hospitality of English recusant women, especially those of the aristocracy. Robert Southwell lived in the Countess of Arundel's London residence, where he set up a press to publish some Catholic books. He had a special relationship with the Bellamy family before he was betrayed by young Anne Bellamy – an episode fictionalized by Spenser in Book V of *The Faerie Queene* in the Samient–Malengin story.[69] Henry Garnet (and many Jesuits and seminary priests who moved about England) relied on the help and protection of the widowed Anne Vaux and her sister Elizabeth,[70] who was a patroness of the Jesuit John Gerard.[71] John Percy, S.J. (alias Fisher the Jesuit) converted the Countess of Buckingham and lived in London under her protection.[72] Henry More, the new Jesuit Provincial in late Caroline England, relied on the help of Lady Arundel.[73]

Such relationships, however, were interpreted maliciously by those wishing to slander Jesuits and the Catholics with whom they were associated. One of the anti-Jesuit Appellants wrote of their special relationship with women:

As all heresies began with talkative women, (these of nature being as flexible to yeeld, as credulous to beleeve) so Silly women more devout than discreet (as alwaies in extreames, either Saints or Devils,) poore soules do mightily dote and run riot after them, among these they title tatle, and lull babies a sleepe, and the ignorant multitudes of the Jesuits do use the most women gospellers, trumpetters of their praise, & with these women tatlers & women Gospellers, the Secular Priests are much troubled: but in the end, their fraud will appeare, when these hot Ladies shall lay their hands a little heavier on their hearts, with mea maxima culpa.[74]

Other anti-Jesuit slanders poured from the pens of the Appellant writers at the turn of the century. Anthony Copley, for example, retails a common libel about Robert Persons as the 'mis-begotten [son] of a ploughman' who 'demeaned himselfe ... in begetting two bastards male and female upon the bodie of his owne sister betweene his age of seventeene and three and twentie'.[75] In the polemical give-and-take following the assassination of Henry IV of France, one French anti-Jesuit writer, whose work was translated into English, attacked the King's Jesuit confessor for his pandering and sexual license.[76]

In *A Foot out of the Snare*, the apostate John Gee retails a story of Jesuit adultery:

> A certaine Catholicke collapsed Ladie ... departed from her husband (yet living) and went over to Bruxels, and was admitted into the order of Nunnerie, I meane, a Nunne at large, one of the uncloistred sisters of the order of Saint Clare, and there shee remained til there appeared in her some passion incompatible with Nunship. She came over into England a companion with a religious Jesuite, since of great note, F.D. [Francis Drury?] and remaining afterwards an inlarged Nunne in London, was (as it seemeth) more visibly taken with a disease befalling that sexe, called flatus uterinus: and thereupon, that this matter might bee carried the more cleanly, it was given out, that shee was possessed with an evill spirit, which did make her belly to swell like a woman with child. Certaine it is many were deluded by this occasion: and the practice of the Priests to hide her blemish, and gull poore people, was lewd and abominable. For a certaine Jesuite (whom I could also name, being a smug, spruce, liquorish, young fellow, a fit man to bee called Father (forsooth) at every word, & of no high stature ...) put on the Ladies or such like womanish apparel, with a Vaile over his face: & that some found Ignaro's about the Towne might be perswaded of the Priests power for the casting out of Divels, they were suffred to come to her chamber, where were two other Jesuites (provided for the purpose, to act their parts in this Comedie); who no sooner fell to their prayers, and began to use their exorcising spells, but thereupon the supposed Ladie began to utter her mind in Italian, Latin, and Greeke: which much astonished the standers by, they little dreaming of this deceit.[77]

This account not only highlights the Jesuits' alleged abuse of the women who trusted them, but also their theatrically skilled deceiving of the wider public through staged 'exorcisms'. In a subsequent work, Gee recounts several stories of women's being deceived by Jesuit-contrived 'apparitions': he describes a Jesuit attempt to proselytize a Protestant servant, Mary Boucher, by means of a faked appearance of her dead godmother come from Purgatory to advise her to become a Catholic and a nun.[78] The 'second Comodie of a Female Apparition' is staged by the Jesuits Fisher and Wainman to convert Mrs Frances Peard, an orphan with £1,000; they succeed in getting control of her money (10–25). Gee exposes how by 'creeping sly stealth the Master-Gamesters the Jesuites doe drive the female Partridges into their Nett by the helpe of the setting Dogge of sneaking Visions, and Phantasmes' (23).

There is an interesting story that appears in different versions of a work translated from the French into English as *A Short Treatise Touching some Very Secret and Close Studies and Practises of the Jesuits*.[79] In the course of criticizing the Jesuits for their adoption of disguises, the writer retails a story about the ways Jesuits seduce women into the subterranean vaults of their houses for bacchanalian revels. The wily porter of the Jesuit house supposedly keeps all sorts of male and female apparel not only to allow Jesuits to disguise themselves in order, for example, to 'haunt Brothell houses, abandoning themselves to all dissolution & excesse', but also to entice poor women into debauchery in the Jesuit house itself:

> … for that which others in the secret places, and Chancells of their Temples, cannot attain by auricular confessions: this fellow easily obtaineth by flattering and sundry sorts of allurements, especially amongst the poorer sorts of widowes and women …. Now when this most impure Porter, hath once drawn them into his net, though before they were sluttish, in their torne and worne apparell, yet doth he daintily adorne them with other which he hath in a readinesse, and leadeth them by divers turnings and windings … to the Reverend Lord and Father. And these things are done, not by day light, but when it is somewhat late in the evening, & after that they spend the whole night in gormandies, & dancing …. they have for these purposes, certain safe or seeled, or if you will, places under the ground, as they had, which in times past at Rome were consecrated to Venus, whose beastly prostituting of themselves, to the lust and wantonesse of the flesh was so great, that the Senate fearing the wrath of the Gods for it, did utterly overthrow that Stue or brothell house …. (3)

Following this with a description of the Jesuits' underground torture chambers where they enact a diabolical theater of cruelty and engage in black magical arts of prognostication, the writer thus creates some of the outlines of the horrors later fictionalized in the Gothic novel.

In *Ignatius his Conclave*, the anti-Jesuit prose satire written in the context of the protracted Oath of Allegiance controversy following the Gunpowder Plot, John Donne portrays Jesuits as Machiavellian 'innovators', threats to the modern nation-state because of their support for papal temporal supremacy and deposing power, their practices of equivocation, mental reservation and of not keeping faith with heretics, their international spying and manipulation, their questioning of the ideology of monarchy,[80] and their sanctioning of invasion and regicide for changing a state's religion.[81] In his speech in Hell, Donne's Ignatius boasts that 'states-men of our Order, wiser then the rest, have found how much this Temporal jurisdiction [of Popes] over Princes, conduces to the growth of the Church'.[82] He is proud that Jesuits have taken advantage of their familiarity with political leaders 'to know times, and secrets of state' (51). He argues that their theory of 'Mentall Reservation, and Mixt propositions' (55) gives them the flexibility to lie for political ends. Competing with the 'innovator', (the republican) Machiavelli, for evil pre-eminence, Ignatius says that the Jesuits' political theories and practices are more subversive and anti-monarchical than his:

> all his bookes, and all his deedes, tend onely to this, that thereby a way may be prepared to the ruine & destruction of that part of this Kingdome, which is established at Rome: for what else doth hee endeavour or go about, but to change the forme of common-wealth, and so to deprive the people ... of all their liberty: & having so destroyed all civility & re-publique, to reduce all states to Monarchies; a name which in secular states, wee doe so much abhor. (55, 57)

In this dystopian fiction, the Jesuits, as internationalists and imperialists, even prove bad citizens of Hell, so they are considered for exile to the 'new world, the Moone' to set up another state ruled by Ignatius, a polity that might serve as a base from which they 'may beget and propagate many Hells & enlarge [their] Empire' (81). The moon is a good place for Jesuits because, says Ignatius,

> a woman governes there; of which Sex they have ever made their profite, which have attempted any Innovation in religion .... Why

may not wee relie upon the wit of woemen, when, once, the Church delivered over her selfe to a woman-Bishop.[83] And since we are reputed so fortunate in obtaining the favour of woemen, that woemen are forbid to come into our houses; and we are forbid, to take the charge of any Nunnes ... why should we doubt of our fortune with this Queene, which is so much subject to alterations and passions? (83, 85)

Thomas Middleton's *A Game at Chesse* exploits the popular beliefs about the relationship of Jesuits and women. This anti-Jesuit, anti-Spanish play was written in the wake of the popular celebration of the failure of the proposed 'Spanish Match' for James I's son Charles, whose return from Spain (with the Duke of Buckingham) set off unprecedented popular celebration in London.[84] It illustrates not only some of the conventional charges against Jesuits, but also foregrounds the association of Jesuits and women as a particularly dangerous one. Its Induction presents a diabolical (recently canonized) Ignatius Loyola as a model Machiavellian politician, whose followers are 'all true labourers in the work/Of the universal monarchy'[85] sought by the King of Spain. They work their way into the houses and courts of aristocrats and monarchs to learn their secrets and manipulate them;[86] they are disguisers, equivocators and advocates of king-killing;[87] they are associated with homosexuality.[88]

Ignatius has as a spiritual 'secular daughter / That plays the Black Queen's Pawn' (Ind. 46–7) – that is Mary Ward, the woman who established (on the model of the Jesuits) an uncloistered teaching order that functioned both on the Continent and in England. In the play's first scene, which demonstrates the attempted seduction into Catholicism of the White Queen's Pawn by a Jesuit (the Black Bishop's Pawn), this female Jesuit assists in the evil business. In the sexualized language of this anti-Jesuit propaganda, the Black King writes to the Jesuit tempter of the White Queen's Pawn 'to require you by the burning affection I bear to the rape of devotion, that speedily upon the surprisal of her, by all watchful advantage you make some attempt upon the White Queen's person, whose fall or prostitution our lust most violently rages for' (2.1.20–5). In the play's allegory (since King James's Queen Anne has been dead for several years), the White Queen may signify either the English Church or the English people left vulnerable to Jesuit temptation. The Black Bishop's Pawn, a gelding,[89] after being refused the kiss he requests to seal the bond of the White Queen's Pawn's 'Boundless

obedience' (2.1.38), acts on his desire to 'possess' (1.1.204) her by
attempting to rape her, revealing himself as an 'arch-hypocrite'
(2.1.147) and the members of his order as habitual breakers of the
vows of poverty, chastity, and obedience (2.1.87–8). In the sexual-
ization of international politics figured in the dramatic allegory, the
fall of the Palatinate and of James's daughter and son-in-law is
attributed to Jesuit subversion. The failure of the Spanish Match
became another Protestant Providential deliverance – even though
the negotiations for a substitute French Catholic spouse began
immediately and the French match, especially in the period of
Charles's 'prerogative rule' when Queen Henrietta Maria (after the
death of Buckingham) had a strong influence on the King's deci-
sions, provoked strong objections to court Catholicism and new
waves of anti-popery and anti-Jesuit paranoia.[90]

Phineas Fletcher's Spenserian epic, *The Locusts, or Apollyonists*,
portrays the Jesuits as the devilish masters of papal treacheries in
the world.[91] In a scene of consultation in Hell, Ignatius, 'in hell
Apollyon, / On earth Equivocus,'[92] argues that the diabolical and
Catholic forces should switch from open conflict to a more subtle
means of subversion. This involves getting at the Protestant male
Christian through his weaker spouse. He explains that his Jesuits
have worked their way into the favor of women to accomplish their
purposes. They have

… with practicke slight
Crept into houses great: their sugred tongue
　　Made easy way into the lapsed brest
　　Of weaker sexe, where lust had built her nest,
There layd they Cuckoe eggs, and hatch't their brood unblest.

There sowe they traytrous seed with wicked hand
'Gainst God, and man; well thinks their silly sonne
To merit heaven by breaking Gods command,
To be a Patriot by rebellion.
And when his hopes are lost, his life and land,
And he, and wife, and child are all undone,
　　Then calls for heaven and Angells, in step I,
　　And waft him quick to hel; thus thousands die,
Yet still their children doat: so fine their forgerie.

(Canto II, st. 34–5)

Fletcher makes the Jesuit Cardinal Bellarmine the originator of the
Gunpowder Plot, the son of Loyola who leads the forces of the
Whore of Babylon or the 'Beast' against Protestant nations, particularly the 'blessed Isle' of England (and Scotland). In his speech in a
papal conclave, Bellarmine reiterates the Jesuit strategy:

> … nothing more our Kingdome must advance,
>   Or further our designes, then to comply
>   With that weake sexe, and by fine forgerie
> To worme in womens hearts, chiefly the rich and high.
>
> Nor let the stronger scorne these weaker powres;
> The labour's lesse with them, the harvest more:
> They easier yeeld, and win; so fewer houres
> Are spent: for women sooner drinke our lore,
> Men sooner sippe it from their lippes, then ours:
> Sweetly they learne, and sweetly teach: with store
>   Of teares, smiles, kisses, and ten thousand arts
>   They lay close batt'ry to mens frayler parts:
> So finely steale themselves, and us into their hearts.

(Canto IV, st. 21–2)

He illustrates the point with the examples of Samson and King
Solomon, both of whom John Milton also criticizes for their
uxoriousness.[93]

Fletcher's short epic has been long recognized as one of the literary influences on Milton's *Paradise Lost*:[94] one can easily see how its
portrayal of Hell and of devils had a strong impact on the
Protestant poet-prophet. In Milton's poem, I would suggest, the
seduction of Eve takes place in the context of anti-Catholic and anti-
Jesuit polemic. A diabolical disguiser who is a skilful rhetorical
seducer succeeds in enticing his female victim into idolatrous,
superstitious practice and alienating her from both her husband
and from the faith in which they have grounded their marital relationship. The impassioned poet, who associated Catholicism with
the pagan East, with witchcraft, idolatry and devil-worship, made
use of the culturally ingrained codes and language of anti-
Catholicism and of its recurrent anti-Jesuit subset. If the Jesuit was
the arch-hypocrite, arch-traitor and Machiavellian and diabolical
antagonist of the 'godly' Protestant, what better model could he

have found for the character of Satan? And what better precedent
for subverting the Protestant male could he have found than in the
assault of the Jesuit 'seducer' on the carnal female spouse? Once the
weaker Eve is seduced from true faith and obedience, her uxorious
husband follows.[95] Although Milton was not writing a traditional
epic of nationalistic celebration, he exploited English cultural codes
and ideological fantasies that characterized both Catholic women
and the priests (especially the Jesuit priests) who ministered to
them as alien to English Protestant identity. And this component of
English national mythology has had a long life in English and
American culture.

NOTES

1. 'Anti-Popery: the Structure of a Prejudice', in *Conflict in Early Stuart
    England: Studies in Religion and Politics 1603–1642* (London and New
    York: Longman, 1989), 82.
2. The 1559 Act of Supremacy (1 Eliz. I, c.1), 'An Act restoring to the
    Crown the ancient jurisdiction over the state ecclesiastical and spiri-
    tual, and abolishing all foreign power repugnant to the same',
    sharply contrasted (royal) English from 'usurped foreign power and
    authority' (*The Tudor Constitution: Documents and Commentary*, ed. and
    introduced by G. R. Elton [Cambridge: Cambridge University Press,
    1965], 363).
3. As early as 1535 a royal proclamation commanded Anabaptists to
    leave the country under pain of death: *Tudor Royal Proclamations*, ed.
    Paul L. Hughes and James F. Larkin, C.S.V., 3 vols. (New Haven and
    London: Yale University Press, 1964–69), 1: 227–8. See also Queen
    Elizabeth's proclamation of 22 September 1560 ordering the deporta-
    tion of Anabaptists (ibid., 2: 148–9).
4. See Alexandra Walsham, *Church Papists: Catholicism, Conformity and
    Confessional Polemic in Early Modern England* (Woodbridge, Suffolk:
    The Royal Historical Society and The Boydell Press, 1993).
5. The main laws were the 1559 Act of Uniformity (I Eliz. I, c.2), which
    included a one shilling weekly fine for recusancy; the 1563 'act for
    the assurance of the Queen's Majesty's royal power over all estates
    and subjects within her Highness's dominions' (5 Eliz. I, c.1), which
    entailed loss of property for first refusal to take the oath of allegiance
    and death for a second refusal; the 1571 'act against the bringing in
    and putting in execution of bulls and other instruments from the see
    of Rome' (13 Eliz. I, c.2) and 'Act whereby certain offences be made
    treasons' (13 Eliz. I, c.1), the former of which also left anyone leaving
    England for more than six months liable to forfeiture of lands and the
    latter of which covered not only those who plotted Elizabeth's death
    or overthrow, but also those who dealt openly with the legitimacy of

her rule or with the royal succession; the 1581 'act to retain the Queen's Majesty's subjects in their due obedience' (23 Eliz. I, c.1), which made treasonous those who drew subjects from their allegiance to the queen or to the Church of England and dramatically increased the fine for recusancy to £20; the 1585 'act against Jesuits, seminary priests and such other like disobedient persons' (27 Eliz. I, c.2), which made being a seminary priest or Jesuit a capital crime (confirming in law the royal proclamation of 1582 [Hughes and Larkin, 2: 488–91]); and the 1593 'act against popish recusants' (35 Eliz. I, c.2), which ordered Catholics to register themselves with local authorities and to keep within five miles of their homes and which also made conforming husbands pay the recusancy fines of their wives. See Elton, 410–32, and J. E. Neale, *Elizabeth I and Her Parliaments, 1559–1581* (London: Jonathan Cape, 1953), 116–21.

6. The first Douai missionaries arrived in England in 1574 and the first Jesuit missionaries in 1580.
7. The most important loyalty oaths were the Elizabethan Oath of Supremacy and the early Stuart Oath of Allegiance.
8. *The Court of King James the First*, ed. John S. Brewer, 2 vols. (London: Richard Bentley, 1839), 1: 86–7.
9. For an extensive treatment of this topic see Frances Dolan, *Whores of Babylon: Gender and Catholicism in Seventeenth-Century Print Culture* (Ithaca and London: Cornell University Press, 1999).
10. *Vox Regis* (1624), 13–14. For a discussion of Scott's work, especially his anti-Hispanicism, see William S. Maltby, *The Black Legend in England: The Development of Anti-Spanish Sentiment, 1558–1660* (Durham, NC: Duke University Press, 1971), 102–8.
11. *Paradise Lost*, 1.444–6, in John Milton, *Complete Poems and Major Prose*, ed. Merritt Y. Hughes (New York: Odyssey Press, 1957). For a discussion of Milton's portrayal of the recusant Catholic spouse as a threat to the Protestant husband, see Cedric C. Brown, 'Milton and the Idolatrous Consort', *Criticism* 35 (1993): 419–39.
12. See the Geneva Bible gloss on Revelation 17: 4: 'This woman is the Antichrist, that is the Pope with the whole bodie of his filthy creatures, as is expounded, ver. 18, whose beauty onely standeth in outwarde pompe & impudencie and craft like a strumpet.'
13. See John N. King, *English Reformation Literature* (Princeton: Princeton University Press, 1982), 381–7.
14. See John N. King, *Spenser's Poetry and the Reformation Tradition* (Princeton: Princeton University Press, 1990), 91–7.
15. David Norbrook, 'Macbeth and the Politics of Historiography', in *The Politics of Discourse: the Literature and History of Seventeenth-Century England* (Berkeley: University of California Press, 1987), 82. In the context of the discussion of the succession question in the Parliament of 1563, Mary's non-Englishness was stressed: Sir Ralph Sadler referred to her as a 'foreign prince' (quoted in Neale, 1: 104).
16. 'A Letter to Queen Elizabeth', in *Miscellaneous Prose of Sir Philip Sidney*, ed. Katherine Duncan-Jones and Jan Van Dorsten (Oxford: Clarendon Press, 1973), 48.

17. Samuel Butler, *Characters and Passages from Note-Books*, ed. A. R. Waller (Cambridge: Cambridge University Press, 1908), 62.
18. See Deborah Willis, *Malevolent Nurture: Witch-Hunting and Maternal Power in Early Modern England* (Ithaca: Cornell University Press, 1995), 118–22, and Garry Wills, *Witches and Jesuits: Shakespeare's* Macbeth (New York and Oxford: The New York Public Library and Oxford University Press, 1995).
19. Anthony Weldon's *Secret History of James I*, which concentrates on the Robert Carr/Frances Howard affair and marriage and on the murder of Sir Thomas Overbury, has an ongoing anti-Catholic theme, sometimes inserted by way of the popular rumours that circulated at various stages of the scandal. The crypto-Catholic Earl of Northampton and his niece are prime targets of this account, Carr himself portrayed as being seduced through the charms and witchcraft of the poisonous Catholic woman. For a discussion of Frances Howard's demonization as a (crypto-)Catholic woman, see David Lindley, *The Trials of Frances Howard: Fact and Fiction at the Court of King James* (London and New York: Routledge, 1993), 49, 165.
20. She is associated with Catholic Mariolatry (1.2.72–86, 90). Charles the French Dauphin is charmed by her and practises a kind of idolatry towards her (1.2.144–5). Joan is identified as a 'witch' (1.5.21; 3.2.38), 'damned sorceress' (3.2.38), 'vile fiend and shameless courtezan' (3.2.45) and 'railing Hecate' (3.2.64). The full treatment of Joan as a witch comes in the third scene of Act 5, in which she calls on her magical powers and the evil spirits that have assisted her (5.3.2–12).
21. See, for example, Robert Southwell's letter dealing with Catholic women expelled, or in fear of being expelled, by their Protestant husbands (Thomas M. McCoog, S.J., ed., 'The Letters of Robert Southwell, S. J.,' *Archivum Historicum Societatis Jesu* 63 [1994]: 10). In the Parliament of 1593, members debated the problem of recusant wives of Protestant (or church papist) husbands (see Neale, 2: 280–97).
22. Henry Garnet addressed women in his 'Treatise of Renuniciation': 'your husbands over your soul have no authority and over your bodies but limited power' (quoted in Marie Rowlands, 'Recusant Women 1560–1640', in *Women in English Society 1500–1800*, ed. Mary Prior [London and New York: Methuen, 1985], 165). Robert Persons, S. J., refers to Catholic wives' being stronger than their husbands (L. Hicks, S. J. [ed.], *Letters and Memorials of Father Robert Persons, S. J.*, vol. 1, *Catholic Record Soc.* 39 [London: John Whitehead & Sons, 1942], 62). Robert Southwell praised Catholic widows for their 'virile hearts' ('Letters', ed. McCoog, 4).
23. 'Mary Claridge' [Katharine Longley], *Margaret Clitherow (1556?-1586)* (New York: Fordham University Press, 1966), 139, points out that the only Catholic woman executed for her faith previously had been Margaret Pole, Countess of Salisbury, who was killed in 1541. See also the second edition of this biography, *Saint Margaret Clitherow* (Wheathampstead, Herts.: Anthony Clarke, 1986), which corrects some of the information of the first edition – particularly Clitherow's

age at marriage (18, not 15) and the date of her execution, 25 March 1586.

24. *An Abstract of the Life and Martirdome of Mistris Margaret Clitherow* (Mackline, 1619). This radical abridgement of John Mush's biography concentrates on her arrest, imprisonment, arraignment and execution.
25. Claridge, 54, points out that Mush, before he went abroad for seminary training, had been a servant of Dr Thomas Vavasour and his wife Dorothy (a friend of Margaret Clitherow), two strong Yorkshire Catholics.
26. On the influence of Greek romance on hagiography in the sixteenth century, see Helen White, *Tudor Books of Saints and Martyrs* (Madison: University of Wisconsin Press, 1963), 279–90.
27. See 'A True Report of the Life and Martyrdom of Mrs. Margaret Clitherow', in *The Troubles of Our Catholic Forefathers Related by Themselves*, ed. John Morris, vol. 3 (London: Burns and Oates, 1877). Citations of Mush's biography are from this text.
28. An earlier confessor had been William Hart, who was tried and executed in 1583 (Claridge, 60). Claridge states that he was 'the priest who perhaps more than any other influenced Margaret Clitherow in both life and death' (94).
29. For a discussion of how Margaret Clitherow was attracted into the cult of martyrdom associated with Jesuit spirituality, see Claire Cross, 'An Elizabethan Martyrologist and His Martyr: John Mush and Margaret Clitherow', in *Martyrs and Martyrologies: Papers Read at the 1992 SummerMeeting and the 1993 Winter Meeting of The Ecclesiastical History Society*, ed. Diana Wood (Oxford: Blackwell Publishers for The Ecclesiastical History Society, 1993), 271–81.
30. Claridge, 182, corrects Morris's use of the word 'harlotry' here.
31. In another account (published from manuscript by Morris as 'Notes by a Prisoner in Ousebridge Kidcote') there is a description of the slanders of the Protestant ministers who tried to convert the martyr in her last days: 'when they saw they could by no means prevail, they used slanderous speeches against her, and said she was reported to be of evil demeanour with priests, using more familiarity with them than with her husband …' (Morris, 3: 309).
32. See Claridge, 113.
33. Ibid., 141, quoting from manuscript a phrase censored from Morris's text.
34. Ibid., ix, notes that Mush's biography, which circulated in manuscript in Catholic circles, inspired Jane Wiseman, 'when arraigned on the same charge as Margaret Clitherow … to follow the same course' and it also inspired Mary Ward, who founded an religious order active in the world in education and works of charity.
35. She was a convert to Catholicism who maintained a house for Jesuits in London and who died for her faith. See Henry Garnet's 11 March 1601 letter about her (letter to the Jesuit General, Arch. S.J. Rom., Anglia 172–83 – I am grateful to Thomas McCoog, S. J., who is editing Garnet's letters, for providing me with an English translation of this document).

36. Like Clitherow, she was sentenced to death after refusing to plead, then imprisoned, then finally executed in 1598. See *John Gerard: the Autobiography of an Elizabethan*, trans. Philip Caraman (London, New York, Toronto: Longmans, Green & Co., 1951), 52–4.

37. Henry Foley, S. J., *Records of the English Province of the Society of Jesus*, vol. 4 (London: Burns and Oates, 1878), 102, calls her Henry Garnet's 'patroness'. She and her sister kept several houses which the Jesuits used as a bases of operations, one in Baddesley Clinton in Warwickshire, another in London, and one in White Webbs at Enfield (see Rowlands, 158 and Foley 4: 84). See Garnet's letter to Anne Vaux of 3 April 1606.

38. She was Southwell's protector and 'especiall frende' (to whom he dedicated his *Epistle of Comfort*).

39. See *The Life of the Most Honourable and Vertuous La. Magdalen Viscountesse Montague* (St Omer, 1627). Largely protected against persecution because of her nobility and old age, she 'maintained three Priests in her house, and gave entertaynment to all that repayred to her' (26), making the Mass and the sacraments available to her family, servants and neighbors, so that her house was called 'Litle Rome' (29). Richard Smith, who later became the Bishop of Chalcedon, the head of the English secular clergy, wrote her biography as a model story of the (noble) recusant Englishwoman, who finally died exuding the 'odor of sanctity.' She was (literally) a towering figure in the Catholic Montague family. See also *An Elizabethan Recusant House, Comprising the Life of the Lady Magdalen, Viscountess Montague (1538–1608)*, ed. A. C. Southern (London: Sands, 1954).

40. The 'female Jesuit' who established her own order of uncloistered religious women that worked in England (and on the Continent) until it was suppressed in 1631. See Henriette Peters, *Mary Ward: a World in Contemplation*, trans. Helen Butterworth (Leominster, Hereforshire: Gracewing, 1994).

41. She was a descendent of Sir Thomas More who became a Benedictine nun and wrote *The Holy Practises of a Devine Lover or The Sainctly Ideots Devotions* (Paris, 1657).

42. See Elizabeth Cary, Lady Falkland, *The Tragedy of Mariam The Fair Queen of Jewry with The Lady Falkland: Her Life by One of her Daughters*, ed. Barry Weller and Margaret W. Ferguson (Berkeley, Los Angeles, London: University of California Press, 1994) for her biography and a discussion of her place in recusant women's literature.

43. For a good discussion of Henrietta Maria's court, see Caroline Hibbard, 'The Role of a Queen Consort: the Household and Court of Henrietta Maria, 1625–1642', in *Princes, Patronage, and the Nobility: The Court at the Beginning of the Modern Age c.1450–1650*, ed. Ronald G. Asch and Adolf M. Birke (London: The German Historical Institute and Oxford University Press, 1991), 393–414.

44. The Jesuits backed off a policy of active resistance in the last years of Queen Elizabeth's reign, though their reputation as activists persisted, re-energized by the government's successful association of the Jesuit superior, Henry Garnet, with the Gunpowder Treason. See

Peter Holmes, *Resistance and Compromise: the Political Thought of the Elizabethan Catholics* (Cambridge: Cambridge University Press, 1982), 205–23. On anti-Jesuitism as a particularly strong form of anti-Catholicism, see Carol Weiner, 'The Beleaguered Isle: A Study of Elizabethan and Early Jacobean Anti-Catholicism', *Past and Present* 51 (May 1971): 27–62, esp. 36–9, 43–4; see also 'The Myth of the Evil Jesuit' in Arnold Pritchard, *Catholic Loyalism in Elizabethan England* (Chapel Hill: University of North Carolina Press, 1979), 175–91.

45. See his *Dialogue betwixt a Secular Priest, and a Lay Gentleman…* (Rhemes, 1601). Queen Elizabeth's proclamation of 5 November 1602 banishing all Jesuit and secular priests made a distinction between the Jesuits, as 'men altogether alienated from their true allegiance … and devoted with all their might to the King of Spain' (Hughes and Larkin, 3: 251), and secular priests opposing the Jesuits, but it nonetheless mandated the expulsion of all Catholic priests' – leaving only the slim possibility that those priests who were willing to turn themselves in to the government and take a loyalty oath might be spared exile or punishment. The kind of toleration hoped for by the Appellants was out of the question.

46. William Barlow, *An Answer to a Catholike English-man* (1609), B2. For a particularly virulent attack on Persons, see the anti-Jesuit Appellant Anthony Copley's *Another Letter of Mr. A.C. to his Dis-Jesuited Kinseman* (1602).

47. R. Doleman, pseud., *A Conference about the Next Succession to the Crowne of Ingland* ([Antwerp], 1594). Persons may have co-authored this work with others. For a discussion of the hostile attitudes of English Protestants to Persons and to other Jesuits, see Victor Houliston, 'The Fabrication of the Myth of Father Parsons', *Recusant History* 22.2 (October 1994): 141–51.

48. *A Sparing Discoverie of our English Jesuits.* (n.p., 1601), a2.

49. Thomas James, *The Jesuits Downefall …* (Oxford, 1612), 3.

50. *Vox Populi. or Newes from Spayne …* (1620), A4^v.

51. See *Aphorismes. Or, Certaine Selected Points of the Doctrine of the Jesuits, with a treatise concerning their secret practises and Close studies* (1609), 15–16.

52. Supposedly, the Gunpowder Treason was a Jesuit plot from the start, undertaken because the Jesuits could not get what they wanted from new new king: '… this treason may properly be called Jesuiticall, as pertaining to the Jesuites … for they were the chiefe plotters and devisers thereof' (*Aphorismes*, 23). Thomas S. Nowak, 'Propaganda and the Pulpit: Robert Cecil, William Barlow and the Essex and Gunpowder Plots', in *The Witness of Times: Manifestations of Ideology in Seventeenth Century England*, ed. Katherine Z. Keller and Gerald J. Schiffhorst (Pittsburgh, PA: Duquesne University Press, 1993), 34–52, 264–7, points out in his discussion of William Barlow's sermons on the Essex Rebellion and on the Gunpowder Plot, that the Jesuits were propagandistically connected with both. In the case of the second conspiracy, however, the first Paul's Cross sermon 'insists that the plot was not a Catholic conspiracy at all, but the work of a few lone

fanatics' (48), but 'the subsequent Gunpowder sermons [over the next five decades] made slight use of Fawkes, preferring to blame the whole affair on the Jesuits and ... the Pope' (49). For a useful discussion of the Gunpowder Plot's reverberations in the literary texts of the time, see Wills's *Witches and Jesuits*.

53.   See Maltby, *The Black Legend*.
54.   For a discussion of the influence of French anti-Jesuit/anti-Spanish writing on England, see Lisa Ferraro Parmelee, *Good Newes from Fraunce: French Anti-League Propaganda in Late Elizabethan England* (Rochester: University of Rochester Press, 1996). Jean Lacouture, *Jesuits: a Multibiography*, trans. Jeremy Leggatt (Washington, DC: Counterpoint, 1995), 352, calls Paris 'the world capital of elegant Jesuit bashing' and Etienne Pasquier, the jurist who unsuccessfully represented the University of Paris's case against the Jesuits' petitioning to get their own school, as 'the true begetter of Jesuitophobia, the man who raised the phenomenon to the level of a literary genre'. Paquier's most influential anti-Jesuit work was published in English in 1602 as *The Jesuites catechisme*.
55.   This was simultaneous with the appointment of the Bishop of Chalcedon as ecclesiastical authority for England.
56.   Quoted in Jenny Wormald, 'Gunpowder, Treason, and Scots', *Journal of British Studies* 24 (April 1985): 147.
57.   This loyalty test was designed to produce self-incriminating evidence of (potential) treason by posing the hypothetical case to Catholics of a papally ordered invasion of England and asking whether the individual Catholic's loyalty would be to the Queen or the Pope.
58.   See Perez Zagorin, 'England and the Controversy over Mental Reservation', in *Ways of Lying: Dissimulation, Persecution, and Conformity in Early Modern Europe* (Cambrdige, MA: Harvard University Press, 1990), 186–220, Steven Mullaney, *The Place of the Stage: License, Play and Power in Renaissance England* (Chicago and London: University of Chicago Press, 1988), 116–34, and Janet E. Halley, 'Equivocation and the Legal Conflict over Religious Identity in Early Modern England', *Yale Journal of Law and the Humanities* 3 (1991): 33–52. Southwell was the first English Jesuit to use equivocation and the practice of mental reservation during his imprisonment, interrogations and trial. Garnet wrote his notorious treatise on equivocation, which circulated in manuscript, to defend Southwell's use of it. See Garnet's letter to Persons, 22 April 1598 (Stonyhurst Coll. P.552). A manuscript copy of the treatise, with Garnet's corrections (in anticipation of its publication) and with the marginal notes of Sir Edward Coke, who prosecuted Garnet after the Gunpowder Plot, is to be found in the Bodleian Library, Oxford among the Laudian manuscripts (No. 968 (E.45), 2821 – noted by Frank L. Huntley, 'Macbeth and the Background of Jesuitical Equivocation', *PMLA* 79 [1964]: 391).
59.   See pp. 113–14. Mariana defended the latter in his notorious *De Rege et Regis Institutione* (Toledo, 1599) – see Sidney Anglo, 'More Machiavellian than Machiavel', in *John Donne: Essays in Celebration*, ed. A. J. Smith (London: Methuen, 1972), 375. For a discussion of

Jesuit attitudes towards tyrannicide, see Thomas H. Clancy, S.J., *Papist Pamphleteers: The Allen–Persons Party and the Political Thought of the Counter-Reformation in England, 1572–1615* (Chicago: Loyola University Press, 1964), 96–106.

60. The Jesuits' association with the political assassinations of William of Orange in 1584 and the French King, Henry III, in 1589 are omitted.

61. J. C. H. Aveling, *The Handle and the Axe: The Catholic Recusants in England from Reformation to Emancipation* (London: Blond & Briggs, 1976), 77.

62. John Bossy, *The English Catholic Community 1570–1850* (New York: Oxford University Press, 1976), 182–94, points out that the numbers of Catholics grew steadily in the first half of the seventeenth century.

63. Thomas Scott, the Puritan polemicist who strongly opposed the Spanish Match, referred to Jesuits and those influenced by them as 'the Hispaniolated, and Romanized, natures in England' (*Vox Dei. The Voyce of God* [1623] in *Vox Populi, Vox Dei.Vox Regis.Digitus Dei et al.* [n.p., n.d.], 83.

64. See John W. O'Malley, S.J., *The First Jesuits* (Cambridge, MA: Harvard University Press, 1993), 147–9. On women and boys as dangerous occasions of scandal for Jesuits, see the set of instructions to Campion and Persons at the start of the English Jesuit mission: 'Familiar conversation with women, even the best of them, will be a thing to be shunned, as also with boys, thus preserving the decorum and gravity due to our state of life' (Persons, *Letters*, 320).

65. The sermon was printed as *A Counter-Plea to an Apostataes Pardon. A Sermon preached at Paules Crosse* (1618), cited in Millar MacClure, *The Paul's Cross Sermons 1534–1642* (Toronto: University of Toronto Press, 1958), 240. It did not go unnoticed that Queen Anne had a Scottish Jesuit confessor, Robert Abercrombie. For this information and for a discussion of Anne of Denmark's Catholicism, see Albert J. Loomie, S. J., 'King James I's Catholic Consort', *HLQ* 34 (1970–1): 303–16. Queen Anne was not the only woman close to throne about whom James had to worry. In 1602 James I expressed concern about the possibility that the Jesuits had converted Arabella Stuart, who was too close for comfort to the line of royal succession (*Letters of King James VI & I*, ed. G. P. V. Akrigg [Berkeley, Los Angeles, London: University of California Press, 1984], 191). In Caroline England, Protestant critics of the regime attacked 'the French Queen and her Jesuites' (*Jesuites Plots and Counsels Plainly discovered To the most unlearned* [1642]) – this, despite the fact that Henrietta Maria had less to do with Jesuits than with the Capuchins who arrived at her court in 1630 and the Oratorian priest who was her confessor (Hibbard, 'Role of a Queen Consort', 404).

66. [H. Compton,] *The Jesuites Intrigues* .... (London, 1669), 35–6.

67. *The Jesuits Character* .... (1642), A2^v–A3.

68. *The Letters of John Chamberlain*, ed. Norman Egbert McClure (1939; reprint, Westport, CT: Greenwood Press, 1979), 1: 392. I owe this reference to Donna Hamilton, who cites it in her book, *Shakespeare and the Politics of Protestant England* (New York and London: Harvester Wheatsheaf, 1992), 177.

69.   See Elizabeth Heale, 'Spenser's Malengine, Missionary Priests, and the Means of Justice', *RES*, n.s. 41 (1990): 171–84. Heale cites John Baxter's *A Toile for Two-Legged Foxes* (1600) as an anti-Jesuit work that utilizes come of the stock imagery found in Spenser's account.

70.   See Philip Caraman, *Henry Garnet, 1555–1606 and the Gunpowder Plot* (New York: Farrar, Straus & Co., 1964), 39, 129, 263.

71.   Foley 4: 110.

72.   Caroline Hibbard, *Charles I and the Popish Plot* (Chapel Hill: University of North Carolina Press, 1983), 66.

73.   Ibid., 66.

74.   James, *The Jesuits Downefall*, 41.

75.   Copley, *Another Letter*, G1ᵛ.

76.   *Anti-Coton, or A Refutation of Cottons Letter Dedicatorie: lately directed to the Queene Regent, for the Apologizing of the Jesuits Doctrine, touching the killing of Kings* (London, 1611), 66.

77.   John Gee, *The Foot out of the Snare* (1624), 61–2. Gee then describes how the Jesuits repeated this performance in other venues to deceive the gullible.

78.   *New Shreds of the Old Snare* (1624), 1–8. Further citations are in the text. Jesuit trickery in staged exorcisms are the especial target of Samuel Harsnett's *A Declaration of Egregious Popish Impostures* (1603). See the edition and commentary of F. W. Brownlow in *Shakespeare, Harsnett, and the Devils of Denham* (Newark: University of Delaware Press and London and Toronto: Associated Universities Presses, 1993).

79.   This is appended to *Aphorismes*. Other versions were printed as *Discoverie of the most secret and subtile practises of the Jesuites* (1610) and 'A Discoverie of the Secret Designes and Bloodie Projects of the Society of Jesuites of later yeares' (in *Two Spare Keyes to the Jesuites Cabinet* [1632], 39ff.).

80.   In *Ignatius His Conclave*, Donne associated Jesuit anti-monarchical attitudes with Protestant democratic resistance theory: he has Ignatius in Hell mention Knox, Buchanan and Goodman favourably (77). It was argued in the Star Chamber trials of Presbyterians in 1591 that they and the Jesuits posed similar threats to the state. See John Guy, 'The Elizabethan Establishment and the Ecclesiastical Polity', in *The Reign of Elizabeth I: Court and Culture in the Last Decade* (Cambridge: Cambridge University Press, 1995), 129. For a discussion of Catholic resistance theory in its contemporary context of political thought, see Holmes, 147–60. In the seventeenth century, however, Jesuits came to be associated with the strong defence of royal absolutism, so that it is not surprising to encounter in a republican, pro-Parliament pamphlet of 1642, the assumption that they are 'utterly against Parliaments, and all Government where Commons have any hand… . they laboured these 100. yeares as stories tell us, to bring people every where to slavery, and Kings to be absolute' (*Jesuites Plots and Counsels*, 2).

81.   For a discussion of Donne's association of Jesuits with Machiavellianism, see Anglo's essay in Smith, 349–84.

82. John Donne, *Ignatius His Conclave*, ed. T. S. Healy, S.J. (Oxford: Clarendon Press, 1969), 43. Further citations are within the text. Healy points out that the three reprintings of Donne's anti-Jesuit work came at politically significant times: 'That of 1626 corresponds to the first year of a new reign when, under a young monarch and his Catholic queen, there was a suspicion of a sharp rise in Catholic activity. The second reprinting came when that suspicion had become a self-evident conclusion from the conduct of the Court and the arrival in London in 1634 of Gregorio Panzini as papal observer. The third and last reprinting of the century came in 1680 in the middle of the stirs provoked by Titus Oates' (xxvii).

83. This is the mythic Pope Joan, a favourite target of Protestant scurrility. See C. A. Patrides, '''A Palpable hieroglyphick'': The Fable of Pope Joan', in *Premises and Motifs in Renaissance Thought and Literature* (Princeton: Princeton University Press, 1982), 152–81.

84. For a discussion of the political context of this play, see Thomas Middleton, *A Game at Chesse*, ed. R. C. Bald (Cambridge: Cambridge University Press, 1929), 1-18 and passim; Margot Heinemann, *Puritanism and Theatre: Thomas Middleton and Opposition Drama under the Early Stuarts* (Cambridge: Cambridge University Press, 1980), 151–71, and Thomas Cogswell, 'Thomas Middleton and the Court, 1624: A Game at Chess in Context', *HLQ* 47 (1984): 273–88. See the discussion of the popular celebrations accompanying Charles's and Buckingham's return in David Cressy, *Bonfires and Bells: National Memory and the Protestant Calendar in Elizabethan and Stuart England* (London: Weidenfeld and Nicolson, 1989), 93–109.

85. Thomas Middleton, *A Game at Chesse*, ed. T. H. Howard-Hill (Manchester and New York: Manchester University Press, 1993), 1.1.50–1. Further citations are from this text.

86. See 1.1.53–62, 109–15.

87. See, for example, 2.2.182 and 4.2.53–7, 111–32.

88. The Black Knight's Pawn says the Black Bishop's Pawn wears an 'epicene chasuble' (1.1.232). In *Ignatius His Convlave*, Donne associates sodomy with 'Ecclesiastique Princes' (39, 41, 43) and retails the false tale of Pier Liugi, Pope Paul III's son, who was supposed to have assaulted the Bishop of Fano (see Healy's notes, 123). Healy notes that Barnabe Barnes in *The Devil's Charter* (1607) has Pope Alexander VI try to seduce, then kill a young male courtier. Peter Lake, 'Anti-popery,' 75, remarks: 'for many Protestants buggery became an archetypically popish sin, not only because of its proverbially monastic provenance but also because, since it involved the abuse of natural faculties and impulses for unnatural ends, it perfectly symbolized the wider idolatry at the heart of popish religion.'

89. This would appear to be a code for celibacy and, possibly, homosexuality.

90. See Caroline Hibbard's discussion of the Habernfeld Plot and anti-Jesuit paranoia (*Charles I and the Popish Plot*, 157-62).

91. Jesuits and missionary priests, in the Biblical language of Revelation 9: 3, were called 'locusts' and 'venomed wasps' (*Letters of James I and*

VI, ed. Akrigg, 205) in Protestant discourse. In one of his sermons, Launcelot Andrewes described Jesuits as a monstrous locusts, 'a kind of creatures who have a man's face, woman's hair but lion's teeth, and their tails the stings of scorpions' (*Ninety-Six Sermons* [Oxford: J. H. Parker, 1841–43], 5: 75, quoted in Alvin Kernan, *Shakespeare, the King's Playwright: Theater in the Stuart Court, 1603–1613* [New Haven and London: Yale University Press, 1995], 75). John Gee refers to Jesuits also as 'the Locusts of the wildernesse, with their Scorpion-like tayles' (*The Foot out of the Snare*, 24). Alison Shell, 'Catholic Texts and Anti-Catholic Prejudice in the 17th-century Book Trade', in *Censorship and the Control of Print in England and France, 1600–1910*, ed. Robin Myers and Michael Harris (Winchester: St. Paul's Bibliographies, 1992), 43, points out 'Jesuits were often compared to the locusts of the Apocalypse.' See also Michael Questier, '"Like locusts over all the world": Conversion, Indoctrination and the Society of Jesus in late Elizabethan and Jacobean England', in Thomas M. McCoog, S.J., ed., *The Reckoned Expense: Edmund Campion and the Early English Jesuits* (Woodbridge, Suffolk: The Boydell Press, 1996), 265–6.

92.   Canto II, st. 9. I use the edition of this poem in *The English Spenserians: The Poetry of Giles Fletcher, George Wither, Michael Drayton, Phineas Fletcher, and Henry More*, ed. William B. Hunter, Jr. (Salt Lake City: University of Utah Press, 1977). Further citations are within the text.

93.   In his polemical assault on the pending match between Queen Elizabeth and the Catholic Duke of Alençon, John Stubbs had also used Solomon and Samson in a discussion of the evils of a mixed marriage (*John Stubbs's Gaping Gulf with Letters and Other Relevant Documents*, ed. Lloyd E. Berry [Charlottesville: University Press of Virginia for The Folger Shakespeare Library, 1968], 10).

94.   See J. B. Broadbent, *Some Graver Subject* (London: Chatto & Windus, 1960), 96, 126, 131, 183, and David Quint, *Epic and Empire* (Princeton: Princeton University Press, 1993), 270–81 (both cited by Wills, 174). For a discussion of the influence of the Gunpowder Plot and of Gunpowder Plot commemorative sermons on Milton's poetry, see Stella Purce Revard, *The War in Heaven* (Ithaca, NY: Cornell University Press, 1980), 87–107.

95.   See Cedric Brown's discussion in his article of the 'idolatrous consort' and its recurrence as a motif in Milton's work, culminating in *Samson Agonistes*, a poem in which Dalila, the foreign wife of a true believer, must be rejected by her godly spouse for her false religion.

2

Robert Persons and the Writer's Mission

Ronald Corthell

In *Authority and Representation in Early Modern Discourse* Robert Weimann argues that 'early modern England produced a vital and articulate setting within which traditional versions of authority could be intercepted by or subjected to the "imaginary puissance" (and empowerment) of the writer's, reader's, and interpreter's conscience'.[1] Catholic polemical writing does not typically figure in such accounts of what Weimann calls the 'reformation discord in authority', and, indeed, it would seem unlikely that a position identified with the papacy would contribute to the story of author-ial empowerment that Weimann tells. Catholic writers undoubtedly located authority in an institution that precluded the believer's own discursive practice.[2] 'What reason, rule, or foundation, have any of these men', writes Robert Persons of his Protestant adversaries, 'to beleeve their owne opinion, more then others, but only self will and fansie?'[3] While Persons undoubtedly subscribes to a position on reli-gious authority that differs profoundly from that of his opponent in controversy, his controverting nonetheless embeds him in the dis-cursive struggles of the late sixteenth century. His dismissal of the self-authorization of (Protestant) discourse must be examined in the light of his particular position in ideological debate and not treated as a transparent statement of a monolithic Catholic belief-system – such a belief-system, that is, as Protestant polemicists were given to representing as the Catholic threat.[4] As a missionary and writer, Persons might invoke the central institutional authority of Rome, but this authority was obtained through the arts of courtship and argumentation and it was reproduced from positions of varying intellectual and geographical distance from the center, at first in England and later on the Continent.[5] His writings, generated out of the changing circumstances of the English Mission, produce historically contingent 'reasons, rules, and foundations' for an English Catholic subject position.

The writings of Persons develop important arguments on questions of authority and obedience to both civil and ecclesiastical power, including theories of resistance to each. His work is characterized by a powerful, overtly ideological style of historical argumentation that responds to the changing conditions for English Catholics and represents a variety of Catholic subject-positions, from a divided recusant subject of power, to a subversive critic of Elizabethan politics, to an imaginary subject of a newly 'reformed' England. The ebb and flow of these arguments during the reign of Elizabeth has been carefully chronicled by Peter Holmes, building on the foundational work of John Bossy.[6] A major debate among these and other historians of English Catholicism has to do with the question of continuity and change in Catholic ideology over the course of Elizabeth's reign, Bossy emphasizing change that is to a considerable extent influenced by the Jesuit mission, Holmes and others stressing continuity. I do not address the historiographical controversies about Persons and the mission with a view to settling them; rather, I want to begin by picking up on separate points made by Bossy and Christopher Haigh, Bossy's chief opponent in the controversy over the history (and historiography) of Catholicism in early modern England. First, Bossy writes that the Catholic mission was a movement energized by a new generation of activist clerks (i.e., scholars) for whom Catholicism 'appeared not as a withdrawal from the Elizabethan order in favour of something older, but as a reaction against it in favour of something better'.[7] What deserves the further attention of literary scholars is the prominence of writing and publication among the activities engaged in by these humanistically educated priests. In his fascinating letters to superiors on the Continent, Persons repeatedly stresses the need for learned priests, 'well trained in Controversy' and 'familiar with polite letters' ('illi in humanioribus sunt literis exercitati'). For, he writes, '[T]here is nothing which helps and has helped and will protect in the future and spread our cause so much as the printing of Catholic books, whether of controversy or of devotion.'[8] Persons exemplifies the controversial writer described by David Loewenstein; he 'assumes an active and dynamic role in the historical process, which he attempts to shape and direct through his polemical discourse.'[9] The second point extends Loewenstein's observation to include not only the influencing of the historical process through polemical writing but also a production of the historical process as a discourse of controversy. Haigh, who would agree on the clerkly thesis of Bossy, vigorously disputes the notion that this band of heroic clerks succeeded in creating a 'vibrant new Catholicism of a devoted minority' that emerged at the end of the Tudor period. Rather, Haigh suggests, the new clerks succeeded in creating a *story* of Elizabethan Catholicism, beginning with the writing of Persons himself, who tells a 'fairy story' of the English Mission's effect on the Catholic community; that story 'has become part of the received historiography of Tudor England, accepted by Protestant historians explaining what they see as the popular appeal of the Reformation and by those Catholics who, like Parsons [*sic*], wish to disown the ramshackle medieval Church'.[10]

What impresses the 'lay' reader of this material is the intertwining of historical and historiographical controversies. Robert Persons's case for English Catholicism was to a considerable extent a revisionist argument about the history of England, and his writing bristles with examples culled from the historical record that he found in medieval and Tudor chronicles and the works of French and English historians. What is more, Persons was at the same time also engaged in writing a history-in-the-making account of the mission in letters and other pamphlets, an account that proved to be his most enduring success. Haigh, the modern professional historian, writes to extricate the story of post-Reformation English Catholicism from confessional biases, using the methods of modern historiography to debunk Persons's 'fairy story' and produce a reliable alternative. He nonetheless finds it necessary to identify himself as 'a non-Catholic historian' before emphasizing that it is not Persons and his fellow missionaries he wishes to criticize but *historians* 'who for 380 years have believed Robert Parsons' [*sic*] fairy story'.[11] In the history of religion in England, history and religion remain entangled enough to require a confessional aside in the production of scholarly authority.

The story that interests me is a subtext in Haigh's critiques of Bossy's discontinuity thesis, a historiographical tradition which, we have seen, Haigh traces to 'its origins in the polemical needs of post-Reformation writers'.[12] It is Weimann's story of the dispersal of 'authority and representation' into scholarly discourse. In the case of Persons's writing it is a story riddled with contradictions – between the claims of Catholic tradition as the privileged origin of authority and the practice of writing polemics whereby authority

appears 'as a *product of discursive activity*', between appeals to institutional 'authority derived from power and the power of a new,
subjective type of author-ity in the uses of discourse'.[13] Weimann
notes that this new discursive production of authority 'was not
confined to a Protestant context'.[14] I wish to suggest that the Jesuit
mission to England, operating at a number of sites and forced to
respond to shifting relations with power and changing political
conditions on the ground, so to speak, was another such context.
The Mission created Persons the *Catholic* writer but also Persons the
Catholic *writer*.

Writing and publishing were established as central activities of
the Mission before its pastoral work began in earnest.[15] En route to
the shires, after having met Catholic leaders in London to explain
the goals of the Mission, Edmund Campion and Persons were
approached by a Catholic prisoner, Thomas Pounde, who had
bribed his jailors in order to reach the missionaries and persuade
them to prepare a document that would accurately represent the
Mission and its purposes against the inevitable 'malignant reports'
that would be circulated by the authorities should Campion and
Persons, as was likely, be captured.[16] Although both men prepared
such documents, it was Campion's *Letter to the Council*, 'the great
bragge and challenge' as it was called by his opponents in controversy, that achieved notoriety after being unwisely circulated by
Pounde and obtained by the authorities. It appeared in print thanks
to the ironic controversialist convention of publishing your opponent's text with your refutation – in this case, in a pamphlet
by Meredith Hanmer entitled *The great bragge and challenge of
M. Champion a Iesuite* (1581), which, along with another anti-mission
work, was in turn answered by Persons in *A Brief Censure uppon two
bookes written in answere to M. Edmonde Campions offer of disputation*
(1581).

The titles of these books refer to one of the leading themes of
Campion's text, a call to scholarly and public debate of doctrinal
points controverted between Catholics and Protestants. Thomas M.
McCoog has discussed the roots of such 'challenges' in the
Protestant tradition and its profound influence on the training of
English Catholic clergy.[17] Evidence of such training is pervasive in
the *Letter*. While the third article mentions more traditional pastoral
charges – 'to preach the Gospel, to minister the Sacraments, to
instruct the simple, to reform sinners' – it is the last of this series –
'to confute errors' – which preoccupies Campion; in articles five, six,

seven, and eight Campion expands upon the call to disputation, confident that 'no one Protestant, nor all the Protestants living, nor any sect of our adversaries (howsoever they face men down in pulpits and overrule us in their kingdom of grammarians and unlearned ears) can maintain their doctrine in disputation'.[18] The fifth article specifies 'iii sortes of indifferent and quiet audiences':

> *the first* before your Honours, wherein I will discourse of religion, so far as it toucheth the common weale and your nobilities; *the second*, whereof I make more account, before the Doctors and Masters and chosen men of both Universityies, wherein I under-take to avow the faith of our Catholike Church by proofs innu-merable ... ; *the third* before the lawyers, spiritual and temporal, wherein I will justify the said faith by the common wisdom of the laws standing yet in force and practice. (154)

If the Queen, with her 'notable gifts of nature, learning, and princely education', would attend such a conference or hear a few of Campion's sermons, 'possibly her zeal of truth and love of her people shall incline her noble Grace to disfavour some proceedings hurtful to the Realm, and procure towards us oppressed more equitie' (154–5). And, once the Privy Council 'shall have heard these questions of religion opened faithfully', it will in its wisdom 'dis-countenance error when it is bewrayed, and hearken to those who would spend the best blood in their bodies for your salvation' (155).

This belief in the power of scholarly disputation to resolve deep-seated religious and political conflicts is also an abiding theme in Persons's writing. In the dedication of *A Brief Discours contayning certayne Reasons why Catholiques refuse to go to Church* (1580), one of his earliest and most influential pieces, he too suggests three kinds of conference: 'breefe scholasticall argumentes'; speeches on each side, either instantaneous or 'uppon studye, to aunswere the same'; or preaching before the Queen herself, 'our soverayne Princesse and mother'.[19] One reason for the repetition of the challenge is sug-gested in Persons's *Epistle of the Persecution of Catholickes in Englande* (trans. 1582) where he complains of a device whereby the author-ities forced Catholic prisoners to write out their opinions and then passed injunctions against 'such books as those, whiche they them-selves before had urged the Catholiques to write'.[20] This Catch-22, like other Protestant representations of Catholics and like the textual practice of controversy mentioned above (that is, of literally

containing an opponent's text within one's own response), seems to
support Stephen Greenblatt's oft-criticized thesis about the production and containment of subversion by establishment discourse.[21]
On the other hand, the missionaries' challenge to debate can be said
to function as a symbolic act of resistance to such strategies of containment, in the equivocal sense of symbolic action described by
Fredric Jameson (following Kenneth Burke). Campion's 'Challenge'
was produced in anticipation of his imprisonment, that is, in anticipation of his inability to act any longer; it was, in Jameson's phrase,
'at one and the same time the accomplishment of an act and the
latter's substitute, a way of acting on the world and of compensat-
ing for the impossibility of such action all at once'.[22] One of
Campion's hagiographic biographers captures this sense of symbolic action, following Persons in constructing the composition of
the 'Challenge' as a heroic act of grace under fire: "'Campion,' says
Persons, 'being a man of singular good-nature, and easy to be per-
suaded to whatever religion or piety inclined towards, rose from
the company [including Persons and Pounde], took a pen, and
seated himself at the end of the table, where in less than half an
hour he wrote the declaration which was soon to be most
famous.'"[23] In his stirring rhetorical performance Campion 'challenged' not only the authorities to whom he ostensibly directed his
letter, but also Catholic subjects divided by conflicting loyalties to
Church and State. In the confident writing of Campion, and
perhaps in Persons's writing about that writing as an act of saintly
sprezzatura, the reading subject could reconcile these conflicts and
regain a sense of unity and resolve.

   Like Campion's 'Challenge', Persons's *Brief Discours* (often cited
as the *Reasons of Refusall*) is also both a polemic and a piece of missionary writing, directed as much at Catholics as at the Elizabethan
authorities. The aims in addressing these two groups tend to work
at cross-purposes. On the one hand, the book defends recusancy
against the official charge that refusing to go to church constitutes a
political act against the interests of the State. Persons's defense is
part of a continual dispute among English Catholics and between
some Catholics and the Protestant authorities over the political
content of Catholicism in an English setting. In article 4 of the
'Challenge' Campion proclaims: 'I never had mind, and am strictly
forbidden by our Father that sent me, to deal in any respect with
matter of State or Policy of this realm, as things which appertain not
to my vocation' (154). Holmes points out that, indeed, both Gregory

XIII and the Jesuit leadership had in 1580 instructed Persons and the missionaries to avoid politics and enabled them 'openly and fully to express their loyalty to the Queen'; in *A True, Sincere and Modest Defense of English Catholics* (1584) William Allen responded to Burghley's allegations of Catholic political insurgency in *Execution of Justice in England* (1583) by insisting that the English Mission had only the spiritual goal of ministering to English Catholics.[24] Thus Persons maintains in the *Discours,* and recusants argued before the authorities, that refusing to comply with the Act of Uniformity, which required church attendance on Sundays and holy days, is not a political act but a 'signe distinctive betwixt religion and religion' (17). Catholics who refuse to attend church remain loyal subjects of the realm.

In support of an argument for toleration of Catholic recusancy, Persons offers a variety of exercises in historical and ideological per-pectivism that, somewhat paradoxically, foreground the cultural variability of religion while also asserting the absolute and universal privilege of conscience in religious matters. For example, he argues that 'if a Gentile [by which I think he means a non-Jew or a non-Christian] should for feare, saye or sweare that there were a Messias ... yet unto the doer, it should be a damnable sinne, because it seemed nought in his judgement and conscience'; for this reason, he notes, Catholics do not enforce their religion, even in the Indies and Turkey (**iy^{r-v}).[25] To those who would urge an occasional church attendance for convenience sake, Persons counters with a hypothetical example of early Christians agreeing to go along with the Jewish religion; surely, he implies, we would not expect such time-serving on the part of that heroic community. But recent history, more than historical imagination, provides an object lesson in the dangers of forced religious observance, for it was not long ago that Protestants found themselves to be 'recusants' in Catholic countries; thus, in demanding church attendance, they contradict their own practice elsewhere (52^v).

This perspectivism threatens to open onto the ideological dimension of religious experience. By this I mean only that Persons seems to appreciate the degree to which holding a religious belief places the believer in a political position – one, in fact, that can circulate between persons of different faiths, depending on time and place (one can be a Catholic or a Protestant recusant); in the confessional wars, what goes around comes around. This realization, however, does not seem to affect the certitude and conviction of controversial writers. Persons could use historical perspectivism to argue a point with his Protestant opponents, but in addressing his Catholic readers, he could be uncompromising in his insistence that 'onelye the Catholycke Religion is truth, and that al other new doctrines, and religions, are false religions, as all new gods are false gods' (3ᵛ).

As Alexandra Walsham points out in her study of church papists, 'recusancy propaganda [including, prominently, the *Discours*] ... collapses any uneasy distinction between 'devotional' and 'polemical' writings'.[26] Framed as an answer to a letter received from 'A Gentleman in England, towching the late imprisonment of Catholiques ther', but actually composed and published in England (at the secret press set up by Persons outside London), the *Discours* on 'why Catholiques refuse to goe to Church' was actually a discourse on why Catholic gentlemen should stop going to church. Bossy supports the view of some scholars that, because the constraining force of loss of family property 'did not arise until after the statute of 1581', the Catholics, and Catholic gentry in particular, whom Persons addresses were attending church to avoid excommunication – put more affirmatively, out of 'a positive attachment to the general life of the community'. Where the gentry lived by an unarticulated disinction between public and private life, which included a liberty of conscience as well as a sense of 'a sphere of public religious activity in which the Queen had the right to take such steps as she saw fit' and expect dutiful compliance from her subjects, Persons and the Mission represented Elizabeth's government as a repressive regime, claiming that Catholic subjects 'did things under constraint which actually they did from choice'.[27] Persons challenges the implicit distinction by which the Catholic gentry lived; he is telling these lay Catholics that it will not do to blame Elizabeth or evil counsellors for their conformity, that the 'private' religious commitment must control the public observance of religion as well.

According to Walsham, pro-recusancy tracts like the *Brief Discours* 'embodied a reassertion of clerical mastery over individuals who ... impertinently supposed they could better assess their spiritual health than the official custodians of their souls'.[28] But in seeking to rehabilitate church papists, Walsham may be confusing two kinds of 'clerical mastery'. To be sure, Persons was a Jesuit priest, and he and his fellow 'missionaries' were engaged in a project of reclaiming the lost souls of the English Catholic laity. But his assertions of authority are generally based not on sacerdotal privilege but on the production of arguments informed, so it is claimed, by superior scholarship; he frequently displays what might be construed as a scholar's disregard for uninformed interpretation of scripture by both 'Sun-shyne doctors' and lay readers.[29] Persons fashions himself not as a priest but as a writer – of advertisements, apologies, censures, conferences, directories, discourses, discoveries, epistles, memorials, treatises, 'ward-words' and 'warn-words', to draw from titles of his works. What missionary resistance writers like Persons were about was the production of texts for a *discourse* of recusancy in the sense of a social practice whereby Catholics are enabled to signify themselves as Catholic subjects.[30]

The nine reasons of refusal set forth by Persons display a high degree of redundancy and have as their common goal the preservation of a unified subject position. A simple listing of the reasons underscores Persons's central concern about the potential division or contamination of the Catholic subject who attends church services; in going to church Catholics risk a variety of threats to their integrity, including infection, scandal, schism, participation (God might interpret attendance to mean consent to heretical practices), dissimulation ('trecherie to God almightie, and a very dangerous matter') and exposure to a 'noughty service' (33ᵛ). The reasons may all be reduced to one: church attendance is 'a signe distinctive betwixt religion and religion'. Within the Protestant hegemony, Persons argues, church attendance marks one as a Protestant while refusal to attend church is the mark of Catholicism. It is imperative, then, for Catholics to signify who they are by means of their recusancy, for 'what doth make a thing to be a proper and peculiar signe, but the judgment and opinion of men?' (17). Walsham sneers at this 'theory of subjectivity' whereby 'what in heretics' prejudiced perception was the earmark of a 'papist' naturally and necessarily became 'the proper and peculiar signe of a true Cathol[i]que', but one could also argue that Persons here displays an understanding of the embeddedness of subjectivities in social process.[31] This understanding can coexist with a belief in the absolute authority of individual conscience in determining the rightness or wrongness of an action. As noted earlier, Persons uses the hypothetical case of a nonbeliever who, for fear of retribution, affirms a Messiah; 'yet unto the doer, it should be a damnable sinne, because it seemes nought in his judgment and conscience' (**iy). Affirming a savior signifies that one is a Christian; one cannot be both a believer and a nonbeliever. Private religious commitment and public religious observance are never, for Persons, independent of one another. In the *Brief Discours*, religion and religious identity are produced as signifying practices.

In something like a Liar's Paradox, Persons's tenth 'reason of refusall' reprises the perspectivism I have already noted above. Catholics should refuse to go to church because infidels and heretics have practiced and promoted the same kind of nonconformity. In forcing church attendance, Protestants 'goe quit against their own doctrine and example' (52^v–3). If this reason be allowed, however, what becomes of the 'signe distinctive betwixt religion and religion'? As Walsham observes, 'abhorrence of conformity constituted a region of ideological common ground'.[32] Two answers to this question are implied in the *Brief Discours*. First, as a missionary might be well situated to notice, signs can only be 'distinctive' within a specific discursive context. Refusing to go to church would not, in England in 1580, signify a commitment to Protestantism. Recusancy, it is important to remember, was a practice advocated in response to specific conditions and statutes, and it was often promoted, as in the *Brief Discours*, in the context of a plea for toleration that would, presumably, lead to a change in those conditions and in the practice of recusancy. Second, in making these pleas for toleration, Persons insists that Catholics are different from Protestants. The book opens by suggesting in the dedication that Catholicism produces more obedient subjects than the sects of Luther and Wyclif, and it closes with another reminder of the Catholic doctrine of obedience to secular power. Granting Catholics the freedom to practice their religion would not affect their reverence for the secular authority embodied in the Queen. This portrayal of Catholicism as allied with authority and tradition is also supported by Persons's representation of the Catholic Church as the mother of Protestants, Puritans and 'howsholders of Love', besides all other newly born sects in England, and the Queen as mother of her Catholic children.

In the process of explicating the Mission's ideology of political non-resistance, which denied a link between religious and political practice, Persons rather astonishingly implies a link – namely, that Catholicism produces loyal political subjects. Both Mission ideology and Persons's interpretation of it were critiqued by another Catholic writer, Alban Langdale, who answered the *Brief Discourse* by arguing that church attendance was not a 'signe distinctiue' between Catholic and Protestant but 'betwene a trew subiect and a rebbell'. Langdale reasons that since many Puritans also refuse to attend and since many who regard themselves as Catholics (known to Protestants as 'church papists') do attend Protestant services, recusancy cannot be the signifier of the true Catholic.[33] Each Catholic must 'weighe his owne case' in deciding whether attendance was 'in his owen nature a thinge indifferent' and warranted by circumstances.[34] As Lowell Gallagher notes, 'both Persons and Langdale, advocating opposite kinds of behavior, were asserting a distinction [between religious and political spheres] that in practice could not hold'[35] and that, as I have noted, does not even hold in Persons's own text. Persons refuses to acknowledge the political aspect of church attendance, while Langdale ignores its religious significance.[36] The Elizabethan authorities, I assume, would not have been reassured by either position.

How, then, does one decide what going to church signifies, since Catholics themselves were apparently divided on the issue? There are really two ways of answering the question, both of them implied in Persons's 'Reasons'. On the one hand, individual Catholics must search their consciences to determine whether, under specific circumstances, church attendance might signify something other than a religious allegiance. We know that in their pastoral work the missionaries used casuistry to allow for occasional church attendance under certain conditions; Holmes has identified Persons, in fact, as a co-author of one such casuistical pastoral manual.[37] But again, Persons belonged to a new generation of clerks who emphasized creativity and change over more traditional duties associated with pastoral care; as Bossy points out, Cardinal Allen proposed that the missionaries 'must not wait for better times, but make them',[38] and in the case of Persons, this activism took the form of writing and publishing books. In print, 'that forum in which the politics of early modern religion was increasingly being played out',[39] books like *A Brief Discours* created the Catholic as a subject of discourse – a subject whose religious practice was a 'signe distinctive betwixt religion and religion' and whose position was 'authorized' by the clarity and force of writers like Persons.

In the mid-1580s, partly owing to developments in France and partly to increasing levels of suppression in England, Persons abandoned in print the original Mission ideology of indifference to politics.[40] His name has long been associated with the brilliant satirical dialogue best known by the title *Leicester's Commonwealth*, which attributes the persecution of Catholics along with a multitude of other ills entirely to the tyrannical manipulations of the Earl of Leicester, portrayed as a consummate stage-Machiavel intent on putting himself or the Earl of Huntington on the throne. Although Persons was certainly involved in the publication and dissemination of this work, modern scholars have strongly challenged his authorship.[41] We are on firmer ground with 'R. Doleman', the pseudonym Persons used for *A Conference about the next succession to the crowne of Ingland* (1594). A powerful work that demonstrates how commitment to a minority religious position could produce both political fantasies and solid critique, the *Conference* is cast in the favorite humanist form of learned dialogue and continues the trend I have been noting of a dispersal of authority into scholarly discourse.

Historiography is Persons's scholarly discourse of choice. By addressing the *Conference* to the Earl of Essex, who is thanked for 'favours receaved from your noble ancestors', Persons boldly politicizes his own excursion into English history. The *Conference* is at once a bizarre historical argument for the claims of the Infanta to the English Crown and a brilliant historical justification of the right to resist a bad ruler and alter the succession. The second part of the treatise includes an extended reading of the history of the English succession since the Conquest, with particular emphasis on 'the great and generall controversie and contention betweene the two houses royal of Lancaster and York'. Noting the historiographical struggle for control over the story of Bolingbroke's takeover, Persons foregrounds historical writing as itself a form of political discourse:

> And truly if we looke into diuers histories recordes and authors which have written of this matter, we shal find that euery one of them speaketh commonly according to the tyme wherin they liued, for that al such as wrote in the tyme of the house of Lancaster, they make the title of Lancaster very cleare, and vndoubted, but such others as wrote since that tyme (whiles the house of Yorke hath held the scepter) they haue spoken in far different manner.[42]

This historicizing of historiography is consistent with Persons's outlook on forms of government as human creations devised to meet particular historical challenges. In Chapter 7 of the first part of the *Conference* Persons reviews Hebrew, Spanish, French and

English examples of altered successions, emphasizing that 'the realme of Ingland hath had as great varietie, changes and diversitie, in the races of their kinges, as any one realme in the World' (I, 178). At the same time, Persons asserts his own scholarly objectivity; given the political agendas of his sources, he writes, 'the best waye I suppose wilbe, not so much to consider what historiographers do say according to their affections, or interests, as what reasons, and profes be alleged of euery side, for that by this, we shal more easely come to iudge where the right or wrong doth lye' (II, 57). Thus, Persons implies, a political conflict re-presented in an historiographical controversy can be resolved by the application of an historical method of 'reasons and profes' which, in turn, serves another political interest.

This historical argument, which draws in large part on the works of Polydore Vergil (who is identified by Persons as a Lancastrian), Holinshed, and Stow, authorizes a theory of political resistance. In a nuanced reading of 1 Peter 2: 13, Persons follows the Rheims New Testament – 'Be subject therefore to every human creature for God, whether it be to king, as excelling, or to rulers as sent by Him to the revenge of malefactors' – which glossed the term 'creature' as indicating that temporal rulers are creatures and receive their authority from the commonwealth.[43] Arguing against theories of absolutism, Persons locates the Prince as a subject: 'al law both natural, national, and positiue, doth teach vs, that Princes are subiect to law & order, and that the common wealth which gaue them ther authority for the common good of al, may also retrayne or take the same away agayne, if they abuse it to the common evel' (I. 72). His reading of the historical sources reveals that the Commonwealth has traditionally conferred this authority on the monarch through the coronation oath, a kind of social contract whereby 'both the Prince and subiect do come to know and agree vppon their duetyes and obligations the one towards the other' (I, 81).

Persons views the writing and reading of history as ideologically informed practices; historiography becomes the subject of controversy. Medieval and Tudor Chronicles, as well as court histories like Polydore Vergil's, could be searched to support an argument for the Infanta. What is more, counter-histories of Catholicism in England needed to be written in order to refute the Protestant reading of English history represented in such works as Francis Hastings's *Watch-word to All Religious and True-hearted Englishmen*, which drew heavily on Foxe's *Book of Martyrs*. In his *Treatise of the Three*

Conversions of England from Paganism to Christian Religion (1603) Persons attempts an exposé of 'the notorious falshood, shifts & sleights' of 'the Fox'.[44] Finally, a history of the present, of the Mission itself, was needed; indeed, as Haigh implies in his dismissal of Persons's triumphal 'fairy story', writing the history of the Mission was, in a manner of speaking, the Mission itself.

What I am describing as a dispersal of Catholic authority into the discourse of historical controversy is balanced in Persons's writing by a countervailing dream of an end of history and of discourse. This imaginary aspect of his resistance writing is most fully exemplified by the 'Memorial of the Reformation of England', a work composed in 1596 and thus at the end of the period of Elizabethan Catholic political resistance. Described as 'an ecclesiastical Utopia' by the anti-Jesuit lay Catholic Anthony Copley, who never read it, the 'Memorial' was in fact a master-plan for the recreation of English society after the imagined restoration of Catholicism.[45] The book is divided into three parts, the first 'Touching the whole Body [of England]', the second concerning the clergy, and the third the laity; the divisions reflect Persons's belief that 'one principal cause' of the religious crisis in England 'hath been the Emulation and Disunion' of the clergy and the laity, and that the reunion of these groups would require the settling of disputes 'about Jurisdiction, Possessions, Revenues, Duties, Prerogatives, Exemptions, and the like' between the temporal and spiritual parties, but also the fashioning of a modern clergy prepared to deal with the challenges of recreating English society. Richly detailed in its suggestions for reforming a wide range of institutions and practices, with particular emphasis on the educational system, the 'Memorial' is, in J. J. Scarisbrick's words, 'a grand design for a theocracy – blatantly clerical, triumphalist and ultramontane, but something new, and something beyond any previous order'.[46]

Something like this form of political imagination had been defended in the opening pages of *Leicester's Commonwealth*. Disputing the government's charges of treason against religious minorities, the work distinguishes between a 'direct' impugning of the state in an article of religious belief and an 'indirect' form of treason characterized by a hidden desire for a change of state favorable to one's religious position: religious minorities, both Papist and Puritan, 'do wish (no doubt) in their hearts that they had a prince and state of their owne religion', but this secret wish, which could be construed as treasonous, should only be punished when it issues in actions against the state.[47] It was, of course, fear of precisely such hidden desires that contributed to repressive measures against minorities.

Like Campion's 'Challenge', the 'Memorial' seems not to have been intended for immediate publication; indeed, Holmes suggests that, given European Catholicism's shift towards a preference for peace and non-resistance at the time of its composition, the tract is 'almost a pipe-dream: what to do if the restoration comes rather than when it comes'.[48] It did not come until 1685 when, according to Edward Gee, who published the book in 1690, a copy was presented by a Jesuit to the Catholic James II upon his accession. In the time-honored tradition of controversial writing, Gee published Persons's text as a piece of *anti*-Catholic propaganda, with the additional title of *The Jesuit's Memorial for the Destruction of the Church of England*, and included 'Animadversions' following each chapter of the first part of the 'Memorial', a life of Persons, and a history of the Jesuit mission.[49]

William Watson, an anti-Jesuit secular priest who never read the 'Memorial', accused Persons of making 'a Puritanian division of the ecclesiastical estate' in the tract, and while Watson's specific accusations of Puritanism were sheer fantasies, Scarisbrick has detailed similarities between the 'Memorial' and Puritan notions of reformation.[50] Indeed, the 'Memorial' matches in several important respects characteristics of utopian writing recently described by James Holstun in his study of Puritan utopias of the seventeenth century. Holstun argues that 'the rebirth of utopian writing in the Renaissance is the product of a new encounter between a body of texts and a subject matter: the displaced population'.[51] While Jesuit writing in this vein is typically associated with the missions in New Spain, the English Mission entailed a similar encounter. I have noted how in Persons's work the displaced Catholic subject is reclaimed through a reading and writing of English history, including the history of the Mission itself. In the 'Memorial' this historical approach is counterbalanced by utopian themes that Holstun gathers under the Weberian concept of rationalization – 'that process by which an array of preexistent particulars is ordered, sorted into manageable groups, submitted to a procedure, and above all made *calculable*'.[52] This process has, following Weber, generally been associated with aspects of the Protestant ethic, and Holstun tends to uphold Weber's distinction between Protestant

and non-Protestant Europe, noting that while '[we] can certainly
see a rational critique of custom in the writings of the Roman
Catholic utopists' (by whom he means More, Machiavelli in *The
Discourses*, and Campanella), 'these writings remained largely unrealized, suggesting that, as Weber argues, the impulse to rationalize
encountered greater customary resistance in non-Protestant
nations'.[53] The context of the 'Memorial' was, of course, somewhat
different from that assumed in Holstun's statement. The author was
a radical activist writing against both a Protestant establishment
and, it turned out, the silent (and sometimes not so silent) majority
of his co-religionists in England. What is more, his efforts
in England were often constrained by political developments and
ideological shifts on the Continent. The plans for the true reformation of England remained unrealized because of conflicts and
changes within Catholicism, both English and ultramontane, as well
as the Protestant resistance to ultramontanism, and not simply
because of a monolithic Catholic traditionalism.

Persons's vision is aggressively reformist, not traditionalist; his
appeal is not to the antiquity that draws Donne's satirical type of
the English Catholic, 'Mirreus', who seeks true religion

> ... at Rome, there, because hee doth know
> That shee was there a thousand yeares agoe,
> He loves her ragges so, as wee here obey
> The statecloth where the Prince sate yesterday.[54]

On the contrary, Persons's rhetoric moves with a passion and zeal
we tend to associate with radical Protestantism. 'Considering the
present State of *England*, under Persecution', Persons envisages reformation 'as the Reformation or Purification of Gold as when it
cometh out of the fiery Furnace, without corruption, dregs or rust:
for so God himself compareth his True Church, and all his Elect
after their probation by the Fire of Tribulation' (12). In creating this
true reformed church, Catholics should 'look upon the Apostles and
their Successors, and upon the Primitive Church that had the force
of Christ's Spirit stirring and hot in them' (13). It is also, perhaps, a
mistake to emphasize too strongly, as Scarisbrick does, the ultramontanism of the 'Memorial'. Persons, in fact, stresses the
Englishness of his true reformation: 'the Reformation of *England*,
after this long and sharp Persecution, ought to be very perfect, full
and compleat, not respecting so much what some cold Catholicks

use to do in other Countries, where Spirit is decay'd, and Corruption crept in, as what may be done or ought to be done in *England'* (13). In a fascinating critique of the Council of Trent, Persons admits that 'it was constrained to accommodate it self in many things to the capacity of that decay'd State of Christendom which then they found'; yet even this diluted medicine, he notes, has been rejected 'by reason of the general Corruption grown into Men's Lives and Customs, for purging whereof even unto the quick, it is supposed that God hath sent this Fire of Heresie into Christendom' (13–14). Whereas the Council tried to 'repair an old ancient House', an English Catholic king and Parliament will be able 'to begin of new and to build from the very foundation the external face of our Catholick Church, and to follow the Model which themselves will chuse' (15–16). In something of an inversion of ultramontanism, Persons imagines that this new English Church will 'be a pattern of true Christianity to the rest of the World' (16). Unlike the Puritan utopists studied by Holstun, however, Persons backs away from millennialism. If the model of reformation chosen by the English is 'a good and perfect' one, Persons writes, 'it will endure at least for a time'. This measured projection is consistent with Persons's self-presentation throughout his career: he is an historian not a prophet.

The 'Memorial' contains a wealth of practical recommendations for the remaking of the English Church, and society. Some of these were learned through the mistakes made during Mary's reign, which is repeatedly used as a negative example in the 'Memorial'. Persons writes of negligence and 'shuffled up' arrangements during the Marian restoration, including, prominently, the continued holding of former church properties by non-Catholics and the failure to discipline lapsed clergymen ('many Priests that had fallen and married in King *Edward's* Days, were admitted presently to the Altar, without other satisfaction than only to send their Concubines out of Men's sight'). The restoration was a game of musical chairs; or, as Persons described it, 'the matter went as a Stage-Play, where men do change their Persons and Parts, without changing their Minds or Affection' (20–1). Persons's envisaged restoration will entail the reclamation of both the infrastructure of the English Church as well as the hearts and minds of the English people. This two-fold project can be illustrated in the proposal for dealing with Church properties, whereby 'first God's Justice and the Church's Right in a certain sort should be substantially satisfied, and the

Possessor's Conscience assured, which is the principal' (54). Resolute heretics will be required to leave these properties, while those whose consciences have been 'assured' may continue occupation by paying an annual rent. All such lands and proceeds from lands would be 'assigned to some common Purses and Treasury' (55), administered by a Council of Reformation, to support 'good Colleges, Universities, Seminaries, Schools, for increasing of our Clergy, as also of divers Houses of other Orders, that do deal more in preaching and helping of Souls' (57).

The Council of Reformation, which Persons supposed would require four to six years to complete its work, is perhaps the single most 'utopian' feature of the 'Memorial'. Its power and responsibilities would be virtually unlimited, embracing every facet of religious life from the national to the parish level. The Council would administer the true reformation of England in a highly systematic manner, based on clearly established needs and priorities. Abbey lands, for example, must not be returned to the monastic orders that originally held them, 'for that the Times and State of *England* are far other, and different from that they were, when these Lands were given; and consequently do require different provision and disposition of things, conformed to the present necessity and utility of the Realm' (56). This kind of rationalization also characterizes Persons's critiques and proposals for universities, colleges and even grammar schools; all facets of the educational enterprise – from curriculum to classroom design, from academic apparel to the appointment of porters to name just a few – are reviewed for their efficacy, and new ideas, such as colleges dedicated to research or to a disciplinary specialty, are proposed for the advancement of knowledge (new for England, that is – Persons enjoys displaying his cosmopolitanism and frequently makes mention of the broad European scope of his experience).

Consistent with this utopian rationalism is Persons's detailed plan for dealing with 'schismatics' ('close or weak Catholicks, that have fallen, denied, or dissembled their Religion') and 'heretics' (i.e., Protestants) at the outset of the Catholic reformation. Like the rational schemes of other early modern utopists, those of Persons can seem eminently sensible, unbelievably idealistic and, finally, unattractive. Persons is concerned, again apparently because of the Marian experience, that the individual's reconciliation to the church be accomplished with all 'due measure of Consideration' (31). It might be best, he writes, 'that Men of Ability and Capacity only should be employed, in receiving of these Reconciliations at the beginning'; what is more, 'some particular form were to be prescribed how it should be done, especially in great Persons, and Subjects of great importance' (33). Persons is willing to countenance, 'considering the present State of the Realm', a limited period ('some **few** *Years*') of toleration,

> with **particular Conditions** and Exceptions, that no meetings, assemblies, preaching or perverting of others be used, but that such as be quiet and modest People, and have never heard perhaps the grounds of Catholick Religion, may use the freedom of their Consciences, to ask, learn and to be instructed for the space prescribed, without danger of the Law or of any inquiry to be made upon them. (33–4)

The benefits of this procedure include bringing into the open and treating what 'otherwise would be dissembled and more infested', relaxing the working conditions 'for the true Conversion of Hereticks', and producing for the Prince knowledge of 'what Disposition of People he had within his Realm' (34–5).

In detailing the particular method for converting heretics Persons reverts to the now familiar topos of Campion's 'Challenge' – the formal debate, in this case a week-long series of debates, in Latin, 'in *London, Oxford, Cambridge,* or some other fit place, where all the Heads of Heresies might most conveniently have recourse' (36). In the characteristic manner of utopian writing, Persons imagines in considerable detail how such an event might be staged (literally, as 'There may be two high Seats, Stages, or Scaffolds appointed so as all may hear, and see' [37]). Each side, that of the Catholics and that of the 'Hereticks', will select three or four scholars to present its case, one of whom on each side will serve as chief presenter and another as notary. On alternating days one side will argue a previously announced point of controversy and be answered by the other side. The assistant debaters of each team will be permitted to make additions or changes to the presentation of the chief presenter. Notaries for both sides will compare notes after the presentation by each side until they reach agreement on what was actually said. A moderator for the debate, appointed by 'the Prince', will also, periodically and at the end of each day's proceedings, cause the notaries 'to read out aloud the Arguments, Answer, Reply, or Distinction, that hath been given' (39). After the week of public debate, the proceedings will be 'publickly shewed in Print, for the satisfaction of such as could not be present' (40).

Persons recommends one additional 'publick satisfaction' that would engage a leading scholar or prelate in comparing the writings of two opponents in controversy; works by a pair of opponents who wrote in English would be examined in a public forum in London, while those of Latin controversialists would be analyzed in Oxford or Cambridge. What is interesting about this exercise is its focus on the question of scholarly authority:

> the manner of this Conference might be, that one in Pulpit, or publick Audience, should read some Paragraph out of one of them, and confer presently the Authors which he citeth, and whether he citeth them truly or no; and to let the places be read publickly out of their own Authors; which may be prepared to be there present, and then the answer of the other might be read, and Authors also that he alledgeth; and for more indifferency of this Examination or Collation, there might be two Learned Men appointed, one of each side, a Protestant and a Catholick, to see that no fraud or injury be done to any Party, but only the Books examined sincerely. (42)

Religious conflicts are here subjected to the formal procedures of scholarship, including the use of expert referees to assure objectivity and the careful checking of sources; religious authority is thus produced by means of authoritative scholarship, meaning the accurate citation and honest use of authors.

Persons explicitly invokes Campion's earlier call to debate and constructs his imaginary disputations 'so as the ability of both sides, in opposing and answering the same thing, shall be seen; which the Protestants never durst permit to Father *Campion* and his Company, in their feigned Disputations' (37). But it is important to note that the context for the debate projected in the 'Memorial' has changed dramatically from the context of Campion's 'Challenge'. Persons is imagining a time when his currently oppressed religious minority will control the ideological state apparatus. There would presumably be no need to guard against marginalization and misrepresentation by the Protestant other, since Catholics would be in a position to regulate religious discourse. Persons writes, of course, with a total conviction of the rightness and truth of his cause; he knows ahead of time who must win the debate. Nonetheless, this religious conviction coincides to a considerable, if not surprising, degree with a faith in *scholarly* discourse as a means of reaching and choosing the truth; following the protocols of scholarly debate, learned men will conduct an indifferent examination of contested evidence, 'and seeing that the truth is but one, and cannot but appear by this collation', they will lay these controversies to rest. Although limited to the deliberations of only highly qualified experts, this phase of Persons's Catholic Reformation resembles the Protestant Reformation in its discursive production of religious authority, which, according to Weimann, 'became a product of writing, speaking, and reading, a result rather than primarily a constituent of representation'.[55]

On the other hand, it must be noted that Persons sharply limits this period of scholarly debate. There is some inconsistency about the time allotted to reconciliation; 'toleration' of the qualified sort described above may extend over a few years, yet the formal debates will take place over the course of one week! In any case, Persons does not envisage a Miltonic process of continual scholarly discussion in the public arena; once the truth is discerned, public disputation will end and private, informal interactions and social pressures will turn people away from heresy and towards Catholicism (43). He also limits the application of the scholarly method described above to those 'that have been deceived by error, and are of a good nature, and think they do well, and do hold a desire to know the truth, and follow the same, and finally do hope to be saved as good Christians, and do make account of an honest Conscience, though they be in Heresie' (43–4).[56] As 'for others that be either wilful Apostates, or malicious Persecuters, or obstinate Perverters of others, how they may be dealt withal, it belongeth not to a Man of my Vocation to suggest.' Ultimately, resisters will have to be turned over to government authorities, who are admonished to rule, like God, 'by Rewards and Chastisements': 'as he hath had a sweet hand to cherish the well-affected, so hath he a strong arm, to bind the Boysterous, Stubborn, and Rebellious' (44). These qualifications in the 'Memorial' create an effect similar to that Greenblatt describes in the reader of More's *Utopia*; an initial sense of flexibility and liberty is seriously undermined as the text unfolds.[57] The last act of the Council of Reformation will be the creation of 'some good and *sound manner of Inquisition* established for the conservation of that which they have planted' (98).[58] Persons's Catholic reformation shares in the Protestant Reformation's 'legacy of discord' which, Weimann asserts, 'was linked to the need to negotiate vital interests ideologically, to shift the medium through which power was appropriated from that of violence and tradition to that of discourse and argument'.[59] But although Persons recommended beginning the process of reforming England with a public argument, it was envisaged in the 'Memorial' as an argument to be won once and for all and enforced with violence.

The unpublished 'Memorial' constructs an imaginary subject unified and sustained by 'reformed' political, economic and educational institutions. By the time he published his next book, Persons, reluctantly and with his usual sense of historical contingency, has resigned himself to the 'legacy of discord'. As Elizabeth's reign approaches an end and controversies over the succession intensify, toleration seems the best goal. In *A Temperate Ward-word to the Turbulent and Seditious Wach-word of Sir Francis Hastings* Persons rips his opponent for claiming that England is a country at peace with itself except for the seditious activities of Jesuits: 'This is not a contention about *Terra Virginea*, where only we must beleeve *Sir Walter Rawleighes* Relations.'[60] Persons's strategy is to present Hastings as an opportunistic Puritan who flatters the Queen while sensing that a Puritan takeover of England is imminent. Catholics, on the other hand, are portrayed as the children of estranged parents, the Queen and the Pope: 'But now our sayd two parentes are fallen at debate, for which all their Catholique subiectes, who are children to them both, are hartelie sorie' (54). The political opportunism of Puritans is matched by their reliance on 'self will and fansie' in matters of religious belief (6); Puritan insistence on the primacy of scripture begs a host of questions concerning canonicity, translation, and interpretation (5). This attempt to drive a wedge between dissident Puritans and loyal Catholics is undermined by a recognition of their shared belief in the sovereignty of conscience. Puritans, he charges, conveniently forget their belief in the sovereignty of conscience in order to attack Catholics for exercising it (78); Marian Protestants, like Elizabethan Catholics, experienced the split between conscience and 'external obedience of his prince and naturall love of his country' (82). While once again insisting that Puritans like Hastings pose a greater threat to Elizabeth than do Roman Catholics, Persons nonetheless finds common cause with them. Turning to an idea that resembles the 'indirect treason' introduced in *Leicester's Commonwealth*, he insists that every subject has the right to 'inward desyres' for change; indeed, if one were able to open up the soul 'many thowsand inward sores and ulcers would be discovered, that now lye hidden, and is expedient that so they should remayne' (78–80).

This powerful image of an afflicted and politically charged Elizabethan inwardness is balanced by a closing vision that combines the national myth of a merry England with Persons's characteristic internationalist outlook and belief in scholarly disputation. This is to be a 'ioyful state' made up of 'al sorts of people merry, contented, loving and confident', where, 'as in Germany and other places', 'freely and confidently men might confer, and eche man shew his reason without feare, and heare an other mans argument without suspistion of fraud or violence to be used' (128). The goal remains the elimination of 'differences of religion', but these 'more easily perhaps would be taken away and union brought in' (128) by a process of free and open debate.

As a brilliant polemicist, Persons was centrally engaged in the discursive production of authority in post-Reformation England, yet his writings are also marked by an 'inward desyre' for an authority beyond discourse. The particular kind of 'author-ity' produced by his work derives from the coincidence of Mission activity and writing. For that first eventful year in England he is constantly on the run, forced to write in the priest-hole and publish from the secret press.[61] Then, in exile on the Continent, he is consumed with business, the *'principium negotium'* regarding the English Crown that he and Father General Aquaviva refer to in their correspondence about England, but also the business of writing. Indeed, all his business and his connections to England and to Rome are heavily dependent on his writing. Bossy has written about the toll exacted on Persons by this incessant activity.[62] But the evidence of Persons's writing also leaves no doubt that he was empowered by his doubly 'decentred' position. And the isolation seems to have produced a compensatory vision. The hope was that the Mission would one day produce 'a perfect Reformation of their Country'; so too, the writing that could only emerge out of 'the differences of religion' might one day produce a union. Persons's dream is a Catholic dream but it is also a writer's dream. When the dream failed, one could still write a 'fairy story' about the Mission, a story to be controverted in another time by another set of clerkly opponents.

NOTES

1. Weimann, *Authority and Representation in Early Modern Discourse*, ed. David Hillman (Baltimore and London: Johns Hopkins University Press, 1996), 29.
2. Weimann notes that in reformation discourse 'the location of authority ... was moved from any court of appeal given prior to the act of writing (and listening or reading) to what ... emerged, and was to be responded to, in the processing of discursive practice itself' (17).
3. Persons, *A Temperate Ward-word to the Turbulent & Seditious Wach-word of Sir Francis Hastings* (1599), 6.
4. On the representation of Catholicism as a vast, 'tightly controlled and conspiratorial' system, see Carol Z. Weiner, 'The Beleaguered Isle: a Study of Elizabethan and Early Jacobean Anti-Catholicism', *Past and Present* 51 (1971): 27–62, and Lacey Baldwin Smith, *Treason in Tudor England: Politics and Paranoia* (Princeton: Princeton University Press, 1986), 61–3.
5. In his new biography, Francis Edwards, S.J. writes admiringly of Persons's skill as a courtier while also capturing something of the complexity of his situation: 'With no more than the authority of superior of the Jesuit mission to England and subject to provincials wherever he resides, he becomes the advisor and confidant of princes and ambassadors, and the point of liaison for high political schemes taking him through most of western Europe except Germany' (*Robert Persons: the Biography of an Elizabethan Jesuit, 1546–1610* [St. Louis: Institutes of Jesuit Sources, 1995], 55). For a nuanced study of Persons's difficult relationships with superiors and patrons, see John Bossy, 'The Heart of Robert Persons', in *The Reckoned Expense: Edmund Campion and the Early English Jesuits*, ed. Thomas M. McCoog, S.J. (Woodbridge: Boydell Press, 1996), 141–58. I am grateful to Arthur Marotti for bringing these books to my attention.
6. Peter Holmes, *Resistance and Compromise: the Political Thought of the Elizabethan Catholics* (Cambridge: Cambridge University Press, 1982); I have followed Holmes's general outline of developing Mission ideology. Bossy's major contributions include 'The Character of Elizabethan Catholicism', *Past and Present* 21 (1962): 39–59, and *The English Catholic Community 1570–1850* (London: Darton, Longman & Todd, 1975). See also J. C. H. Aveling, *The Handle and the Axe* (London: Blond and Briggs, 1976), and Christopher Haigh, 'The Continuity of Catholicism in the English Reformation', *Past and Present* 93 (1981): 37–69, and 'From Monopoly to Minority: Catholicism in Early Modern England', *Transactions of the Royal Historical Society*, 5th Series, 31 (1981): 129–47. This is, perhaps, the place to acknowledge the influence of Bossy's writing on my characterization of the missionary writer.
7. Bossy, 'The Character of Elizabethan Catholicism', 44.
8. *Letters and Memorials of Father Robert Persons, S.J.*, vol. 1, ed. L. Hicks, S.J. (London: Catholic Record Society, 1942), 62, 106, 114, 107. Persons describes the distribution of Catholic books in a letter of August 1581

which he printed in his edition of Nicholas Sanders's *De Schismate Anglicano*, published in Rome in 1586; see *Letters and Memorials*, 1:85.

9. Loewenstein, *Milton and the Drama of History: Historical Vision, Iconoclasm, and the Literary Imagination* (New York: Cambridge University Press, 1990), 5.

10. Haigh, 'From Monopoly to Minority', 129, 147, 130. Haigh argues that the Jesuits fostered a seigneurial, as opposed to congregational or parochial, system of Catholicism, and that this resulted in the *loss* to the Church of the majority of Catholics while the gentry were then credited, by Persons et al., with *saving* Catholicism: '"The English Catholic Community", as brilliantly characterized by John Bossy, was not the successful product of a missionary triumph in the face of Protestantism and persecution. It was a rump community, the residue of a process of failure and decline in which whole regions and social groups were neglected and betrayed by the heroes of Robert Parsons' [*sic*] story' ('From Monopoly to Minority', 132). Haigh's argument about the failure of the Mission to capitalize on the residual strength of Catholic traditions is perhaps supported by Eamon Duffy's powerful study, *The Stripping of the Altars: Traditional Religion in England, c. 1400–c. 1580* (New Haven: Yale University Press, 1992), which portrays the triumph of Protestantism in England as the forcible imposition of a minority ideology on an unconvinced Catholic majority.

11. Haigh, 'From Monopoly to Minority', 147.

12. Haigh, 'The Continuity of Catholicism', 38.

13. Weimann, 'Discourse, Ideology, and the Crisis of Authority in Post-Reformation England', in *The Yearbook of Research in English and American Literature*, vol. 5 (Berlin: De Gruyter, 1987), 122, and '"Bifold Authority" in Reformation Discourse: Authorization, Representation, and Early Modern "Meaning"', in *Historical Criticism and the Challenge of Theory*, ed. Janet Lemarie Smarr (Urbana: University of Illinois Press, 1993), 168.

14. Weimann, *Authority and Representation*, 65.

15. On this point, see also Nancy Pollard Brown, 'Robert Southwell: The Mission of the Written Word', in *The Reckoned Expense*, 193–213.

16. I am following the account given in A. C. Southern, *Elizabethan Recusant Prose 1559–1582* (London: Sands and Co., 1950), 149–50. On the circumstances of publication and character of the statements prepared by Campion and Persons, see also Thomas M. McCoog, S.J., '"Playing the Champion": the Role of Disputation in the Jesuit Mission', in *The Reckoned Expense*, 119–39.

17. See McCoog, '"Playing the Champion"', 119–23.

18. *Letter to the Council*, in *Elizabethan Recusant Prose*, 154. References to the *Letter* are taken from this reprint and noted in my text.

19. *A Brief Discours Contayning certayne Reasons why Cathliques refuse to goe to Church* (Douai, 1580), 'Dedicatorie', n.p. References to this work will appear in my text.

20. *An Epistle of the Persecution of Cathlickes in Englande*, trans. (from French) G.T. (1582), 106.

21.   Greenblatt, 'Invisible Bullets', in *Shakespearean Negotiations: The Circulation of Social Energy in Renaissance England* (Berkeley and Los Angeles: University of California Press, 1988). On various strategies of representation of the Catholic threat, see Weiner, 'Beleaguered Isle', and Anthony Milton, *Catholic and Reformed: The Roman and Protestant Churches in English Protestant Thought 1600–1640* (Cambridge: Cambridge University Press, 1995).

22.   Jameson, 'The Symbolic Inference: Or, Kenneth Burke and Ideological Analysis', in *Representing Kenneth Burke, Selected Papers from the English Institute*, n.s. 6, ed. Hayden White and Margaret Brose (Baltimore: Johns Hopkins University Press, 1982), 88–9. See also Jameson's discussion of symbolic action in *The Political Unconscious: Narrative as a Socially Symbolic Act* (Ithaca: Cornell University Press, 1981), 78–82, *et infra*. On contradictions and their imaginary resolution in Campion's *Letter to the Council*, see my '"The secrecy of man": Recusant Discourse and the Elizabethan Subject', *English Literary Renaissance* 19 (1989): 272–90.

23.   Southern, *Elizabethan Recusant Prose*, 150, quoting Richard Simpson's biography, *Edmund Campion*, rev. edn (London: John Hodges, 1896). See also Persons's admiring accounts of Campion's extemporaneous rhetorical brilliance in his unpublished 'Life of Campian', summarized by McCoog in '"Playing the Champion"', 126.

24.   Holmes, 42. The Execution of Justice in England *by William Cecil and* A True, Sincere, and Modest Defense of English Catholics *by William Allen*, ed. Robert M. Kingdon (Ithaca: Cornell University Press, 1965).

25.   On the paradoxes and problems of conscience, see Lowell Gallagher, *Medusa's Gaze: Casuistry and Conscience in the Renaissance* (Stanford: Stanford University Press, 1991) and Katherine Eisaman Maus, *Inwardness and Theater in the English Renaissance* (Chicago: University of Chicago Press, 1995), 15–24.

26.   Walsham, *Church Papists: Catholicism, Conformity and Confessional Polemic in Early Modern England* (Royal Historical Society: Boydell Press, 1993), 26. Although he does not explicitly make this point, Anthony Milton implies a similar blurring of genres in anti-papal Protestant polemic of the earlier 1600s: 'a hatred of popery was seen as a positive manifestation of true religion, a testimony of the individual's commitment to God', and even 'one of the signs of election' (35, 36).

27.   Bossy, *English Catholic Community*, 124–5.

28.   Walsham, 27.

29.   See, for example, *A Temperate Ward-word to the Turbulent and Seditious Wach-word of Sir Francis Hastings* (1599), 12, 16; *The Warn-word to Sir Francis Hastinges Wast-word* (1602), L15^v.

30.   On discourse as social practice, see Robert Hodge and Gunther Kress, *Social Semiotics* (Ithaca: Cornell University Press, 1988), 5–6 *et passim*.

31.   Walsham, 34, quoting from *A Brief Discours*, 15–18. It is also worth noting that the social theory of signification (and identification) stated here receives a much more nuanced treatment in Persons's writing on equivocation, though even there he is extremely chary of playing fast and loose with the act of signification. See *A Treatise*

Tending to Mitigation towardes Catholicke-Subiects in England (1607), 275ff.

32. Walsham, 38.
33. The passage from Langdale's *A trestise to prove that attendance at the Protestant church was in itself no sin* (1580) is reprinted in Southern, 143.
34. Southern, 143. My comments on the Persons–Langdale exchange are indebted to Gallagher, 85–7. Gallagher proves a full account of the 'circumstances' cited by casuists that would warrant attendance at church.
35. Gallagher, 87.
36. They were not alone in this refusal; both Cardinal Allen and William Cecil, in the tracts mentioned above, denied what Weimann calls the 'intricate, changeful, and paradoxical' connections between religion and politics that permeated the English Reformation (Weimann, *Authority and Representation*, 53). Cecil's denial of any government attempt to meddle with religious beliefs occurs in the context of an argument supporting the justice of a statute requiring observance of a state religion; Allen's claim of purely spiritual motives, notes Wallace MacCaffrey, just as obdurately 'refuses to admit any link between the pastoral ministrations of the seminarians and the political intentions of the Papacy towards England' (*Queen Elizabeth and the Making of Policy, 1572–1588* [Princeton: Princeton University Press, 1981], 138).
37. Holmes, *Resistance and Compromise*, 102, and Holmes, ed., *Elizabethan Casuistry* (London: Catholic Record Society, 1981).
38. Bossy, 'Elizabethan Catholicism', 46.
39. Walsham, 71.
40. A fascinating part of the story of Persons's political activities, including his possible advocacy of a plot to assassinate Queen Elizabeth, is brought to light by Bossy in 'The Heart of Robert Persons', a careful and thoughtful study of his correspondence with Claudio Aquaviva, General of the Society of Jesus.
41. See D. C. Peck, ed., *Leicester's Commonwealth: The Copy of a Letter Written by a Master of Art of Cambridge (1584) and Related Documents* (Athens: Ohio University Press, 1985), esp. 13–32. Holmes accepts the work without comment as Persons's; Bossy, in 'The Heart of Robert Persons', is 'now inclined to think' that Persons wrote the book as well as publishing and distributing it (116).
42. See *A Conference about the Next Succession to the Crowne of Ingland* (1594), Part II, 56. Further citations to this edition are noted in my text by part and page number.
43. On this point, see Holmes, *Resistance and Compromise*, 148–9.
44. *A Treatise of the Three Conversions of England from Paganisme to Christian Religion* (1603), **2, 133.
45. Copley's phrase in his *Answer to a Letter of a Jesuited Gentleman* (1601) is quoted by J. J. Scarisbrick, 'Robert Persons's Plans for the "True" Reformation of England', in *Historical Perspectives: Studies in English Thought and Society in Honour of J. H. Plumb*, ed. Neil McKendrick

(London: Europa Publications, 1974), 34. The attacks of Copley and others on the 'Memorial' came in the context of the 'Archpriest controversy': the opposition by a group of priests known as the 'Appellants' to the appointment of George Blackwell as 'archpriest' or superior of the Mission. The Appellants strongly opposed the Jesuit theory and practice of resistance and used the 'Memorial', which they had not read, as evidence of a Jesuit plot for the overthrow of the Elizabethan regime. On the Appellants and the Archpriest Controversy, see Holmes, *Resistance and Compromise*, 186–204, and Arnold Pritchard, *Catholic Loyalism in Elizabethan England* (Chapel Hill: University of North Carolina Press, 1979), 192–201.

46. Scarisbrick, 39.
47. *Leicester's Commonwealth*, 67.
48. Holmes, *Resistance and Compromise*, 165.
49. See the dedication to Gee, ed., *The Jesuit's Memorial, for the Intended Reformation of England* (London, 1690). References to this edition of the 'Memorial' will appear in my text. Like the 'Memorial', *Leicester's Commonwealth* and *A Conference about the Next Succession* also survived their immediate contexts to be recycled into the controveries of a later time. See the reissues of *Leicester's Commonwealth* (1641) and *A Conference about the Next Succession* (1681).
50. The Appellant Watson's *Decacordon of Ten Quodlibeticall Questions* (1602) is quoted in Scarisbrick, 36; on Persons and Puritanism, see 39–41.
51. James Holstun, *A Rational Millenium: Puritan Utopias of Seventeenth-Century England and America* (New York: Oxford University Press, 1987), 34.
52. Ibid., 18.
53. Ibid., 22.
54. Satire III, Lines 45–8 in *The Complete English Poems of John Donne*, ed. C. A. Patrides (London: J. M. Dent, 1985), 226.
55. Weimann, *Authority and Representation*, 5.
56. On the honest conscience and its paradoxes, see Gallagher, ch. 2.
57. See Greenblatt, *Renaissance Self-Fashioning: From More to Shakespeare* (Chicago: University of Chicago Press, 1980), 40–1.
58. The phase of inquisition also marks a return of ultramontanism. England should follow the example of Spain or Italy or a combination of them both, but in some particulars, Spanish procedures 'are so necessary as without them, no matter of moment can be expected'; this includes papal delegates to oversee operations in England (99).
59. Weimann, *Authority and Representation*, 64.
60. *A Temperate Ward-word to the Turbulent and Seditous Wach-word of Sir Francis Hastings* (1599), 3. References to this work appear in my text.
61. On the 'Greenstreet House Press' set up by Persons, see Southern, *Elizabethan Recusant Prose*, 349–59 and Brown, 195.
62. By late 1585 'after three years or more of *negotia*, political or other, he was in some kind of a state of incipient breakdown' ('The Heart of Robert Persons', 155). See 148–53 on the '*principium negotium*' in the Persons–Aquaviva correspondence.

3

Parasitic Geographies: Manifesting Catholic Identity in Early Modern England

Julian Yates

On 17 July 1581, Edmund Campion, one of the founding fathers of the Jesuit Mission to England, was found hidden in a priest-hole at Lyford Grange, in Berkshire. Anthony Munday's account of the apprehension provides details of the search, but devotes most energy to an elaborate character-sketch of Campion. He examines Campion's upbringing, education, flight abroad, entry into the Society of Jesus, return to England, and opposition to the Queen, and discovers therein the genealogy of a traitor. This genealogy, however, amounts to more than a parental or pedagogical failure: it reveals a tale of travel, of flight, return and concealment. 'Neither remembering his dutie to God, loyaltie to his Prince, nor loove to his countrey: but hardening his hart more and more in that divellish obscuritie of life' (A2^v–A3),[1] Campion leaves England for the Continent and then returns home in order to 'seduce the hartes of her [the Queen's] looving Subiectes' with his 'perverse perswasions … till God at length made knowen this wicked and abhominable' course (A4^v). Munday's account of Campion's 'course' discloses an England infested by hidden traitors, by subjects who have deviated from the truth of a Protestant England towards Rome.

The job of the pursuivants, informers and propagandists who formed the strands of the state's embryonic intelligence system was to reveal the paths of these dissenting subjects, to apprehend the offenders, and so to root out the hidden intentions and secret location of England's Catholic community. Faced with the difficulty of manifesting the 'truth' of recusancy, these agents interrogated the

63

sites of recusant practice: the local structures of the Jesuit underground and the resistant figure of the Catholic subject. My aim in
this chapter is to read the practices of priest and pursuivants alike,
as coextensive gestures within a 'social network' organized, as
Michel de Certeau might say, by the 'hidden'.[2] Priest and pursuivant shared a common landscape, the 'topography' or symbolic
'geography' embedded in Munday's description of Campion's life.[3]
This 'geography' constitutes both the imagined space of recusancy
in early modern England and the very real terrain of Catholic resistance. For Catholics, it represented a terrain filled with obstacles, a
landscape that they had to negotiate in secret. For the authorities, it
was the fabric of a realm distorted by the hidden presence of a
Jesuit underground and dislocated by the existence of seminaries,
safe-houses and hiding-places of all kinds. The history of recusancy
and Catholic resistance in England throughout the sixteenth
century may then be read through the contest for control over these
spaces, and in contemporaries' notion that to be a Catholic was to
have a particular relationship to space, to England and its borders.

UNREADABLE BODIES

'A recusant', writes Godfrey Anstruther in the preface to his *Vaux of
Harrowden*, 'is one who refuses',[4] who objects or who resists. In its
more specialized use, the word refers to 'a Papist who refused to
resort to divine worship in Protestant churches'. While this refusal
marked a concerted effort on the part of Catholics to differentiate
themselves from their Protestant fellows and so to articulate the
presence of a viable and, crucially, visible Catholic community, the
authorities read this disobedience as evidence of a more general
and potentially more dangerous refusal of the bonds between sovereign and subject.[5] To the authorities, recusants were men and
women who held themselves apart, whose absence from Church
meant that they assembled elsewhere, that they met in private.
They were men and women who had closed their hearts to the
Queen and thus harbored secret, possibly treasonous, desires. As
Peter Lake notes, to 'many, if not most, educated Protestant English
people of the period, popery was an anti-religion, a perfectly sym-
metrical negative image of true Christianity. Anti-Christ was an
agent of Satan, sent in to the Church to corrupt and take it over
from within.'[6] The 'scandal' of recusancy was not, however, simply

this withholding of self from social and religious rituals. Recusancy was not a negative gesture, a mere 'refusal' of the state, so much as it was an act of assertion, expressing the desire to remain elsewhere and testifying to the fact that there were places, however circumscribed, that lay beyond the state's control. It was the existence of this 'elsewhere' – of the 'secrete caves, dennes, and holes, to which the Romish Foxe, that devoureth the innocent Lambes of Christ's foulde, resorteth daily' as the turncoat and propagandist, Thomas Bell, called them[7] – that contributed to the image of Catholics as a clandestine community working to undermine the realm.

While Queen Elizabeth may not have liked 'to make windows in men's hearts, and secret thoughts',[8] not all of her supporters shared her distaste for mental invasion. Such was the perceived difficulty of decoding Catholic intentions that, some way into *A Toil for Two-legged Foxes* (1600), John Baxter imagined this fanciful solution to the problem. 'When Iupiter had made man,' he observes,

> being delited with such a cunning peece of workmanship, he demaunded of Momus [to] finde fault, what he could spy, in so fine a feature and curious frame, out of square and worthie just reproof: Momus commended the proposition and comely disposition of the lineaments; but one thing (saith he) I like not well, that thou hast forgotten to place a window in his brest through which we might behold whether his heart and his tongue did accord. If a window were framed in the brests of these discontented catholikes, that her Majestie and the state-guiding counsell and all true friends to the kingdom might know their secret intentions … many false hearts would be found lurking under painted hoods, and cakes of foule cancred malice under meale mouthed protestations.[9]

This fantasy of absolute disclosure promises knowledge not merely of 'secret intentions' and 'false hearts' but of the relationship between tongue and heart, between secret meaning and outward appearance. For the master-geometer, with the power to 'square' irregular shapes, to compute the relationship between inside and outside so as to leave no remainder, there were no liars, no traitors, no recusants. By remodelling the body so as to elide the differences between inside and out, private and public, Momus eliminates the very need for surveillance at all. Baxter's fantasy was, of course, never an option for the Queen and her Council: the bodies of her

Catholic subjects remained opaque containers that resisted or re-
coiled from her authority. And so, in the absence of Baxter's 'just
reproof' – in both the juridical and geometric sense of the word –
knowledge of 'secret intentions' could be revealed only through the
continuous and inexact procedure of surveillance. The very inability
of vision to decode the meaning of Catholic bodies meant that more
careful surveillance was essential.

TURNING AWRY

In a letter to Elizabeth I dated 1588, Richard Topcliffe, chief priest-
hunter to the crown, delivered the following assessment of the
Jesuit mission to England. Since 'there be known 8 or 9 Seamenarye
Colledges at least beyond the seas for the nourishment of English,
Irishe, and Scottish youths in treason', he begins, and since 'yt were
known that there dyd arryve yearly from ... 2 Seamenaryes every
yearr about the number of 16 or 18 Seamenarye Priests into
Englande. Now it is thought that there doth arryve from those 8 or
9 Seamm. and Colledges not so few as 40 or 50 Jhezewitts and
Seamenarye Preestes, seedmen of treason.' This line of reasoning
leads him to conclude that 'Englande wil bee overflowen with treasons', for, 'when as the sayme 2 springs of treason, and 4 or 5 times
dooble the number of Springs or Seamenaryes Bee Burste, and so
yearelye fawlle and flowe into England'.[10] What alarms Topcliffe is
not the existence of seminaries on the Continent or the flow of men
and money abroad, but rather the imminent return of an ever-
growing number of priests. This arithmetic progression of returning
'seedmen' will, he thinks, eventually overwhelm the country and
bring both the State and the Anglican Church to ruin.[11]
   It is hardly surprising that, in the wake of the Armada, such a
'flow' of Catholic priests from abroad was identified with Spanish
interference. But, more importantly, Topcliffe's concern with the
growing number of returning priests discloses a significant story of
travel. It is possible to read his letter and deduce a set of movements, of turns, that define what it means to be a Jesuit, a seminary
priest and a recusant. While Topcliffe is obsessed with the return
journey of so many 'seedmen', his fear is predicated on a previous
inward turn towards Rome that produces a trajectory leading out of
England and towards the Continent. This mental, spiritual and con-
sequent physical 'turning' away from the 'truth' of a Protestant

England accords exactly with Michael Questier's observation that every conversion 'demonstrated the existence of a hidden fund of latent popery about which Protestants had every reason to be anxious'.[12]

The publication of Anthony Munday's *English Romayne Lyfe* in 1581, 'discovering the lives of Englishmen at Roome [and] the orders of the English Seminarie',[13] together with his revelations concerning the recently executed traitor, Edmund Campion, in a series of pamphlets, demonstrated that the first of these dislocations began at home. Catholic gentlemen fled abroad to what Elizabeth's proclamation against Jesuits of 1591 described as 'certain receptacles made to live in', where Englishmen are trained to become 'seedmen of treason'.[14] Within the walls of these seminaries, where the diet and 'airs' proved lethal to many, those fugitives who survived were said to be 'transformed', 'Jesuitized' or 'Jesuited'.[15] Whereas 'those that beheld the head of the Medusa were onely turned into stones',[16] these 'lost companions', the reformed fugitive Sir Lewis Lewkenor warned, were transformed 'into shapes much more horrible and monstrous'. They become 'creatures' of Spain, of Rome and of the Pope, who 'maintaines a sort of discontented fugitives in his Seminaries, as it were in so many Cages, where dieting them for the nonce, he easily techeth them what tune hee pleaseth. And having done, sends them home againe, where filling our hedges and our houses with their tunes.'[17]

It was from one such seminary, as Munday tells us, that Edmund Campion returned to England to convert good Protestant subjects away from their religion and their Queen. Following the example of this 'dissembling hippocrite' (A4^v), many other 'altered' English souls returned to England 'by Secrete Creekes, and landing places, disguised, both in their names and persons'.[18] Supplied with stories which explain their movements, they make 'breaches in mens and womens consciences, and so to traine them to their Treasons' and '[harbor] the sayd traiterous messengers in obscure places'.[19] Thus returned, the priests invade the houses of good subjects, insinuating their way into good Protestant households and so 'peturbe the quiet of the Realme ... sow[ing] sedition ... practis[ing] revolts, and ... alienat[ing] the minde of the subjects'.[20] They then 'impoverish the land by transporting ... infinite summes of money into those forraine parts', financing their seminaries with English money.[21] And, as Munday observes, by reconciling even one member of a family to Catholicism, they ensure that 'from Father to Sonne, husband to wife, kinsmen and acquaintance, a number are seduced and brought into theyr detestable dealings'.[22]

Named as parasites in contemporary propaganda-texts, 'two-legged foxes',[23] 'household enemies',[24] 'locusts',[25] 'venemous vipers', 'caterpillars',[26] 'serpents in the bosome',[27] these 'seedmen' were understood to invade both the realm's cycle of production (material goods) and reproduction (good subjects), redirecting them to their own ends, gearing them towards an imminent Spanish invasion. This parasitism represented a network of exchanges, a series of 'flows' which drained the country. Lewis Owen complains that 'an incredible summe of mony' left England each year 'enriching those countries, and empoverishing of their owne'[28] and insists that there was a continuous flow of men and material out of England to the Continent, where it was stored up, reprocessed and then returned in the form of the seminary priest and the Jesuit. To the Queen and Privy Council, these seminary priests and Jesuits were a spatial anomaly, a 'noise' interrupting the 'quiet of the Realme'. They were an offensive remainder, an embarrassment to the perfect geometry of England, its houses and its households. The England these priests travelled, the landscape that bore the trace of their presence, was not merely an inversion of the 'truth' that the Privy Council sought to defend, it constituted a parasitic growth within the realm, sapping its resources and energy.

To be a Jesuit or seminary priest was thus to be a parasite. And this 'parasitic' identity derives from both the strategies that Jesuits employed to win converts and from the measures they adopted in order to defeat the state's mechanisms of capture. They became 'parasites' in the more neutral sense employed by Michel Serres, surviving by inhabiting the threshold between two worlds (the public and the private).[29] The network of seminaries, safe-houses and hiding-places that occupied this threshold world represents this parasitic relation. To the propagandists, the existence of these spaces was the material evidence that Jesuits had invaded the homes of the Queen's subjects. To Catholics, they were the 'elsewhere' that made life possible, a material re-routing of the space and assets of the realm necessary to their survival. To be a recusant was to be part of this parasitic 'geography', to be one who refused, who remained, and also to be perceived as a 'remainder' or unacceptable residue. It became one position within a wider landscape, a series of locations created in order to further the dissemination of returning 'seedmen' that Topcliffe so feared.

From England to the seminary and back again, insinuated into houses, 'obscure places', and harbored by subjects led astray, the Jesuits embodied these spatial aberrations. Their identity is a story of travel, of transformation, of flight and return, of turning. They are an interruption, a toxin, an infection, an invasion: they are an affront to the sovereignty of the state. Like Campion, the names of these men disclose a 'scandalous' history. Merely to have desired to leave England in the first place was, of course, the greatest aberration of all. Of all these dislocations, however, it was the imminent return of 'Jesuitized' gentlemen, the treacherous swerve from the path of true religion first to Rome and then back 'home' as traitors, that gave Topcliffe the greatest cause for concern. In this, he was not alone: Queen and Council shared his concern and so developed a parallel system of detection and capture in order to stem this perceived flow of 'seedmen' and make manifest the treasonous practices of the Jesuit underground.

NETWORKS OF THE HIDDEN

The authorities had begun their attack in 1581 with a twenty pound fine for non-attendance at church services, and followed this measure in 1585 with an Act that prescribed the death penalty for priests ordained since 1559 who set foot in England and for those who harbored them.[30] While, the first provision attacked outward signs of recusancy by punishing public non-attendance at church, the second intruded into the homes of Catholic families and criminalized the maintenance of priests in private. These measures left Catholics in a double-bind. If, as one Jesuit commentator observed, they lived 'publicly', then they became a visible minority considered to be 'either too wealthy, or else too well, to live'; if, however, they lived 'in secret', then they were accused of 'devis[ing] secret conspiracies' and having Spanish sympathies.[31] The overall effect of these two Acts was to empty the realm of any place where Catholics could legally maintain even a minimal religious life. This legislation culminated in the proclamation 'Establishing Commissions against Seminary Priests and Jesuits'[32] of 1591 which created 'certaine Commissioners' whose job it was to guarantee that 'all manner of persons of what degree soever they be … make a present due and particular Inquisition of all manner of persons that have bene admitted, or suffered to have vsual resort, diet, lodging, residence

in their houses'. Anyone 'found unwilling to answere', or whose
answer cast doubt on their obedience, was to be sent to one of the
commissioners to be examined. Moreover 'their answeres [were] to
be put into writing' and kept 'in a maner of a Register or Kalender'.
The state intruded into the space of the household or home and
demanded that everyone be accounted for and give account. In the
process, Queen and Council redrew England as a map of anomalous or insufficient answers, of subjects whose hearts held
'secrets'.[33]

In each case, every move made to drive Catholicism beyond the
bounds of the realm was met by a commensurate move further
underground. As the ports, roads and countryside of England were
transformed into the weave of an ever-tightening net, Catholic
households developed ever more subtle ways of protecting Jesuits
and seminary priests. In a series of meetings held throughout 1585
and 1586, the leaders of the Jesuit mission laid the foundations of an
underground system for meeting, equipping and distributing
priests arriving from the colleges abroad around the country.[34] They
settled the 'problems of distribution and finance … [and of] mobility or stability for priests' that had previously prevented them from
establishing an effective underground movement,[35] and so ensured
that, ten years later, there would be a highly effective system for
receiving priests from the Continent.[36] They also established the
necessity of constructing secret hiding-places in safe-houses and all
major Catholic residences.

In their initial stages, these hiding-places were as simple as the
roof-hide in which Campion was discovered at Lyford, or no more
than a converted guarderobe or privy. Priests fled to the margins of
the house, enacting their symbolic exclusion from the realm in both
statute and proclamation. As pursuivants grew more adept at
searching for hidden spaces, however, the hides became more
complex. Throughout the 1590s and the first decade of the seventeenth century, hiding-places became more numerous, more varied
in design, and moved to less obviously marginal areas of the house.
Under the direction of Richard Holtby and the lay brother Nicholas
Owen, Catholic families built hiding-places 'of several fashions in
several places [so] that one being taken might give no light to the
discovery of another'.[37] Priests moved to hides engineered in stair-
wells;[38] they hid in spaces excavated out of chimneystacks, as at
Braddocks, in Essex;[39] or, as at Harvington Hall, in Worcestershire,
they evaded capture by means of a double-hide which gave

the priest a second hiding-place to move to when the first was discovered by the searchers.[40]

It was hides such as these that led Baxter to compare the life of a Jesuit to that of a fox. 'It is well-known to fox-hunters', he writes,

> that the Fox make[s] his denne in the ground that is hard to dig, as in galt, clay or such earth, the passage into his earth being streight, and going very farre in before it come to his couch, having also many Holes, thorow which to unearth himselfe: Even so it is with this kind, they make their burrowes strong, they have so many streight passages, so many muses, so many winding corners, so many turnings, so many interturnings, and starting holes, that it is a matter full of difficultie to find the couch of a Catholicke, especially of a Priest or a Jesuite.[41]

At Harvington, the Jesuit finally becomes no more than the 'para' in parasite, the sum of all directions, 'turnings' and 'interturnings'. He becomes a dislocation of space which the state seeks to reduce to a single trajectory, a proper name, a physical description.

By the mid-1580s, then, there were two opposed yet coextensive networks for regulating and redirecting the flow of priests who arrived from the Continent. Each proposed mutually incompatible lines of emplotment: one led to the safe-house, the other to the prison. One sought to maximize the yield from the seminaries, or 'seed-banks', abroad. The other committed its resources to interrupting the cycle and channeling the dispersal into its own receptacles: the scaffold, and the prisons which ringed London. The scandal that produced these simultaneous networks was not, however, the obvious fact that throughout the 1580s and 1590s there were still Catholics in England. It was instead the fact that there were subjects who held themselves apart, who sought to maintain both a mental and physical space that lay beyond the reach of the state but within the borders of its authority. While Catholics dealt with the problems of an increasingly hostile state by, as Maus puts it, 'insisting upon a traditional distinction between the domains of secular and ecclesiastical authority, rendering unto Caesar what is Caesar's and reserving for God what is God's',[42] the state responded by refusing to recognize these boundaries. It dismantled the distinction between private and public life, and so sought to bring Catholicism into the open, to make manifest the unreadable hearts of Catholic subjects by enforcing conformity and expelling the Jesuit 'seedmen'.

The task of Cecil's and Walsingham's pursuivants was thus, as Serres would say, to 'deparasite' the realm and so to silence the siren song of the Jesuits and priests who returned from Rome. The 'scandal' of recusancy was thus not so much the beliefs of English Catholics so much as the manner of their existence, the fact that they inhabited the fabric of the realm and did not resist openly. The problem facing Queen and Council, however, was that they were unable to make recusancy fully present, to lay hold of the essence of the movement and so remove its foundations. There always remained the possibility that when they captured a priest they had the wrong man, that the person identified as say 'Campion' might turn out to be someone else altogether. There was also the possibility that his apprehension was just a ruse, a trick to allow the escape of his fellow priests. In these instances, the drive towards certainty, towards a 'silent' realm produced ever more sophisticated forms of detection, an ever more subtle 'network of the hidden'.

A document relating to one Father Thomas Fitzherbert dating from 1594 illustrates the privy council's dilemma exactly. This 'quaint pedigree … furnished … by some government spy' (Fig. 3.1)[43] traces the Fitzherbert family tree and records the whereabouts and supposed loyalty of each family member, which it represents in the form of a numbered circle containing the subject's name, relationship, location and reasons for suspicion. Each circle represents the opaque exterior of a Catholic subject and the state's gloss discloses his or her supposed intentions or identity. The original Fitzherbert's third son, for example, was a 'prieste', his grandson, Richard, 'a feugitive out-lawed and now in prison'. And so the tree proceeds marking the generations with the usual arrows and lines of inheritance. Below each of the circles representing the fugitives or the 'resedew' that have remained in England, are a further series of remarks that publicize the malicious intentions within. Nicholas, now 'a Canonist at Rome … in service with Cardinall Allen', is declared 'A Trator', as are his brothers Francis and George. Anthony Fitzherbert, who had been imprisoned for 'receiving of seminary preests', is declared 'a tratorous fellowe Nowe Enlarge out of Darbye Gaole'; and the descendants of Richard, the 'feugitive', are variously pronounced 'daingeroos', 'trator', or, as in the case of his daughter Anne, 'verye badd and daindgeroos'. The only exception to this catalogue of suspect persons is Thomas Fitzherbert who is

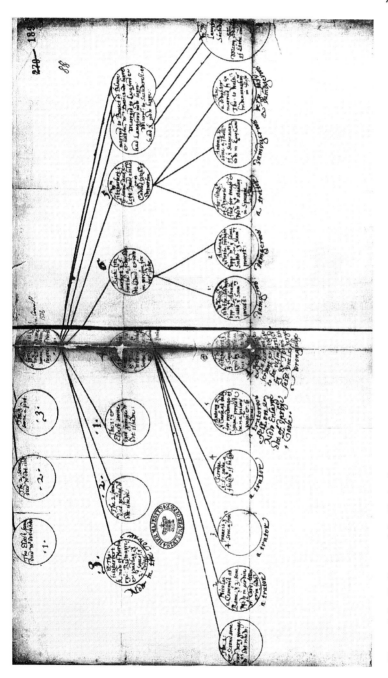

Figure 3.1 Pedigree of the Fitzherberts.

declared to be 'a good subject', as well as 'her majestie's servant', and is 'thoughte to be disinherited by Sir Thomas ... his uncle verye wrongfullye'. Significantly, the circle representing this Thomas Fitzherbert, this 'good subject', is not linked to any other family member by an arrow or line of succession. Instead, he is severed from the family and placed outside the circuit of recusancy that is the Fitzherbert family tree. He is the 'good subject' who should properly inherit his uncle's estates and so become the progenitor of a different, Protestant, family.

This 'petygree' discloses an England made up of anomalous or treacherous subjects. It recalls the movements identified in Topcliffe's letter and enables us to read the network of recusant sites, of folds and ripples in the surface of England, that pursuivants identified in the lives of these men and women. 'Dyvers' live 'beyond sea' while a 'resedew [remains] yet ... in England'; Nicholas lives abroad in a seminary; Anthony receives seminary priests in his home; Thomas is now 'with Stanley in Spaine'. Others have been captured but are now 'at large', or 'now in England'. Each bounded circle marks also a threshold beyond which simple surveillance could not proceed. So many of these suspects are still 'at large', or are have now returned to England and remain unaccounted for. Their movements must be charted, and their circle annotated. Paradoxically, then, the pedigree of John Fitzherbert will be complete not when all the members of the Fitzherbert family have been captured or are dead, but when the figures and marks that it contains have been erased, when there remains only the blank, empty, white space of a realm without recusants, without this treasonous 'resedew'. In the meantime, the 'pedigree' remains a partial map, an interim report on the authorities' success in manifesting the hidden intentions of its Catholic subjects.

VANISHING ACTS

Central to this project of detection was the floating population of agents, pursuivants and informers who formed the strands of the state's web of intelligence-gathering.[44] These men and women monitored houses, ports, crossing-places, bridges, entryways and thoroughfares, relaying a mish-mash of signs that would enable Cecil and Walsingham to track the flow of bodies arriving from the Continent. The transformation of this 'news' into the body of a Jesuit priest or offending Catholic householder was the aim of their labor, but that involved fortuitous timing, betrayal and violence. Moreover, searches required an efficient use of men, an intimate knowledge of the house and its environs, and above all patience. An effective search might require four to five days or more (four days at Braddocks in 1594, four or five days at Scotney Castle in 1598,[45] and eleven days at Hindlip Hall in 1606).[46] Even when intelligence came from a reliable informer in a Catholic house, or by direct observation, the outcome of the search was often dictated by chance.

When, for example, George Eliot and David Jenkins, pursuivants to the Crown, sought to capitalize on their unwitting discovery of a Catholic prayer meeting run by none other than Edmund Campion at Lyford Grange in 1581 by returning to the house with the local Justice of the Peace and a posse of forty or fifty men, they could find no trace of Campion or his fellow priests. Delayed by the gatekeeper for 'the space of half an hour',[47] they entered the house and were met with a series of denials from their class-superiors. In particular, Mrs Yate, the mistress of the house, 'could not be content only to make a plain denial of the said Masses and the Priests: but with great and horrible oaths, forsware the same, betaking herself to the Devil if any such were there'.[48] Mrs Yate's performance was so convincing that Eliot feels it necessary to add that 'if I had not [seen them] with my own eyes, I should have believed her'. Such occurrences were not uncommon; and, when faced with an absolute denial by the householder as well as a Justice of the Peace anxious to preserve local harmony, some searches were discontinued or conducted half-heartedly.

Such were the difficulties inherent to searching a sprawling Elizabethan house that, even when the searchers took the household by surprise, they could not guarantee success. As Baxter comments somewhat ruefully,

> experience hath taughte us, that when it hath been a matter undoubted that a Foxe priest hath been readie to say masse, and therefore his denne hath beene compassed, the terriers have winded him, and all his pretie-trinkets have been found prepared for so great a peece of worke: yet in the ende the foxe would not be found. Perhaps he serves hunters as the fish called the Cuttle serves the fishermen, which when she is like to be taken casteth forth a slimie humor like unto ynke; and so darkening the upper part of the water, and dazeling the fisherman's iies, marres his aime, and escapes danger.[49]

Like the hidden or unreadable heart of the recusant, the Jesuit turned fox and then fish, leaves only traces, fragments that indicate a former location and perhaps a line of flight. Even though the house has been 'compassed,' enclosed by the state's representatives, the priest cannot be found. The pursuivants lose him in the confusion that follows their arrival. The incomplete sacrament, Baxter implies, effects not a transubstantiation but a transformation: the Jesuit-fox turns fish and produces a 'slimie humor' both like and unlike 'ynke'. This 'ynke' which is both inert and organic – implicitly here the 'pretie-trinkets' of the Mass and perhaps even the communion bread – blinds the pursuivants. The invasion of the house itself falls prey to a further parasitic production of debris, of 'noise', from which the pursuivants must filter the whereabouts of the priest.

Rather than allow themselves to be overwhelmed by such debris, Baxter counsels his 'terriers' on how to restore their 'aime' and so 'unkenell' the fox. He instructs them to

> follow the examples of miners, which pursue the signes every way, as they spread in the ground, till they be guided to the trunke or bodie of the metall: even to follow the appearances of suspitions and likelihoods, until it be manifest, what light made the shadow, or what fire the smoke. A candle end not warily snuffed, a few imbers carelessly couched, a few strikes not thorowly quenched, have brought many a household to extreme woe and miserie.[50]

For the pursuivant, space radiates significance: the secret 'spreads in the ground'. Baxter tells the searchers to focus not on the priest but on what he has left behind. They must reconstruct the debris in order to trace the path of the priest and assemble the fragments into a coherent narrative of his flight. Indeed, Baxter predicates the successful apprehension of the priest on a series of narrative operations, a number of strategic conversions. The pursuivants must, he says, follow even the 'appearances of suspitions and likelihoods' and track their multiple possibilities until they end or converge in a singular cause or agent (*a* light, *a* fire, *a* candle). These singular agents then replace the matter of the sign and are exchanged once again for a suspicion, a hermeneutic skepticism. This suspicion itself becomes a trajectory, a movement through space, a repetition and reversal of the priest's line of flight that culminates in his discovery.

At Lyford, Eliot and Jenkins took stock of the situation and immediately began to search for 'secret corners' by sounding the house for hollow spaces. They searched every inch of the house as well as 'the orchards, hedges, ditches'[51] and the moat, moving around the exterior of the house and from room to room, looking for any irregularity or discrepant detail that might indicate a hidden space. This movement through the house reorganizes it, decides its shape and produces the quiet, deparasited realm promised in Elizabeth's proclamation of 1591. These 'terriers' unfold the social and material fabric of the realm, tracing the seams and folds of the hiding-place, opening its parenthetical enclosure and removing the body inside. They are a force of genealogy, bearers of a state-authored narrative that already knows who the priests are and what they represent.

In his account of the events that passed at Lyford in 1581, for example, Munday is interested in matters of space and location only in so far as they relate to the moment of discovery:

[the searchers] being entred with no smal company, sawe walking in the house divers of these that they brought to the Tower: entring farther, up into a Chamber neere the top of the house, which was but very simple, having in it, a large great shelfe, with divers tooles and instrumentes, bothe upon it and hanging by it, which they judged to belonge to some Crossebowe maker. The simplenesse of the place caused them to use small suspition in it, and were departing againe. But one in the company, by good hap, espied a chinke in the wall of boordes, whereto this shelfe was fastened, and through the same he perceived some light, drawing his Dagger he smit a great hole in it, and sawe there was a roome behinde it, whereat the rest staied, searching for some entrance into it, which by pulling downe a shelfe they found, being a little hole for one to creep in at: There they entred and found Edmund Campion, the Jesuit and John Peters and Thomas Saltwell, preestes, standing up very closely. (A6–7)

This progress through the house represents a record of conclusions rather than actions, a progress through unproblematic, exhausted space. In other words, we do not read a description of the search, but of the results of the search. The room is thus 'but very simple' and not worthy of full description. It exists only as a catalogue of the objects on the shelfe, the tools and instruments which, collectively, the pursuivants identify and disregard. Here space appears neutral, even boring – no more than a series of insignificant surfaces.

The 'company' moves on and, in the passage through the door which permits only one person to pass, dissolves into pairs of hands, pairs of eyes. This dissolution of the group into a serialized procession of singular bodies, each of which 'depart[s] againe', localizes the moment of discovery. 'One in the company', writes Munday, 'espied a chinke in the wall of boordes … and through the same he perceived some light'. He sees some sort of hole and then, in a second act of viewing, perceives a light. The 'chinke' does not of itself signify. Instead, the light becomes a sign of discrepancy, an indication of a place beyond, of the 'wall of boordes' as a transitional space and not a terminus. The light that issues forth from this 'chinke' is an address, an invitation to narrative. This light focalizes the scene: it passes through the boards and leaves a trail which the pursuivant's 'rush' towards it with his dagger reverses.[52] By this blow, the 'chinke' becomes a hole which permits actual vision. This act of looking ends the serialized present of the search and galvanizes the group to action. They tear down the shelf and then enter the 'little hole for one to creepe in at'. Inside, they find not a priest-hole, but three priests, or rather three names – Edmund Campion, John Peters and Thomas Saltwell. From this moment of 'discovery' on, Munday ceases to describe the house at all: his interest in space is at an end. We hear of a perfunctory search of a 'dove house' (A7) which yields two more suspects and of an arrest made on the following morning, but there are no more revelations, no more violent intrusions.

There are, however, strategic differences between Eliot's account of the moment of discovery and Munday's. In Eliot's version, Jenkins discovers the hiding-place by piercing the wall with a hammer and not a dagger. Then 'the said Jenkins … called very loudly, and said "I have found the traitors!"; and presently company enough was with him: who there saw the said priests [that], when there was no remedy for them but *nolens volens* courteously yielded themselves.'[53] For a moment, there is the threat of escape, of contest: there are three priests and only one pursuivant. Only when 'company enough' arrives do the priests bow to decorum and politely surrender. In Munday's account, the moment of revelation works differently: the act of naming Campion enforces an immediate identification of this man as the person who, as you will remember, 'neither remembering his dutie to God, loyaltie to his Prince, nor loove to his countrey: but hardening his hart more and more in that divellish obscuritie of life' (A2ᵛ–3), fled to Rome and joined a seminary. A quasi-divine light issues forth from a wall, indicating the location of the priest-hole and so the presence of a hidden body, and there can be no doubt. The men inside this hiding-place may only be Campion, Peters and Saltwell. To be in hiding is to be guilty: to be discovered in a priest-hole is to be a traitor, a conspirator, a Jesuit.

Whereas Eliot's account of the search began with the uncertain circumstances that led to the surprise capture of the very man that the authorities most wanted, Munday's pamphlet already knows all that there is to discover, all that will occur. Whereas Eliot's text proceeds as a linear account of the search, Munday's discloses the 'truth' not of the events that transpired, but of a parasitic geography, of the trajectories that led Campion to Rome and then back to England as a 'seedman' of treason. For Munday, the act of discovery occurs only after a lengthy description of Campion's upbringing, of how, when young, he 'got such a smack of [popery] … that he could never leave it' (A2). This genealogy of a traitor, the life history of a 'household enemy', directly mirrors the parasitic trajectories of Jesuits and seminary priests found in the propaganda texts. Even Lyford Grange itself radiates treachery: it is, as Munday tells us, a 'house well moated about, and from any village or dwelling, halfe a mile and more, [which] hath long borne a reporte, that there was papistrie maintained in it' (A5). What else could such a remote, recusant-owned house be used for other than maintaining priests? Merely to have been a guest there seems already to serve as an admission of guilt.

We have not, as it turns out, been reading a search for Edmund Campion at all, merely the location of a body that will bear his name, and so be held accountable for the story of flight and return that forms the basis of Jesuit identity. The 'work' of discovery complete, we, as readers, take away a list of names, places and personal histories. We discover that Lyford Grange hid three priests, one of whom was 'Campion the Seditious Jesuit', that Jesuits come from Spain, and that Catholic houses contain secret hiding-places. Munday's vision of a house exhausted by the search, of three men whose identities are disclosed by their presence in a hiding place, in the 'elsewhere' of recusant practice, fantasizes an England free of parasites, a realm in which the quiet of a Protestant peace is golden. In the end, however, Munday's text discloses no more than its title communicated to the reader. It merely establishes a 'truth' that, as Lake reminded us at the beginning, 'many, if not most, educated English people' already knew. His account merely confirms that to be 'Campion' is to be a Jesuit, a traitor, a thief, an invader, and a hidden body.

THE LIMITS OF KNOWLEDGE

Munday's account of the search ends not with this moment of reve- lation or discovery, however, but with a scene of writing. At the end of the search, the pursuivants receive instructions from the Privy Council ordering them to escort Campion to London. As Eliot confirms, they spent the night (21 July 1581) at Colebrook, where, according to Munday, 'they met a pursuivant, whose message declared, they put a piece of paper on the head of Campion, whereon was written: Edmund Campion, the Seditious Jesuit'. On the road to London, the pursuivants are told to pause, to interrupt their journey and to attach a piece of paper to one in their company. They then continue their journey towards London, the Tower and the scaffold. Thus annotated, Campion literally becomes an icon that the state parades through the streets of London: he lit- erally comes to embody the narrative of recusancy disseminated by the state. For, if this piece of paper functions deictically (drawing all eyes to him), it also makes legible a specific story about Jesuits, seminary priests and recusants: the man who rides this horse, it insists, who resembles his companions in all other respects, is 'Edmund Campion, the Seditious Jesuit' (A7). He is Campion the traitor, Campion the conspirator, Campion the ingrate. Indeed, by this act of writing, the very name 'Campion' comes to disclose a story of travel and of flight: it embeds a series of false turns, a journey that leads from England to Rome and back. It makes mani- fest the 'truth' of a Catholic identity figured as the 'many turnings and interturnings' that so frustrated Baxter's 'terriers'. On the road to London, his missionary 'circuit' now redirected towards the Tower, Campion's body and name are fixed. Forced to bear the weight of the state's narrative, the semiotically eviscerated bodies of Campion and his fellows become proof-texts of a 'Jesuit' conspiracy and evidence of Catholic resistance. They become tokens also of the futility of such resistance and proof of the efficacy of the state's mechanisms of detection.

While it is tempting to read this act of annotation as Munday's ultimate victory over Campion, as a moment when Baxter's fantasy of transparent bodies is delivered through the agency of a letter, this piece of paper begs more questions than it answers. Whom, for example, did the Council expect to read this note? When was it written? By whom? Whom, in other words, does this piece of paper address? It is not difficult to understand that the authorities might worry about losing so famous a Jesuit as Campion. That they should send out a second set of orders instructing the company to supplement his body with a written sign is, however, more curious. In one sense this act of annotation is entirely redundant. Campion is already marked for death. He is already anchored in the narrative of recusancy disseminated by the state: his parasitic identity is assured. And yet, the state's paranoid act of writing, of physically marking Campion's body, of tying him ever more closely into its narrative, testifies to the instability of this reference. There remains the possibility, it seems, that Campion might simply don a disguise and fade back into the landscape, that he might retreat into another secret hiding-place, or that the real Campion remains at Lyford Grange concealed in some variety of double-hide of the type that Owen built at Harvington Hall.

The very existence of this 'piece of paper' is evidence then of the impossibility of Munday's fantasy of the perfect search. It reveals the symbolic work necessary to fantasize a realm without parasites, and also the impossibility of Munday's fantasy of a closed system of discovery. Even as the 'piece of paper' seeks to sustain this fantasy, to make it real, to render the narrative material, it foregrounds the limitations of the state's knowledge, and the suspectability of all their measures to further parasitic dislocation. Indeed, in the following year all these fears would be proved true: for it was on this very 'piece of paper' that Cardinal Allen, head of the Jesuit college at Douai, seized when disseminating the Catholic 'truth' that Campion represented. In his *Martyrdom of Father Campion and His Companions* (1582), Allen included a series of engravings depicting the annotated martyr on his way to the scaffold,[54] the 'piece of paper' now a sign of the abject fate not of 'Edmund Campion, the Seditious Jesuit', but of 'Edmund Campion, the Catholic Martyr'.

NOTES

1. All references will be to Anthony Munday, *A Breefe Discourse of the taking of Edmund Campion, the Seditious Jesuit, and divers other Papistes, in Barkeshire* ... (London, 1581).
2. De Certeau writes that secrecy 'is not only the state of a thing that escapes from or reveals itself to knowledge. It designates a play between actors. It circumscribes the terrain of strategic relations between the one trying to discover the secret and the one keeping it, or between the one who is supposed to know and the one who is assumed not to know it .... The hidden organizes a social network' (*The Mystic Fable*, trans. Michael B. Smith [Chicago: University of Chicago Press, 1992], 97–8).
3. My use the words, 'topography', or 'geography', does not refer directly to the local or regional studies of post-Reformation Catholicism such as Hugh Aveling, *Northern Catholics: The Catholic Recusants of the North Riding of Yorkshire 1558–1790* (London: Geoffrey Chapman, 1966); John Bossy, *The English Catholic Community 1570–1850* (London: Darton, Longman and Todd, 1975); and Christopher Haigh, *Reformation and Resistance in Tudor Lancashire* (Cambridge: Cambridge University Press, 1975). While I have found these accounts of local Catholic practice invaluable, they tend to treat the landscape as a pre-given terrain which had to be crossed by both priest and pursuivant alike.
4. Godfrey Anstruther, *Vaux of Harrowden* (Newport: R. H. Johns Ltd., 1953), xiii.
5. Peter Holmes, *Resistance and Compromise* (Cambridge: Cambridge University Press, 1982), 83–98, discusses the political, doctrinal and everyday complexities of the practice of recusancy in sixteenth-century England.
6. Peter Lake, 'Anti-Popery: the Structure of a Prejudice', in *Conflict in Early Stuart England*, ed. Richard Cust and Ann Hughes (London and New York: Longman, 1989), 73.
7. Thomas Bell, *The Hunting of the Romish Foxe* (London, 1598), A3ᵛ.
8. Francis Bacon, *Certain Observations Made Upon a Libel Published this Present Year, 1592*, in James Spedding, *Letters and Life of Francis Bacon*, vol. 1 (London: Longmans, Green, and Co., 1890), 178.
9. John Baxter, *A Toile for Two-legged Foxes* (London, 1600), 109–10.
10. Henry Foley, *Records of the English Province of the Society of Jesus*, vol. 2 (London: Burns and Oates, 1878), 355–6.
11. The exact number of priests who were trained abroad and then returned to the English mission is uncertain. John Bossy estimates that 'when Queen Elizabeth died there were three hundred missionary priests in England' (216), but the figures for the first five years of the College at Douai show that 'by 1578 ... fifty-two were "on the mission"' (E. E. Reynolds, *Campion and Parsons* [London: Sheed and Ward, 1980], 24). Patrick McGrath and Joy Rowe conclude that 'in the fifteen-eighties and the fifteen-nineties the number of seminary priests at work in England seems to have fluctuated between 120 and

150 in any one year' ('The Elizabethan Priests: Their Harbourers and Helpers', *Recusant History* 19.3 [May 1989], 209).

12. Michael Questier, *Conversion, Politics, and Religion in England, 1580–1625* (Cambridge: Cambridge University Press, 1996), 8.

13. Anthony Munday, *The English Romayne Lyfe*, ed. Philip J. Ayres, (Oxford: Clarendon Press, 1980), xxx.

14. *Tudor Royal Proclamations*, ed. P. L. Hughes and J. F. Larkin, vol. 3 (New Haven: Yale University Press, 1964), 88.

15. Thomas Bell, *The Anatomie of Popish Tyrannie* (London, 1603), 5.

16. Sir Lewis Lewkenor, *The Estate of the English Fugitives under the Kinge of Spaine and his Ministers* (London, 1596), K1ᵛ.

17. Lewis Owen, *The State of the English Colledges in Forraine Parts* (1626; facsimile edn, Amsterdam and New York: Da Capo Press, Theatrum Orbis Terrarum Ltd., 1968), B1ʳ⁻ᵛ.

18. *Tudor Royal Proclamations*, 3: 91.

19. Ibid., 90.

20. Owen, 123.

21. Ibid., B1ᵛ.

22. Anthony Munday, *A Discoverie of Edmund Campian and his Confederates, their most horrible and traiterous practises, against her Majestie's most royall person, and the Realme* (London, 1582), Civ.

23. Baxter, *A Toile for Two-legged Foxes.*

24. Ibid., 110.

25. Owen, 22.

26. Ibid., 72.

27. Baxter, 149.

28. Owen, 109.

29. Michel Serres, *The Parasite*, trans. Lawrence R. Schehr (Baltimore and London: Johns Hopkins University Press, 1982), 38.

30. 'An Acte against Jesuites, Semynarie Priestes and such other Sundrie Persons', in *Statutes of the Realm*, vol. 4 (1819; rpt. London: Dawson's, 1963), 706–7.

31. Father Richard Holtby, 'On Persecution in the North', in *The Troubles of Our Catholic Forefathers*, ed. John Morris, vol. 3 (London: Burns and Oates, 1877), 120–1.

32. *Tudor Royal Proclamations*, 3: 57.

33. Enforcement of anti-Catholic legislation was capricious at best and varied considerably from county to county. Aveling counsels extreme caution on the subject (112). While Questier remains ambivalent about the degree of conviction that lay behind these measures, he observes that 'the Church Courts, the ecclesiastical commissions, and exchequer', for example 'seem to have been extremely efficient in performing their allotted tasks' (205).

34. Anstruther (155–9) and Philip Caraman (*Henry Garnet 1555–1606 and the Gunpowder Plot* [London: Longmans, Green and Co., 1964], 29–37) provide accounts of these meetings, which involved William Weston, Jesuit Superior, Henry Garnet, Robert Southwell, Lord Vaux, Sir Thomas Tresham and Sir Richard Catesby.

35. Bossy, 204.

36. Edward Oldcorne would supervise the underground across Worcestershire and Richard Holtby would run a similar project in the North (Michael Hodgetts, 'Elizabethan Priest-Holes V – The North', *Recusant History* 13.4 [October 1976]: 256).

37. John Gerard, *A Narrative of the Gunpowder Plot*, ed. John Morris (London: Longmans, Green and Co., 1871), 182–4.

38. The most sophisticated of these stairwell hides has been identified at Sawston Hall, in Cambridgeshire (Michael Hodgetts, *Secret Hiding-Places* [Dublin: Veritas, 1989], 58).

39. John Gerard, *Autobiography of A Hunted Priest*, trans. Philip Caraman (New York: Pellegrini and Cudhay, 1952), 58–71.

40. Hodgetts, *Secret Hiding-Places*, 93.

41. Baxter, 123.

42. Katherine Eisman Maus, *Inwardness and Theater in the English Renaissance* (Chicago: Chicago University Press, 1995), 23.

43. Public Record Office, State Papers Domestic, 12/235/88.

44. It would be a mistake to think of the surveillance and internal security operations of early modern England in terms of a professional or institutionalized police force. Drawing on the work of G. R. Elton (*Policy and Police* [Cambridge: Cambridge University Press, 1972]), John Michael Archer writes that 'the field of intelligence was instead a particularly obscure sector of the greater field of patronage' (*Sovereignty and Intelligence: Spying and Court Culture in the English Renaissance* [Stanford: Stanford University Press, 1993], 5).

45. John Morris records the experience of one Father Blount at Scotney (*The Troubles of Our Catholic Forefathers*, vol. 1 [London: Burns and Oates, 1872], 207–15).

46. Henry Garnet was captured at the end of this search following Gunpowder Plot (Caraman, 330–41).

47. George Eliot, *A Very True Report of the Apprehension and taking of arch-Papist Edmund Campion, the Pope his right hand; with Three other lewd Jesuit Priests, and divers other Lay people, most seditious persons of like sort*, rpt. *The English Garner*, vol. 8 (London: Archibald and Constable and Co., 1896), 213. Eliot's account appeared shortly after Munday's version of the events that passed at Lyford and was an attempt to correct Munday's errors and to answer aspersions cast against Eliot's own reputation, character and beliefs.

48. Ibid., 213.

49. Baxter, 123.

50. Ibid., 174.

51. Eliot, 214.

52. By focalization, I mean the term that Mieke Bal has popularized in order to describe the complexities involved when we speak of 'the point of view' in a literary text (*Introduction to the Theory of Narratology*, trans. Christine van Boheemen [Toronto: University of Toronto Press, 1988], 100–14).

53. Eliot, 215.

54. William Allen, *The Martyrdom of Father Campion and His Companions* (London, 1582).

4

A Qualified Intolerance: the Limits and Ambiguities of Early Stuart Anti-Catholicism

Anthony Milton

One of the more important findings of recent historians of early modern England has been the extraordinary prominence of anti-Catholicism in that society. Violently anti-Catholic language drenched the religious literature being produced, not just by Puritan fanatics, but by the most learned bishops of the Church of England. The Pope was routinely identified as Antichrist by university professors and Puritan artisans alike, while 'to many, if not most educated Protestant English people of the period' (we are told) 'popery was an anti-religion'. Parliamentary debates were often punctuated by clarion calls for more vigorous persecution of Roman Catholics. At a popular level, in years of political crisis such as the early 1640s, a whole series of local communities was seized by hysterical fears that an armed popish rising was imminent. The outbreak of the English Civil War has been blamed in particular on the escalating fears of a popish conspiracy at the heart of Charles I's court directed against Englishmen's religious and civil liberties. In a characteristically subtle study of the phenomenon, Peter Lake has argued that anti-popery occupied an even more fundamental position in the Protestant mind, as popery was perceived '[t]hrough a series of binary oppositions' in which 'every negative characteristic imputed to Rome implied a positive cultural, political or religious value which Protestants claimed as their own exclusive property'. In this way, anti-popery is depicted as 'a "rational response" to situations in which values central' to the Protestant self-image 'came under threat'. Anti-Catholicism thus constituted a fundamental political language and

ideology which enabled contemporaries both to explain and to
identify solutions to the political conflicts of the period'.[1]

It is now transparently obvious that it is impossible to write a
political or cultural history of seventeenth-century England in
which anti-Catholicism does not play an important role: indeed,
recent scholarship has also traced a continuity of such antipathies
right through to the late nineteenth century.[2] It is not the intention
of this chapter to question any of these historical findings.
Nevertheless, there is a danger that historians have perhaps gone
too far: that in seeking to free themselves from anachronistic
assumptions of a country divided by rationally minded constitutional principles, historians have ended up generating an image of
early modern Englishmen as trapped in a stifling anti-Catholic mentality. The more that anti-Catholicism is seen as an expression of
Protestant cultural values, the greater the tendency to assume the
existence of an anti-Catholic ideological straitjacket, from which
Protestant Englishmen were neither able nor willing to escape, and
which impelled them into an allergic response to all things and
people who carried the slightest taint of Roman Catholicism.

Of course, no historians have suggested that anti-Catholicism
represents a truthful picture of Roman Catholicism or its adherents,
and indeed there is a sense in which anti-popery as a political ideology was not a direct response to Roman Catholicism as such at all.
But it should also be emphasized that the starkly polarizing anti-
Catholic ideology that recent historians have depicted was only one
of the ways in which Catholicism was perceived and understood in
this period, and only one of the discourses which an individual
Englishman might choose to adopt when describing and responding to Catholic phenomena. It will be argued here that the precise
significance of anti-Catholicism can only be appreciated when it is
fully contextualized within an early Stuart England in which it was
simply implausible for people to remove themselves from the least
tincture of this contagious 'anti-religion'. For all the occasional
use of a language of binary opposition between the forces of
Protestantism and Catholicism, and alarmist talk of religious conta-
gion, life in Protestant England was in fact littered with Roman
Catholic ideas, books, images and people. English people did not
suffer from a simple allergic reaction to all things popish. But, as
we shall see, it is the very extent of these compromises with
confessional polarities which could at critical times translate anti-
Catholicism's potential for disruption into belligerent reality.

I

It is necessary to begin our analysis with anti-Catholic writings themselves. There can be no doubting the theoretically uncompromising nature of prominent anti-Catholic polemic in England in this period. The Pope was usually identified as Antichrist, and the church as Babylon, destined to fall increasingly into the most abhorrent sin of idolatry, its faith a form of heathenism or anti-religion, its doctrines a form of blasphemy and atheism, and the Reformation justified as the flight of true Christians from Babylon, as foretold in the Book of Revelation. Rome stood as the absolute antithesis of godliness, and its relationship to Protestantism could be expressed in terms of the doctrine of the Two Churches. In this doctrine, the companies of God's elect and reprobate were conceived as belonging to two separate camps or 'churches', the true church and the false, running through history, and many divines were happy to translate this starkly dualistic view directly into the division between the two earthly churches of Rome and Protestantism.

But this starkly antithetical approach was not the only model adopted in English Protestant writings against Rome. One problem with recent accounts of anti-Catholicism has been their decision to concentrate on a particular form of anti-Catholic writing, namely the works of converts from Roman Catholicism.[3] But these represent only one mode of anti-Catholic discourse, and they do not seem to have been a form that was particularly widely read. They rarely seem to have run to second editions, at least one author of such a tract found considerable difficulties in raising sufficient money to publish his work, and many of them also arose from the specific interest (and presumably editorial direction) of one man – Archbishop George Abbot.[4] But English anti-Catholic writings were vastly more wide-ranging and subtle than this particular narrow genre of writing might suggest, and their perception of Rome's errors was not necessarily constructed along the lines of a simple inversion of the positive values of Protestantism.

In fact, early Stuart anti-Catholic polemic – which is so often used to illustrate a starkly anti-Catholic mindset – often presented a far more complex and potentially ambiguous picture of Roman Catholicism than might be assumed. To be sure, at both a popular and elite level, anti-Catholic writers would often discuss the relationship between the Protestants and Rome in terms of the division between the 'true church' of Christ and the 'false church' of

the wicked. But the sort of absolute divisions that this doctrine of
the 'Two Churches' propounded were simply one mode of discussing religious divisions, and did not necessarily underlie all
anti-Catholic polemic. Elsewhere, I have described the degree to
which Laudian perceptions of Rome differed significantly from this
more polarized anti-Catholicism.[5] But my intention here is to focus,
not on those like the Laudians who rejected many of the tendencies in early Stuart anti-Catholicism, but rather on the degree to
which non-Laudians and Puritans were themselves able to deploy
multiple modes of anti-Catholic polemic, and were not limited to
the Manichean extremes described so well by Peter Lake. To
provide an effective refutation of Roman polemicists, English anti-
Catholic controversialists often had to have recourse to rhetorical
strategies which heavily qualified the simple binary oppositions
that typified converts' accounts and the rhetoric of the 'Two
Churches'. Most polemicists – even Puritan ones – recognized that
there was a tactical advantage to be gained by appearing more
moderate and irenical than one's Roman Catholic opponent.
Moreover, many of the theological issues raised by Protestant/
Catholic controversy simply could not yield very easily to the
schematic polarizations and rhetorical bravado of the converts'
accounts. Similarly, a robust line that sought to unchurch Rome
because of her corruptions, or to deny the efficacy of her sacraments, and to glorify the absolute separation made from her, could
run the risk of providing ammunition for native separatists from
the Church of England. As a consequence several modes of anti-
Catholic discourse developed which did not rely on the simple
representation of popery as a satanic inversion of normative
Protestant values.

Rome's status as a Church was a case in point. Outside the 'Two
Churches' argument, it was very rare for Protestant polemicists to
deny absolutely that Rome was a Church of Christ. They were still
forced to recognize that Rome retained the necessary means of
regeneration through the Word and sacraments and also the min-
istry (this was recognized in a practical sense as converted priests
were not reordained), and therefore granted that Rome was *in a
sense* a Church. The English Protestant position on the possibility of
salvation in the Roman communion was also not entirely clear, and
it is possible to find writers of Puritan inclination allowing explicitly
for the salvation of reforming elements within the Roman Church.[6]
One further line of argument that was happily adopted by Puritans

and Calvinist bishops alike seemed by implication to give a still more positive recognition to the Church of Rome. In order to repulse Rome's claim to be *the* Catholic Church on earth, it was argued that Rome was in fact only a particular member of this one Universal Church on earth which erroneously claimed absolute authority, as a part laying claim to the whole (in the manner of the early Christian heretics the Donatists).[7]

The precise nature of the separation that had been made from Rome was not merely depicted as the flight from Babylon. When tackling the Reformation itself, English Protestants increasingly stressed the moderation, orderliness and restraint that had been observed in the ecclesiastical separation. Edmund Bunny had noted in the 1580s (and Puritan writers like Richard Bernard agreed) that, if Protestants wished to avoid the charge of schism, then it was vital that they resist the temptation to agree with Romanists that the Protestants had departed absolutely from Rome. English writers therefore routinely denied that they were guilty of schism by stressing that they had been unwillingly forced to leave a tyrannical Church. The notion that the Church of England had undergone only a limited, qualified separation from Rome became increasingly fashionable. Even a Puritan divine such as Richard Bernard, who was often happy to attack the Pope as Antichrist and to invoke the language of the 'Two Churches', could adopt this other mode of more tactically pacific discourse, writing that

> wee doe not break off from her [Rome] simply, but in some re-spects, that is, as farre forth as she hath forsaken her former selfe: so that if shee would returne to the Catholike Faith and Religion. and forsake her Trentisme, Jesuitisme and Popery ... wee want not charitie towards her, to unite our selves unto her againe.[8]

Rome's doctrines could indeed be attacked as a separate religion altogether, as heathenism, and even as a form of atheism, but polemicists also had to admit that the Church retained the elements of true doctrine and worship (however infected with errors). Again, one favorite line of attack in the early Stuart period was to seek to capitalize on the point that Rome retained some orthodox doctrines, by pointing out how far the Church of England shared many of Rome's doctrines, so that it could be concluded that Rome thereby granted the truth of Protestant doctrines. The most famous example of this approach was William Perkins's *A Reformed Catholike*, in which the author studied all the points currently controverted between Rome and the Protestants, and under each heading described the common ground shared by both Churches before going on to explain the additional points imposed by Rome from which the Protestants dissented.[9] This was an approach that was particularly evident in one form of anti-Catholic polemic that was especially notable for drawing more moderate lines of argument, namely tracts that were directly addressed to recusants. Some of these tracts particularly sought to entice recusants back into the Church of England by providing strikingly moderate accounts of the main points of division between the Protestant and Roman Churches, denying that they represented contrary religions, and insisting that church attendance was a natural extension of the principles that recusants already accepted as Roman Catholics.[10]

Most of these arguments were, of course, merely tactically advantageous polemical and rhetorical strategies. But they were also evidence of the fact that English Protestants (and even those most dedicated to attacking Rome in print) were not confined simply and exclusively to presenting the division between the two Churches and religions in absolute, polarized terms. It was natural, of course, to try to read the doctrinal divisions between the Churches in the same light as the physical separation of Rome and the Church of England, and thus as the division between the true church and the false church. But this did not exhaust the approaches available to English Protestant writers. We can thus observe a multitude of modes of anti-Catholic discourse being employed. We should not assume, however, that these were necessarily competing discourses, or that the more moderate polemical strategies were intended simply to overturn the more absolute 'Two Churches' model that depicted Rome in simple inversionary terms as an anti-religion. Rather, they appear to constitute different modes of discourse which an individual might adopt at different times, for varying effect. Thus William Perkins's *Reformed Catholike* in some respects seemed to adopt a more moderate line, by discussing in detail those elements of doctrine that Rome and the Protestants shared. But it was quite explicitly *not* Perkins's intention to suggest that the two churches were actually similar in their doctrine. He consciously wrote to refute the doctrine 'that our religion and the religion of the present Church of Rome are all one for substance'. Instead, at various points Perkins employed the more absolute, vituperative anti-Catholic discourse, insisting that 'they of the Romane Church have razed the foundation' of Christian faith, beginning his book with an exposition of Revelation 18.4 (the flight from Babylon), and arguing that Rome was not a Church of Christ at all. Nevertheless, while Perkins's rhetorical pragmatism is clear, our postmodernist sensibilities should alert us to the fact that Perkins's readers might have chosen to construe his work differently, as being in conflict with the more vituperative style of anti-Catholic argument. Indeed, Perkins's work could be – and demonstrably was – read by some contemporaries as an irenical, and even ecumenical, tract.[11]

II

Polemical pressures might force anti-Catholic writers towards a more qualified position, but these intellectual compromises only echoed the sort of collaboration made with Roman Catholicism on a daily basis by scholars, politicians, tradesmen and others. For all its polarizing language, there is little evidence that anti-Catholicism created in early modern Englishmen a knee-jerk response to everything Roman Catholic.

In fact, cross-confessionalism was the norm, rather than the exception, in many areas of intellectual enquiry in this period. In logic, philosophy, philology and natural theology, Roman Catholic authors were still among the most important authorities cited by scholars across the doctrinal and confessional spectrum. The logician Jacobus Zabarella has been described as 'the outstanding commentator on Aristotle in the late sixteenth century', and his works, along with those of Franciscus Toletus, regularly appear in surviving scholars' library lists from the period, and in the guides to philosophical study produced even by vehement anti-Catholics such as Thomas Barlow.[12] Similarly, the Spanish Jesuit Francisco Suarez enjoyed a cross-confessional esteem as a philosopher. Suarez's influential *Disputationes Metaphysicae* was a standard text in almost all Protestant universities in the seventeenth century.[13] His writings on law and political theory were hardly any less influential in Protestant England. Such was Suarez's reputation in these fields that, in the parliament of 1628, opponents of the Forced Loan, such as John Pym, struggled to lay claim to the Spanish Jesuit's ideas against Roger Mainwaring's attempts to recruit Suarez's support for royal policies. Similarly, parliamentarian pamphleteers in the 1640s made ready recourse to the writings of the Jesuit resistance theorists.[14] Even the violently anti-Catholic William Prynne was happy to cite approvingly the opinions of the notorious Juan de Mariana when mustering writers against stage plays in his *Histriomastix*, and when tackling the attribution of the play *Christus patiens* Prynne appealed to the writings of 'Baronius, Bellarmine, Lewenclavius, Possevine, with other learned Papists'.[15]

But Catholic authors also were recognized as having much to teach in matters that touched more directly on the conscience. Casuistry and systematic ethics were areas where even a dogmatic Puritan like William Ames was forced to have regular recourse to Roman Catholic writers. For all his obvious distaste, he could not avoid making the grudging confession that 'the Papists have laboured much this way to instruct their Confessors: and in a great deale of earth and dirt of Superstitions, they have some veines of Silver: out of which, I suppose, I have drawne some things that are not to be despised.'[16] Again, the Calvinist Thomas Barlow specifically recommended to students the writings on ethics of famous Roman Catholic scholars such as Gabriel Vasquez (notorious among Protestants for his defense of image-worship), Gregorius de Valencia, Cajetan, Alvarez, and even Johannes Malderus (who had composed a violently critical attack on the Synod of Dort).[17]

Historians have also in more recent years started to grasp the profound influence of Roman Catholic devotional literature in this period. This was a sphere in which Roman Catholic authors reigned supreme.[18] Robert Persons's *The Book of Resolution* was famously and successfully modified for a Protestant readership by Edmund Bunny as *A Booke of Christian Exercise*, and in this form went through no fewer than seventeen printings in two years. But this was simply one of many examples of the popularity of Roman Catholic devotional works among Protestants. The first Earl of Manchester's *Contemplatio mortis et immortalitatis* (also known as *Manchester al mondo*), which went through seven editions in the period 1631–42, borrowed from many other writers, but particularly (and unacknowledged) from St François de Sales's *Traité de l'amour de Dieu*. Other Roman Catholic writings sold well even when their author was identified directly. The devotional writings of the German Jesuit Jeremias Drexelius were extremely popular in England, with the Cambridge scholar Ralph Winterton's edition of

The Considerations of Drexelius upon Eternitie enjoying at least fifteen reprints after its first publication in 1632.[19]

The popularity of Roman Catholic devotional writings in England does not simply attest to the scarcity of English Protestant writings on this topic. It has been suggested more recently that Roman Catholic understandings of effectual evangelical conversion and devotional techniques were in fact very similar to those of evangelical Protestants, however much the different Churches' philosophical and doctrinal rationalizations of such matters might differ. This overlap in perceptions of the grace of conversion, it has been argued, enabled those of an evangelical persuasion in either the Roman or Protestant Church to enter into 'a central evangelical stream of consciousness', which could facilitate conversions between confessional allegiances.[20] This is just one example of how important it is not to be misled by the polarities of confessional polemic into presupposing a yawning gulf in doctrinal belief and religious sensibility between the Roman and Protestant Churches.

Roman Catholic authors were also regularly used in other forms of religious study and writing, most notably in the shape of the bible commentaries that were the bread and butter of preachers and theologians alike. John Selden, with typical acuteness, was recorded as remarking that 'these puritan Preachers: if they have any thing Good: they have it out of popish Bookes, though they will not acknowledge it; for fear of displeaseing ye people'.[21] There is much to support this observation that Puritan authors regularly used Roman Catholic biblical commentaries. Andrew Willet and William Perkins certainly made extensive use of Romanist biblical commentators such as Arias Montanus and Benedictus Aretius.[22] Even in a passage in which he described them as 'the marked ones of Antichrist', the Puritan Richard Bernard admitted freely that

> the learned Papists may shew great skill in the outside, the ryne or barke ... of holy Scriptures, that is, of the Grammar, the Logicke, the Rhetoricke, the naturall Philosophie of the Bible, and such other things to be found there ... which may be called (as it were) the humanitie of the Scriptures; yea they can speake of morall precepts, of duties, of common honesty very excellently; neither can we deny their knowledge in the generall heads of Gospell, wherein wee and they agree, and by profession whereof they be called Christians.[23]

Small wonder, then, that the shelves of Puritan libraries seem to have groaned under the weight of Roman Catholic bible commentaries. The town library of Ipswich, presided over by the famous Puritan Samuel Ward, was fully stocked with Roman Catholic works, including commentaries by famous exegetes such as Aretius, Maldonatus, Arias Montanus and Cornelius à Lapide, and even works by the notorious Tridentine Catholics Alphonsus Salmeron and Joannes de Piñeda, the latter a member of the Inquisition.[24] The library of William Ames contained many of the same works, and especially large collections of commentaries by Toletus and Cajetan. Another Catholic exegete making regular appearances in Protestant library lists and marginal citations was the Spanish Jesuit Benedictus Pererius. His commentary on Genesis in particular was probably the most important, and certainly the most regularly cited, of all those being used by Protestant writers in the seventeenth century, Andrew Willet for one making frank admission of his indebtedness to the Spaniard who had 'taken great paines in this argument'.[25] Indeed, so prominent were Catholic bible commentaries in Protestant libraries that one scholar has suggested that 'the great commentaries of the Renaissance are not only international but also suprasectarian'.[26]

Even on directly doctrinal matters, hardline English Protestants did not read Catholic authors merely in order to refute them. The libraries of Ames and Ward display a clear interest in the writings of the Dominicans in the *De Auxiliis* controversy.[27] The works of the Spanish Dominicans Domingo Bañez and Didacus Alvarez, which appear in both Puritan libraries, adopted a line of argument on questions of free will and predestination which arguably shared a number of similarities with the Calvinist position on these matters. More generally, as has been stressed already, the polarities of confessional polemic can easily exaggerate the doctrinal differences between Roman and Protestant authors, and as a result we may often seriously underestimate the degree of theological borrowing taking place, and the genuine influence that Roman Catholic theologians could have on Protestant divines. If we accept the existence of the vast, unbridgeable doctrinal gulf between Rome and Protestantism that the 'Two Churches' style of anti-Catholic polemic depicted, then it becomes very difficult to explain much of the intellectual history of the seventeenth century.

It is important to remember, then, that the constant anxiety of Puritan writers concerning the availability of popish books should not be taken as evidence that their own libraries were free of such works. Joseph Hall might well agonize over Cardinal Bellarmine's wide readership in England, referring (with, one assumes, some exaggeration) to how 'our very ungrounded artisans, young gentlemen, frail women, buy, read, traverse promiscuously the dangerous writings of our subtlest Jesuits'. But he did nor intend to suggest that the same Jesuits should not form an important part of the reading of any mature, educated scholar.[28] Moreover, even anti-Protestant polemical writings by Romanist divines were greatly sought after by Puritan divines, and London booksellers could command a high price for them. There was also no shortage of publishers who were prepared to publish both Catholic and Protestant works according to demand.[29]

For all the venomous assaults made upon each other in polemical literature, Protestant and Catholic scholars (even clerical ones) do also seem to have been capable of enjoying amicable relations with one other. It may not be surprising that the Laudian Richard Montagu exchanged expressions of mutual esteem with the Jesuits Fronto Ducaeus and Andreas Schottus, and that he sent his own edition of the five books of Eusebius' *Adversus Marcellum Ancyram* to be included in a Roman Catholic edition of patristic works published in 1628.[30] Yet it is striking to find that James Ussher, the implacably anti-Catholic Archbishop of Armagh, exchanged scholarly correspondence and research assistance with David Rothe, the Romanist Bishop of Ossory, and the Franciscan historian Luke Wadding (whom Ussher asked to search out historical materials in the Vatican Library). The Benedictine Augustine Baker also managed to make use of Robert Cotton's library for his history of medieval English monasticism.[31]

The degree of cross-confessionalism in the realm of the arts hardly needs elaboration. In poetry, music, painting, sculpture and architecture, ideas easily permeated confessional boundaries. The works of foreign Roman Catholics in all these fields were admired, and musicians such as Byrd, Bull and Dowland observed only minimal conformity to Protestantism. The works of Rubens and Bernini were famously admired in Charles I's court, while the example of Prince Henry's court is a helpful reminder that a passionate and militaristic Protestant nationalism could coexist with taste for Italianate style and a courtly circle that included a number of Roman Catholic aesthetes.[32]

III

The political world might appear at first sight to be an area where confessional divisions were more acute and serious. Nevertheless, the regularity with which religious language intruded into political argument should not blind us to the extent to which confessional divisions were often disregarded.

Anti-Catholicism and Protestant nationalism were habits of thought which found foreign policy a natural area for comment and exhortation. The attempted invasion by Catholic Spain in 1588, and the later struggles of the Thirty Years' War, could easily be depicted as part of a universal confessional struggle between the forces of the Antichrist and those of the true Protestant religion. Direct military conflict between Catholic and Protestant forces seemed a natural expression and realization of the bellicose imagery of the Book of Revelation, and Puritan authors kept up an unceasing depiction of Europe as a stage upon which the forces of good and evil were locked in inevitable and fatal conflict.[33] Nevertheless, while the confessional conflicts of the sixteenth century had undoubtedly introduced new motives for division and conflict among nations, and provided the ideological basis for a polarizing commentary on political events, they did not simply reshape the world of diplomacy and foreign policy to their will. Whatever the imperatives of confessionalism, those of diplomatic calculation, pragmatism and national self-interest were as vital as they had always been, however much they might choose to clothe themselves in confessional garb whenever possible.

To begin with, diplomatic niceties inevitably demanded an attitude that was not simply conditioned by confessional division. Formal diplomatic precedence was awarded as a matter of course to Spanish and French ambassadors, rather than to those of Protestant countries.[34] The balance of power in Europe also meant that an anti-Spanish foreign policy could rarely be simply an anti-Catholic one, as it usually required the support of the Catholic French. It has more recently been argued that England's alliance with Henry IV's France in the 1590s, combined with a tendency to see the Pope as subordinate to the power of Spain, destroyed straightforward anti-Catholicism and its unitary picture of the forces of Rome. But in fact Roman Catholicism continued to be depicted in anti-Catholic polemic throughout the early Stuart period as a unitary force under the power of the Pope. The foreign policy concerns of the 1590s and

later decades merely reflected the capacity of simply binary oppositions to coexist with a more informed and discriminating perception of political divisions among Roman Catholic countries.[35] In
other words, the discourse of foreign diplomacy presupposed con-
ceptual distinctions and calculations that were alien to the radically
polarizing style of anti-Catholic discourse, but this did not mean
that the one discourse was regarded as simply invalidating the
other.

Even those divines most insistent on a Protestant foreign policy
were not necessarily prepared to sacrifice their careers in its pursuit.
Recent historians (especially Tom Cogswell) have drawn important
attention to the extent of popular hostility provoked by the proposed Spanish marriage for Prince Charles.[36] Nevertheless, while
the significance of this opposition can hardly be understated, it is
important to stress that, for all the strong language deployed, contemporaries did not view the matter merely in inflexible confessional terms. Individual divines did not either refuse all thought of
compromise, or supinely and cravenly support the Catholic marriage, but sought instead to pick their own different routes through
the minefield of conflicting religious, practical and political allegiances. A recent study of John Donne's conduct at this time has
emphasized the careful *via media* that he pursued when called upon
to defend James's policies.[37] More outspoken opponents of the
Spanish Match were also aware of the political dangers of creating
an impression that they were simply incapable of countenancing
the conduct of non-confessional policies. The hardline anti-papist
and convert priest Richard Sheldon was severely reprimanded for
an anti-Catholic sermon that he gave at Paul's Cross in 1622 at the
height of the unrest over the Spanish Match. Yet it would be wrong
to depict Sheldon's position as one of unreflective and absolute
anti-Catholicism. In the form in which it was subsequently printed,
in 1625, the sermon does indeed stress the duty of magistrates to
make war on the Whore of Babylon. Yet Sheldon also explicitly left
room for *raison d'état*. He pointed out that the Christian magistrate
might offer toleration towards peaceable Roman Catholics in the
country 'for some high respects', if he might thereby ensure the
better treatment of Protestants in Catholic countries. The latter was
James's justification for his policy of offering *de facto* toleration of
Roman Catholics as part of the Spanish negotiations. What is
particularly striking about the sermon is Sheldon's opposition to
the 'Neutralizers' who were adopting a moderate line towards

the errors of Rome. Since reason of state demanded that Roman Catholics be tolerated, it was all the more important to Sheldon that the traditional condemnation of Rome's religion should be made with redoubled force. In other words, violent anti-Catholicism was intimately related to a policy of practical toleration: it was precisely *because* Roman Catholics were tolerated in practice that it was vital to attack their religion stridently on the level of theory.[38]

It could be objected that the text of Sheldon's sermon that was published in 1625 might have been more explicit in its allowance of toleration than the sermon originally preached in 1622, and that the deference to *raison d'état* was directed more at justifying the impending French marriage of Charles I. But, if this were true, it would simply introduce a further significant element of compromise into the anti-Catholic position. Despite all the popular hostility to the proposed Spanish Match, the French Catholic marriage that followed swiftly on the failure of the earlier negotiations contained in its marriage treaty many similar articles concerning the toleration of Roman Catholics. Although strong suspicions and fears were certainly entertained about the possible content of the marriage treaty, and the government undoubtedly feared parliamentary unrest on the matter,[39] it is still striking that there was so little popular protest over the marriage itself. The same anti-Catholicism that prompted opposition to the Spanish Match should in theory have mobilized opposition to the French marriage too.

There is a number of possible reasons for the remarkable acquiescence in this Catholic marriage. One lies in the sheer speed with which the marriage was accomplished. In contrast to the long and drawn-out negotiations over the Spanish marriage, the French marriage was concluded swiftly and secretly, and the country presented with what was essentially a *fait accompli*. Deprived of the opportunity to debate the issue, hardline Protestants would seem to have been prepared to knuckle down and accept what had taken place, even if the precise terms of the marriage provided ready ground for argument and dissent. Would a rapid Spanish marriage have disabled Protestant critics in the same way? Another more obvious reason for the acceptance of the French marriage was the fact that it was combined with a French alliance that was necessary for the impending war with Spain. In this context, as Marvin Breslow has noted, Puritan writers were prepared to adopt a very charitable attitude towards Louis XIII, even when he turned against his own Huguenot subjects in the 1620s. In the 1630s, enthusiasts for a war with Spain to restore the Calvinist Palatinate were usually pro-French, and closely associated at court with the Catholic queen Henrietta Maria. Again, a unitary vision of Roman Catholicism was forced to contend with practical requirements for a successful war with Spain that could not be fought with sole reference to confessional allegiance.[40]

Moreover, the other side of the coin of an anti-Catholic foreign policy, namely a union of interest with other Protestant countries, was not necessarily always forthcoming. For most of the population, envy and xenophobia often complicated their dealings with their confessional allies abroad. The Dutch were potentially England's most important Protestant allies, but outside the simplicities of anti-Catholic discourse, even Puritans expressed strong reservations over the arrogance and avarice that supposedly stained the Dutch national character. The ideology of Protestant internationalism could not overcome the fact that the Protestant Dutch were England's principal commercial rivals in many areas of the globe. The anti-Dutch sentiment stirred up at the time of the so-called 'Amboyna massacre' was genuine enough, and while the East India Company had to be careful not to appear anti-Protestant in its condemnation of the Dutch, it felt confident enough to declare in print in 1628 that the Dutch 'as they have infinitly prevailed in the augmentation of their Trade by the declination of other Nations, so they ayme at nothing more now then to weaken the English in their Trafficke, for we onely are their Corrivals, able to keepe them from the absolute dominion of the Seas'.[41] Considerations of national interest and commercial success were not therefore necessarily subordinated to anti-Catholic ideology. After all, even puritanically minded laymen apparently had no qualms in trading directly with the Spanish enemy even at the height of war, and were happy to go to war with the Protestant Dutch in the 1650s.[42]

IV

The practical compromises and adaptations that we have already observed in the areas of anti-Catholic discourse, intellectual scholarship and politics, can also be seen in the way that Roman Catholics were treated at a local level. Historians of both the seventeenth and eighteenth centuries have emphasized the degree to which local office-holders, while opposed to 'popery' in a general sense, were less prepared to prosecute men who were neighbors or friends, or who shared a common social status and interests. While they may have believed in the principle that no Roman Catholic could be a loyal subject, they seem in practice to have known that many Roman Catholic neighbors were politically loyal. As MPs they may have demanded in parliament the fierce execution of recusancy laws in the hottest anti-Catholic language, but as JPs in their counties their vehemence seems to have considerably diminished. Moreover, even at the height of anti-Catholic fears in 1641, a procession of Long Parliament MPs intervened to plead for the exemption of Catholic friends from the rigors of the anti-Catholic legislation.[43] Nor should it be implied that such restraint was only practiced by groups and individuals whose attachment to Protestantism was skin-deep. On the contrary, this practical toleration might often be accompanied by Puritan sentiments. It is interesting in this light to read an exchange of letters between two of Elizabeth's senior ministers in 1584. Writing to Archbishop Whitgift, Lord Burghley had registered his concern at receiving constant complaints that Whitgift's proceedings against nonconforming ministers and preachers were giving great encouragement to papists. In reply, Whitgift made the oft-reiterated point that papists were more encouraged by seeing the encouragement given to the disorderly Puritans, but he then exclaimed: 'O! my Lord, wold to God, some of them which use this argument had no Papists in their families, and not otherwise also countenance them, whereby indede they receave incoragement.'[44]

Whitgift had a point. There were precious few puritanically inclined families in the Elizabethan or early Stuart period which were entirely free of Roman Catholics. Among the families of Elizabeth's most prominent councillors, the daughter of Sir Francis Walsingham, the son of the Earl of Leicester, a grandson of Lord Burghley and a younger son of Lord Buckhurst were all Catholic converts, and even those unimpeachably anti-Catholic bishops George Abbot and Tobie Matthew had close Roman Catholic relations (a nephew and son respectively).[45] Some strongly Protestant gentry families might also have a cadet branch which remained staunchly Roman Catholic. Some of these Roman Catholic relatives might be disowned by their Protestant kinsmen, but family connections *could* often ensure that such cadet branches were shielded from the rigours of the recusancy commissioners.[46] More generally, members of the gentry might also be on friendly terms with local Catholics of the same social status, and would often similarly intervene to protect them from the more severe anti-Catholic legislation. King James complained in 1614 that laws against recusants were not being enforced, partly because some of the judges 'were kin or friends of the papists'.[47] A significant percentage of the higher nobility of England also remained Roman Catholic or crypto-Catholic, and could therefore still hope to wield social power, and (on occasion) trust that their fellow peers in the House of Lords would close ranks if recusancy proceedings threatened the privilege of their order.[48]

Prominent Roman Catholic gentry might also hope to be able to avoid prosecution, or at least the full weight of the penal legislation, by bribing or simply browbeating socially inferior officials or magistrates.[49] The social and potential political importance of Catholics was particularly evident in Yorkshire, and never more so than before a parliamentary election. The correspondence of Sir Thomas Wentworth in the 1620s makes it entirely clear that the Catholics were one of the most important interest groups to which a potential MP had to address himself. It is interesting to note that, despite the undoubted popular following and national prestige that Wentworth had gained from his refusal to pay the Forced Loan, in 1628 he was assured by his friend Christopher Wandesford that he could not be sure of a parliamentary seat unless he was partnered by a local gentleman who was 'gratious with the papists'.[50]

We must be careful not to present too rosy a picture of Roman Catholic fortunes, however. We cannot take at face value the Puritan Richard Bernard's damning indictment of 'allowance, toleration, connivencie, or remisnesse, and paralyticall distemper of the arme of justice' in the treatment of Roman Catholics. On the contrary, more recent research by Michael Questier has emphasized the remarkable efficiency of the government's administrative machinery for enforcing religious conformity upon Roman Catholics. Many Roman Catholics suffered constant and crippling financial penalties, even though the Exchequer was more keen to exploit them as a source of state revenue, rather than to use the laws to secure their permanent religious conformity (as the more vigorous anti-Catholics clearly wished).[51] In Yorkshire, fellow members of the gentry and even kinsmen might still exact penalties for recusancy from Roman Catholics, and in some areas at least, it has been suggested, 'religious antagonism weighed more heavily than class loyalty'. In some cases, of course, vigorous prosecution might have represented, not the subversion of communal ties by confessional divisions, but simply the workings of more traditional rivalry, greed or self-interest.[52] Clearly, patterns of behavior towards Roman Catholics varied enormously with regional differences and the varying social and political complexion of the local elite.[53] Julia Merritt's forthcoming work on Westminster is particularly interesting in this regard, as she presents a subtle and complex picture of the multiple influences that lay behind the treatment of individual Roman Catholics in a single urban community.[54]

The crucial point, however, is that anti-Catholicism did not convert itself in an uncomplicated way into the severe prosecution of local Roman Catholics. The practical accommodations that did take place need not, however, be taken to represent a conscious rejection of Protestant principles. Partly, they simply manifested the interplay of different codes of conduct which were not necessarily confessionally driven. Local community values bound neighbors together, while members of the gentry could feel bound by a code of honor and conduct in which issues of confessional allegiance had no place. The Roman Catholic Petre family gave hospitality to their neighbors regardless of religious allegiance, and the same was presumably true of Protestant gentry.[55] Some preachers, like Joseph Hall, could only throw up their arms in despair at how 'our Romish Samaritans haunt our tables, our closets, our ears ... we match, converse, consult with them carelessly'.[56] But it is also true that a certain amount of civil correspondence with Catholics was even granted specific approval by some divines. William Bedell in his *Examination of Motives* had defended certain forms of civil intercourse with those of differing religions according to a set of careful definitions. Responding to Roman Catholic attempts to dissuade Catholic gentry from attending church, or from any social interaction with Protestants, Bedell instead set out specifically to refute the argument that 'society with those of contrary Religion, hath alwaies been pernicious and unlawfull'. Not only did Bedell deny that Protestantism was 'a contrary religion to the Romane obedience', but he also emphasized that many forms of social interaction would be permissible even if it were such. 'Society' he divided into various aspects: first, a distinction needed to be made between society 'in the duties of religion' and society 'in common life', and second, a distinction made between 'necessary' society and 'voluntary' society. 'Necessary' society, which is 'not at our choice and discretion', Bedell defined very widely: it included 'the society of parents and children, servants and masters, subjects and princes, citizens, neighbours, kinsfolkes, passengers in the same ship, guests at the same table; yea, every man with another, in that hee is a man'. In the relationship between subject and prince, husband and wife, servant and master, 'the Law of God, or man' must be upheld, and civil society was necessary 'even with men of a false religion or wicked life'. 'Voluntary' civil society, 'as of contracting marriage, friendship, familiarity, choosing our habitation and company with whom we consort ourselves' was a different matter, and should not be held with men of a false religion (but was still, according to Bedell, permissible for Protestants with Roman Catholics).[57]

Roman Catholic casuists, too, were prepared to recognize and allow for those occasions when the social demands of the gentry lifestyle and their responsibility to offer hospitality to their neighbors might require Roman Catholic gentlemen to compromise some of their confessional duties. For example, they were permitted to be present at meals in Protestant houses when grace was said, and were allowed to bare their heads when the prayers were uttered – partly to conceal their faith but also, it was revealingly conceded, 'out of civility and politeness. For not to bare one's head when everyone else is bareheaded is a sort of incivility and the act of a bumpkin.'[58] Even though they shared Hall's fear that 'we are easily infected with heresy through familiarity with heretics', the casuists still emphasized that 'we can show them a good deal of familiarity and loyalty without it being too much familiarity', and concurred with Bedell that the natural duty of subjection to superiors meant that it was not sinful for wives, children and servants to serve husbands, fathers and masters in heretical activities (such as preparing meat on fast days).[59]

It should also be remembered, moreover, that while Roman Catholicism may have been depicted in the more extreme anti-Catholic polemic as an increasingly alien, exotic and above all foreign force, there was another type of Roman Catholicism with which early modern Englishmen still maintained some contact. This was a form of Roman Catholicism that was not alien or exotic but familiar, even reassuring, and from which a sense of estrangement had not necessarily been achieved – and that was England's own Roman Catholic past. English Protestant preachers had done their best to create a sense of disjuncture with the past, with their regular invocation of a people newly converted, fleeing the popish Babylon, and destroying the monuments of idolatry. But it is vital not to let the language of violent change and sweeping Protestantization disguise the fact that many of the sermons that eulogized the newly Protestantized Church of England were delivered in parish churches that were still dominated by the images and physical structures of the Catholic past. Local churches still contained medieval and early sixteenth-century monuments with Catholic inscriptions, and for all of the Edwardian and Elizabethan reformations, still contained many pieces of medieval church furniture, including seating and fonts. Much elaborate stonework still survived, as did a great deal of medieval stained glass, which Puritans such as Henry Sherfield were still trying to remove from their parish churches in the 1630s. The high cost of replacing the 'stories in glasse windowes', or their inaccessibility, or even the simple lack of any specifically idolatrous content, helped much old stained glass to remain intact until the iconoclasm of the 1640s, when they were removed along with the newer Laudian decorations.[60] The very structures of the churches themselves were designed for Catholic worship, and the realignment of church furniture and services could not entirely disguise this.

Moreover, all early modern Englishmen in a sense had Roman Catholic neighbors and kinsmen, in the form of their own ancestors. There is ample evidence to suggest that English Protestants were anxious to be reassured that their ancestors who died before the Reformation had been saved, despite having held Roman Catholic beliefs. Archbishop Toble Matthew noted in 1616 that Roman Catholic proselytizers entangled people more in this matter than in any other, while Thomas Morton remarked in the 1620s that in his own experience in dealing with Roman Catholics this particular point was 'the greatest barre and hinderance unto us, for their conversion'.[61] In response, English Protestant divines, and even those who were zealous in their anti-popery, were forced to develop a more positive picture of the pre-Reformation Latin Church, and of the possibilities of salvation within her. This approach is, of course, yet another example of the compromising and softening of anti-Catholic polemic in the face of practical necessity. The more that Protestant divines sought to 'Protestantize' the pre-Reformation Church, the more they reaffirmed the bonds between the present and the Catholic past.[62]

It is important, too, that any study of local attitudes towards Catholicism, at least among the more educated members of society, should allow for a certain degree of simple intellectual curiosity about the forbidden religion. One secular priest missioner, writing to the English secular clergy's agent in Rome Thomas More in 1611–12, noted a growing interest in religious issues among lay Protestants, particularly in matters of religious controversy and cases of conscience. Coming across Roman Catholic books, they would often try to seek out Catholic priests, either out of curiosity or in order to engage in religious debate and controversy.[63]

There is an important sense, therefore, in which early modern English men and women were used to disregarding confessional divisions on a fairly systematic basis. This was made easier, on the local level, because of the way in which popular, polarizing forms of anti-Catholicism increasingly depicted papists as an alien, exotic, but above all foreign force. The more that the adherents of the Roman religion were presented as foreign and demonic, the more incongruous it would seem to apply this model to friends or neighbors (or, indeed, to the country's own past). Even if the formal doctrinal position against Rome was unable to accommodate the notion of a faithful Roman Catholic who yet was also a loyal and dependable subject of the Crown, both the central government and the laity more generally worked on the practical assumption that this was possible, and that 'good papists' both could be and should be easily distinguished from 'bad papists'.[64] 'Bad papists' were more 'Romanized' in their views, and were typically priests, strangers, but above all foreigners. It was foreigners against whom popular opprobrium was therefore most directed, and it was strangers who most often generated the local 'popish scares' in the early 1640s.[65]

The greatest fear of all, however, was that of *unseen* Roman Catholics. Andrew Willet, writing just five years before the Gunpowder Plot, confessed that he wished that all English papists were recusants 'that we might the better take heede of them. But there be many close Papists in England, that are content for a while to temporize. waiting for an houre, which I trust they shall never see.'[66] The scope of this fear is made clear by the motion put in the Addled Parliament (which is chilling in its twentieth-century resonances) that Roman Catholics 'shoulde weare yellowe Cappes and slippers'.[67] Even more worrying for some commentators were those Roman Catholics who not only attended Protestant services, but also took the Oath of Allegiance. The Oath was in a sense a tangible manifestation of the pragmatic assumption of most people that

there were indeed politically loyal Roman Catholics, even if theoretically this was impossible. For those most preoccupied with the theoretical impossibility, however, the prospect of Roman Catholics'
taking the oath was deeply worrying: it made them impossible to
detect, but would also oblige them to carry out some form of vil-
lainy to atone to their confessor for this offence in taking the oath.
As Richard Bernard concluded, quoting the sermon of a friend
(perhaps Robert Bolton), 'conformity to the Oath of allegiance, and
other outward formall satisfaction of the State, concurring with a
resolution to continue in Poperie, is farre more pernicious to the
State, then open and profest Recusancie.'[68]

It was this anxiety over unseen Roman Catholics, rather than
an allergic hatred of Roman Catholicism in the flesh, that would
ironically prove to be 'more pernicious to the State' than anything
else.

V

As we have seen, Elizabethan and early Stuart anti-Catholicism
could present a starkly polarized view of the world, in which true
English Protestants were aligned in direct and hostile opposition to
every trace of Roman Catholicism. But, for all its ideological force,
this was no more than an ideal, prescriptive model. Historians have
more recently retreated from the suggestion that early Stuart
English society was one dominated, not by mere iconoclasm (which
might involve the reformation of images), but by 'iconophobia', in
which people were seized by an allergic reaction to all images,
which they totally repudiated, and were afflicted by a 'visual
anorexia', bereft of visual art. On the contrary, Tessa Watt has
argued that, while images may have been distrusted to a great or
lesser extent, and their religious use circumscribed, they still seem
to have been ubiquitous in early modern England.[69] What is true of
images was arguably true of Roman Catholicism as well. While
there may have been a general fear and wariness of Roman
Catholicism, and at least one mode of anti-Catholic discourse which
represented Catholicism as the diabolical inversion of all the norms
of civilized Protestant society, this does not seem to have created a
society seized by a frantic, allergic response to everything with the
least taint of Rome, and therefore barren of all remnants of Catholic
objects and ideas. Rather, the polarized models of confessional

relations lived in uneasy – perhaps contradictory – coexistence with what might even be called rampant cross-confessionalism in many areas of life and thought. Instead of the 'papophobic' society depicted by some modern scholars, the social and intellectual land-scape of early Stuart England was studded throughout with Roman Catholic physical and intellectual structures and a degree of practi-cal compromise remarkably at variance with the theoretically absolute division between Protestantism and Roman Catholicism.

How should we interpret the *mentalité* of a society riven by such inconsistencies? Clearly, this degree of confessional confusion did not denote the early emergence of a pluralistic, religiously tolerant society: the semantic associations of 'tolerance' in this period were almost entirely negative ones. But historians such as Gregory Hanlon have been tempted by this evidence to reject 'the assump-tion that most contemporaries adhered to both the spirit and the letter of the doctrines they professed or the ideas they expressed'. The complexities and contradictions attendant on the interaction of religious principles with individuals' circumstances could create a situation in which 'culture offered multiple references and multiple choices so that individuals could play simultaneously on several fields of commitment or engagement'.[70] Simple confessional alle-giances might thus be seen as inherently unrealistic and insufficient belief-systems, with anti-Catholicism being unable to encompass and explain the range of incongruities and inconsistencies that dog everyday life. In these circumstances (it would appear) individuals dealt with inconsistency by simply turning a blind eye. Anti-Catholicism was thus simply one among many different ways in which early modern Englishmen depicted their society and its nor-mative values. Just as recent work on the political thought of the period has represented the existence of a variety of political lan-guages, working within carefully defined boundaries, between which people shifted with little sense of incompatibility, so anti-Catholicism represented simply one of many discourses deployed by people to explain, understand and justify their social. political and intellectual activities.[71]

But, in this case, did rigidly unyielding anti-Catholicism really matter, or was it merely an irrelevance, easily sidestepped by moving into different modes of explanation and codes of conduct? There is a danger that the approach described above may exagger-ate people's capacity to live with contradictory beliefs or half-beliefs. While people's belief-systems may not have been entirely coherent, and while religious principles may have been compromised, it was nevertheless the case that people probably felt the need at least to *attempt* to harmonize conflicting ideas, and were happiest when there was the least contradiction between religious principles and daily life. These were ideological inconsistencies which could generate genuine and serious tensions, both within individuals, and in their relationship with others. The fact that the absolute divisions promulgated by anti-Catholicism were often compromised did not invalidate such notions, but rather increased the desirability of strongly anti-Catholic gestures at times of crisis, and this was a fact which could be exploited politically, or even commercially.

Certainly, contemporaries occasionally derived political and even commercial benefit by sliding between modes of anti-Catholicism and manipulating the discontinuities, playing off the one against the other. When Peter Heylyn seized upon Prynne's citation of Mariana to suggest that Prynne therefore approved of the Jesuit's doctrines of tyrannicide, the unscrupulous Laudian polemicist was deliberately embracing the simplistic 'papophobic' position which he would ridicule elsewhere in his own writings. The book trade could also profit from the ambiguous attitudes towards Roman Catholic scholarship. Thomas Goad, a chaplain to the notoriously anti-Catholic Archbishop Abbot, expressed his concern in 1621 that the granting of a monopoly on the importing of all foreign books written by popish authors would lead to a cynical increase in their price 'under colour of hinderinge poysonous bookes'. All divines, he complained, would thus feel the pinch when they tried to purchase works by Roman worthies such as Bellarmine and Maldonatus.[72] Again, the simple 'papophobic' position could thus be invoked as a means of boosting book prices. Selden's famous remark that 'wee charge the prelaticall Clergie with popery to make them odious tho' wee know they are guiltye of no such thing' should not be taken as an accurate description of the anti-episcopal position (Selden was surely hardly a typical politician of the period), but it does demonstrate an awareness of the fact that anti-Catholicism *could* be manipulated.[73]

Nevertheless, these examples should not be taken to imply that the simplistic 'papophobic' position was simply irrelevant or insincere. It was certainly not irrelevant: after all, in the examples provided in the previous paragraph, the use of the more extreme mode of anti-Catholic discourse always triumphed over the more pragmatic mode. To be sure, this polarized view of Catholicism, which presented a simple black-and-white world in which the lines of confessional demarcation were strong, clear and not to be broached, existed within a society in which the same lines were constantly criss-crossed, redrawn, reconceived and tacitly ignored. But this degree of compromise generated very real ideological tensions. Absolute confessional imperatives spoke in a loud, clamoring and simplifying voice, and at times of tension and crisis, their demands were treated with far more anxious concern and respect. Times of political crisis in early Stuart England were also times when the country was seized by a fear of internal betrayal, and it was at these moments that the ignoring of confessional absolutes – however widespread and seemingly tolerable at other times – could become suddenly serious and alarming.

We have also already noted how Puritans were most exercised by fears of *hidden* Roman Catholics. If people feared exotic, unseen Catholics, they also feared fifth columnists, crypto-Catholics, hidden within the Protestant establishment. But how were such hidden Catholics to be detected? One obvious way was to search for evidence of supposed Protestants fraternizing with the enemy and his ideas, in a manner that ran starkly counter to the theoretically absolute division between the two religions. As we have seen, however, the many compromises and complexities in the early Stuart view of Roman Catholicism created a situation in which the confessional polarization to which everyone deferred on the level of theory, was systematically circumvented. This meant that it was very simple indeed to find the necessary 'evidence' that a suspected individual was guilty of temporizing towards the Church of Rome. In a sense, of course, virtually everyone was guilty of such temporizing. But this meant that, once a political crisis had created a temporary popular mood in which people were sensitized to the more absolute, 'papophobic' stance, then it was very easy to feed the fears of confessional betrayal with the evidence of daily compromise with Roman Catholicism by one's political enemies.

In these circumstances, too, it was relatively simple to find suspects deploying other, more subtle modes of anti-Catholic discourse, who could then be portrayed as betraying Protestant orthodoxy. The existence of multiple modes of anti-Catholic polemic can thus help to explain the fact that Laud and his colleagues were frequently charged by their Calvinist opponents with having uttered comments about Rome which anti-Laudian Calvinists and even Puritans had themselves written in different circumstances. I have argued elsewhere that there was in fact a good deal that was novel and distinctive in Laudians' perceptions of the Roman Church. But the specific charges against them were often generated by the presupposition of their crypto-Catholicism, which led their critics to lambast as 'popish' positions which they themselves had often held, or to attach dread significance to the possession of 'popish' books, or 'popish' friends when these were very common.

   If most of English society truly upheld the 'papophobic' version of anti-Catholic discourse which scholars have identified, then there would have been little reason for political conflict. Instead, it is important to recognize that, while violent anti-Catholicism could be a highly potent ideological force in times of political crisis, it was not the only form of anti-Catholicism. Moreover, while confessionally driven anti-Catholicism was a *prominent* discourse in early modern England, it was not the single *dominant* one. It is true that some Laudians in particular seemed to be somewhat immune to its charms. But it would also be wrong to assume that all non-Laudians and Puritans were simply slaves to an unthinkingly antagonistic mindset. This was not true of all the clergy, and it was undoubtedly not true of the laity. If the precepts of anti-Catholicism were the 'politically correct' language of the day which could never openly be challenged without considerable danger, this did not mean that they were not effectively undermined on a daily basis by the norms of intellectual inquiry, political behaviour, commercial calculation and social intercourse. At times of political crisis, however, when men groped for the reassuring certainties and simplicities of extreme confessional regulation, and were fearful of ideological betrayal, it was precisely the fact that anti-Catholicism did not control everyday conduct in society that made its precepts so problematic and divisive.

ACKNOWLEDGEMENT

I am grateful to Julia Merritt for her comments on an earlier draft of this chapter, for allowing me to read over her own forthcoming work on Catholics in Westminster, and for many discussions over several years on this topic.

NOTES

1. P. Lake, 'Anti-popery: the Structure of a Prejudice', and T. Cogswell, 'England the the Spanish Match', in R. Cust and A. Hughes, eds., *Conflict in Early Stuart England* (London and New York: Longman, 1988), 72–106, 107–33; R. Clifton, 'Fear of Popery', in C. Russell, ed., *The Origins of the English Civil War* (London: Macmillan, 1973), 144–67, and 'The Popular Fear of Catholics during the English Revolution', *Past & Present* 52 (August 1971): 23–55; C. Z. Weiner, 'The Beleaguered Isle: A Study of Elizabethan and Early Jacobean Anti-Catholicism', *Past & Present* 51 (May 1971): 27–62; P. Christianson, *Reformers and Babylon* (Toronto and Buffalo: University of Toronto Press, 1978); A. J. Fletcher, *The Outbreak of the English Civil War* (London: Edward Arnold, 1981), 407–19 and passim; C. Hibbard, *Charles I and the Popish Plot* (Chapel Hill: University of North Carolina Press, 1983).
2. See, most recently, C. Haydon, *Anti-Catholicism in Eighteenth-Century England* (Manchester: Manchester University Press, 1993).
3. Lake, 'Anti-popery', 74–9, 98 n6; Clifton, 'Fear of Popery', 148–9.
4. Magdalen College, Oxford MS 281/22 (petition of James Wadsworth to William Herbert, Earl of Pembroke, n.d.); M. C. Questier, *Conversion, Politics and Religion in England, 1580–1625* (Cambridge: Cambridge University Press, 1996), 47–8.
5. A. Milton, *Catholic and Reformed: the Roman and Protestant Churches in English Protestant Thought, 1600–1640* (Cambridge: Cambridge University Press, 1995), chs. 1–7.
6. Ibid., 134–9, 161–2.
7. Ibid., 139–41.
8. Edmund Bunny, *A Treatise Tending to Pacification* (1586), 79–81, 83, 93; Richard Bernard, *Looke beyond Luther* (1623), 44; Milton, *Catholic and Reformed*, 323–8, 340–2.
9. Milton, *Catholic and Reformed*, 176–8.
10. For examples, see Edmund Bunny, *A Briefe Answer* (1589); John Dove, *A Perswasion to the English Recusants* (1603); William Bedell, *An Examination of Certaine Motives to Recusansie* (Cambridge, 1628).
11. William Perkins, *A Reformed Catholike* (1634), A2, A3^v, 1–9, 293–4; F. G. M. Broeyer, 'De Irenische Perkins–Vertaling van de Arminian Everard Booth (1577–1610)', *Nederlands Archief voor Kerkgeschiedenis* 71–2 (1991): 177–210; Jean Hotman, *Syllabus aliquot synodorum et colloquiorum* (Strasbourg, 1628), D1^v–2^v.
12. M. Feingold, 'The Humanities' and 'The Mathematical Sciences and New Philosophies' in N. Tyacke, ed., *History of the University of Oxford*, vol. 4: *Seventeenth-Century Oxford* (Oxford: Clarendon Press, 1997), 294–6, 403.
13. L. E. Loemker, *Struggle for Synthesis* (Cambridge, MA: Harvard University Press, 1972), 20, 48, 119; J. Platt, *Reformed Thought and Scholasticism: the Arguments for the Existence of God in Dutch Theology, 1575–1650* (Leiden: E. J. Brill, 1982), 155, 159, 166–8, 229–31.

14. J. P. Somerville, *Politics and Ideology in England, 1603–1640* (London and New York: Longman, 1986), 77, 129, 237.
15. *Documents Relating to the Proceedings against William Prynne in 1634 and 1637*, ed. S. R. Gardiner, Camden Society, 2nd ser., vol. 18 (Westminster: Camden Society, 1877), 7, 12, 41.
16. William Ames, *Conscience, With the Power and Cases Therof* (1639), 'To the Reader'; K. L. Sprunger, ed., *The Auction Catalogue of the Library of William Ames*, Catalogi redivivi no. 6 (Utrecht: HES, 1988), 6–7. Azorius and Azpilcueta are obvious examples of casuists who were influential in the thinking of Ames and other Protestants.
17. Feingold, 'The Humanities', 322.
18. T. Birrell, 'English Catholic Mystics in Non-Catholic Circles', *The Downside Review* 94 (1976): 60–81, 99–117, 213–28; R. McNulty, 'A Protestant Version of Robert Persons' First Book of the Christian Exercise', *Huntington Library Quarterly* 23 (1959–60): 271–300; B. S. Gregory, '"The True and Zealouse Service of God": Robert Parsons, Edmund Bunny, and *The First Booke of the Christian Exercise*', *Journal of Ecclesiastical History* 45 (1994): 238–68; V. Houliston, 'Why Robert Persons would not be Pacified: Edmund Bunny's Theft of *The Book of Resolution*', in T. M. McCoog, ed., *The Reckoned Expense: Edmund Campion and the Early English Jesuits* (Woodbridge, Suffolk: Boydell, 1996), 159–77.
19. A. F. Allison, 'The "Mysticism" of Manchester Al Mondo: Some Catholic Borrowings in a Seventeenth-Century Anglican Work of Devotion', and J. M. Blom, 'A German Jesuit and his Anglican Readers: The Case of Jeremias Drexelius (1581–1632)', in G. A. M. Janssens and F. G. A. M. Aarts, eds., *Studies in Seventeenth Century English Literature: History and Bibliography* (Amsterdam: Rodopi, 1984), 1–11, 41–51.
20. Questier, *Conversion*, ch. 4; P. F. Jensen, 'The Life of Faith in the Teaching of Elizabethan Protestants' (D.Phil. thesis, Oxford, 1979).
21. F. Pollock, ed., *Table Talk of John Selden* (London: Quaritch, 1927), 23; Sprunger, 6–7.
22. Willet, *Hexapla in Exodum* (1608), A6; J. C. H. Aveling, 'The English Clergy, Catholic and Protestant, in the 16th and 17th Centuries', in J. C. H. Aveling, D. M. Loades and H. R. McAdoo, *Rome and the Anglicans* (Berlin: De Gruyter, 1982), 94, 123.
23. Richard Bernard, *A Key of Knowledge for the Opening of the Secret Mysteries of St Johns Mystical Revelation* (1617), 100–1.
24. J. Blatchly, *The Town Library of Ipswich* (Woodbridge, Suffolk: Boydell Press,1989).
25. Sprunger; Arnold Williams, *The Common Expositor* (Chapel Hill: University of North Carolina Press, 1948), 33–4; Andrew Willet, *Hexapla in Genesin* (Cambridge, 1605), 'Certaine Directions to the Reader'.
26. Williams, 34.
27. Sprunger; Blatchly, 78, 84, 88.
28. *The Works of … Joseph Hall*, ed. P. Wynter, 10 vols. (Oxford: Oxford University Press, 1863), 5: 11.

29. T. Watt, *Cheap Print and Popular Piety* (Cambridge: Cambridge University Press, 1991), 51–2; Sheffield University Library, Hartlib MS 29/3, 20, 32ᵛ.

30. Richard Montagu, *Diatribae upon the First Part of the Late History of Tithes* (1621), 74, 127; J. Klemke, *Patricius Junius ... Mitteilungen aus Seinem Briefwechsel* (Leipzig: M. Spirgatis, 1898), 37–8, 52–3; *Ecclesiae Londino-Batavae Archivum*, ed. J. H. Hessels, 3 vols. in 4 (Cambridge: Cambridge University Press, 1887–98), 1: 862; *The Correspondence of John Cosin*, ed. G. Ornsby, Surtees Society 52, 55 (Durham: Andrews & Co., 1868–72), 1: 47, 52, 53, 57–8, 61, 64; *Lucae Holstenii Epistolae ad Diversos*, ed. J. F. Boissonade (Paris: Biblipolio graeco-latino-germanico, 1817).

31. N. Vance, *Irish Literature* (Oxford: Blackwell, 1990), 42–3; T. A. Birrell, 'The Reconstruction of the Library of Isaac Casaubon', in *Hellinga: Festschift* (Amsterdam: Israel, 1980), 61.

32. J. C. H. Aveling, *The Handle and the Axe: the Catholic Recusants in England from Reformation to Emancipation* (London and Tiptree, Colchester: Blond & Briggs, 1976), 124–5; R. Strong, *Henry Prince of Wales and England's Lost Renaissance* (London: Thames & Hudson, 1986); K. Sharpe, *Politics and Ideas in Early Stuart England* (London and New York: Pinter, 1989), 288–90.

33. S. Adams, 'The Protestant Cause: Religious Alliance with the West European Calvinist Communities as a Political Issue in England, 1585–1630' (D.Phil. thesis, Oxford, 1973); P. Lake, 'The Significance of the Elizabethan Identification of the Pope as Antichrist', *Journal of Ecclesiastical History* 31 (1980): 161–78.

34. *Finetti Philoxenis: Some Choice Observations of Sir John Finett* (1656).

35. J. Lock, '"How many Tercios has the Pope?" The Spanish War and the Sublimation of Elizabethan Anti-Popery', *History* 81 (1996): 197–214. There is no evidence to support Lock's suggestion that some divines' changing opinions concerning the anti-Christianity of the Pope derived partly from a loss of the sense of the predominance of the papal Antichrist on the Catholic side in the face of Spain (213).

36. T. Cogswell, *The Blessed Revolution: English Politics and the Coming of War, 1621–1624* (Cambridge: Cambridge University Press, 1989) and 'England and the Spanish Match'.

37. J. Shami, '"The Stars in their Order Fought against Sisera": John Donne and the Pulpit Crisis of 1622', *John Donne Journal* 14 (1995): 1–58. I am very grateful to Professor Shami for providing me with a copy of this important article.

38. Richard Sheldon, *A Sermon Preached at Paules Crosse* (1625), 31, 41–3, 45; Milton, *Catholic and Reformed*, 59–60.

39. C. Russell, *Parliaments and English Politics, 1621–1629* (Oxford: Clarendon Press, 1979), ch. 4.

40. M. A. Breslow, *A Mirror of England* (Cambridge, MA: Harvard University Press, 1970), ch. 5; R. M. Smuts, 'The Puritan Followers of Henrietta Maria in the 1630s', *English Historical Review* 93 (1978): 25–45.

41. Breslow, 85–95; *The Petition and Remonstrance of the Governor and Company of Merchants of London, Trading to the East Indies* (1628), 25;

Milton, *Catholic and Reformed*, 504–6. I deal with the East India Company's ideology in more detail in my 'Marketing a Massacre: the Amboyna Incident and the Moulding of English Public Opinion', in P. Lake and S. Pincus, eds., *The Public Sphere in Early Modern England* (Manchester: Manchester University Press, forthcoming).

42. P. Croft, 'Trading with the Enemy, 1585–1604', *Historical Journal* 32 (1989): 281–302.

43. J. P. Kenyon, *The Popish Plot* (London: Heinemann, 1972), 5–8; Haydon, 11–13; J. Miller, *Popery and Politics in England 1660–1688* (Cambridge: Cambridge University Press, 1973), 16–17, 58–9; Russell, *Parliaments*, 69, 120, 154–5, 195–6; and *The Fall of the British Monarchies 1637–1642* (Oxford: Clarendon Press, 1991), 234n, 421–2.

44. John Strype, *The Life and Acts of John Whitgift*, 3 vols. (Oxford: Clarendon Press, 1822), 3: 108.

45. M. Questier, 'Clerical Recruitment, Conversion and Rome c.1580–1625', in *Patronage and Recruitment in the Tudor and Early Stuart Church*, ed. C. Cross, Purvis Seminar Studies/Borthwick Studies in History 2 (York: Borthwick Institute, University of York, 1996), 82–3.

46. T. Cogswell, *Home Divisions* (Manchester: Manchester University Press, 1998). Note also the case of Walter Hastings in R. Cust, 'Honour, Rhetoric and Political Culture: The Earl of Huntingdon and his Enemies', in S. D. Amussen and M. A. Kishlansky, eds., *Political Culture and Cultural Politics in Early Modern England* (Manchester: Manchester University Press, 1995).

47. M. Jansson, *Proceedings in Parliament 1614* (Philadelphia: American Philosophical Society, 1988), 7. Roman Catholics were allowed by the casuists to act as magistrates: P. J. Holmes, *Elizabethan Casuistry*, Catholic Record Society 67 (London: Catholic Record Society, 1981), 50–1.

48. Russell, *Fall*, 213, 331, 340, 472.

49. F. Heal and C. Holmes, *The Gentry in England and Wales 1500–1700* (Basingstoke, Hampshire: Macmillan, 1994), 156–8.

50. *Wentworth Papers 1597–1628*, ed. J. P. Cooper, Camden Society, 4th ser., vol. 12 (Westminster: Camden Society, 1973), 287.

51. Bernard, *Key*, B7ᵛ; Questier, *Conversion*, ch. 6.

52. H. Aveling, *Northern Catholics: Recusancy in the North Riding* (London: Chapman, 1966), 204, 207, 210–11; J. T. Cliffe, *The Yorkshire Gentry* (London: Althone Press, 1969), 174–5.

53. Cliffe, 209. The same appears to be the case in France. Gregory Hanlon's recent study of Layrac-en-Brulhois in Aquitaine found a good deal of practical toleration between Catholics and Protestants on a local level, with Huguenots continuing to act as auditors for municipal accounts, and cross-confessional exchanges in loans and other contracts, apprenticeships, the hiring of finanicial agents, godparents, and the witnessing of marriages and wills: G. Hanlon, *Confession and Community in Seventeenth-Century France* (Philadelphia: University of Pennsylvania Press, 1993), 98–116. But contrast this with the remarks of Philip Benedict, '"Un roi, une loi, duex fois": Parameters for the History of Catholic–Reformed Co-existence in

France, 1555–1685', in O. P. Grell and R. Scribner, eds., *Tolerance and Intolerance in the European Reformation* (Cambridge: Cambridge University Press, 1996), 84–93.

54. See J. F. Merritt, *A Courtly Community? The Transformation of Early Modern Westminster 1525–1642* (Manchester: Manchester University Press, forthcoming).

55. F. Heal, *Hospitality in Early Modern England* (Oxford: Clarendon Press, 1990), 171–2.

56. Hall, *Works*, 5: 11. See also Thomas Taylor, *Two Sermons* (1624), #1, 12–14.

57. Bedell, *Examination of Motives*, epistle dedicatory, 1–6.

58. Holmes, *Elizabethan Casuistry*, 71.

59. Ibid., 122–3, 119.

60. Watt, 137–8, 172–3.

61. *The Whole Works of James Ussher*, ed. C. R. Elrington, 17 vols. (Dublin: Hodges and Smith, 1847–64), 15: 91–2; Thomas Morton, *The Grand Imposture of the (now) Church of Rome*, 2nd edn (1628), 414.

62. Milton, *Catholic and Reformed*, 133, 161, 285–95.

63. Aveling, *Northern Catholics*, 251–2. See also A. Shell, 'Catholic Texts and Anti-Catholic Prejudice in the Seventeenth-Century Book Trade', in R. Myers and M. Harris, eds., *Censorship and The Control of Print in England and France 1600–1910* (Winchester: St Paul's Bibliographies, 1992), 33–57, at p. 49.

64. Milton, *Catholic and Reformed*, 251–60.

65. Clifton, 'Fear of Popery', 165; Lake, 'Anti-popery', 93–4.

66. Andrew Willet, *Synopsis Papismi* (1600), 619.

67. *Commons Debates 1621*, ed. W. Notestein, F. H. Relf and H. Simpson, 7 vols. (New Haven: Yale University Press, 1935), 7: 636.

68. Bernard, *Key*, B2ᵛ–C2.

69. P. Collinson, *From Iconoclasm to Iconophobia* (Reading: University of Reading, 1986) and *The Birthpangs of Protestant England* (Basingstoke, Hampshire: Macmillan, 1988), ch. 4; Watt, 132–9, 177.

70. Hanlon, *Confession*, 11.

71. G. Burgess, *The Politics of the Ancient Constitution* (University Park: Pennsylvania State University Press, 1992).

72. *Documents Relating to William Prynne*, 7, 12; Bod. Tanner MS 290, f. 46 (Goad to Samuel Ward, 9 January 1621).

73. Selden, *Table Talk*, 99.

5

'Out of her Ashes May a Second Phoenix Rise': James I and the Legacy of Elizabethan Anti-Catholicism

John Watkins

Throughout Elizabeth's final months, aristocrats, privy councillors and foreign ambassadors anticipated her death as an opportunity for change. Although their expectations differed, even the most conservative members of the ruling elite hoped that things would be different under her successor. Some longed for personal advancement, others for a different managerial style, and still others for sweeping changes in the realm's foreign, domestic and religious policies. According to the Venetian envoy Giovanni Carlo Scaramelli, grief over Elizabeth's decline was less evident among her ministers than eagerness for fresh leadership. Writing to the Doge and Senate a few days before Elizabeth's death, he suggested that James's accession was already a *fait accompli*: 'It is, however, a fixed opinion that the Ministers, being convinced that this Kingdom is strong rather in reputation than in actual forces, are resolved not to be governed by a woman again, but to give the Crown to the King of Scotland.' According to Scaramelli, Cecil and his partisans attributed England's weakness to the incompetence of female magistracy, and they took measures to ensure a male succession and the recovery of diplomatic and military strength.[1]

Scaramelli predicted that the new regime would derive its security from greater religious tolerance. Although Elizabeth had supposedly tried to eradicate English Catholicism, Scaramelli reported that it was 'held for certain' that James would 'permit the rights of the Roman Catholic Church' after his accession. Throughout his correspondence, he attributes Elizabeth's anti-Catholicism neither to genuine piety nor to political expedience but to womanish paranoia. Whereas a later dispatch recounts her deathbed regret for having spent her life 'at war with Pontiffs and princes', James would supposedly adopt the wiser course of making peace with both the papacy and England's small but influential Catholic population. Praising James for his masculine prudence, Scaramelli notes that he will have to persist in his Calvinism 'at least for some time', since 'the majority many times over in these kingdoms of England, Scotland, and part of Ireland are absolutely alienated from allegiance' to the Catholic Church. But Scaramelli also notes that there are many 'chiefly among the nobility and the women who have the true religion in their hearts'. Even if James does not convert, he will undoubtedly repeal the punitive measures that condemn these otherwise law-abiding subjects as traitors.[2]

James's secret correspondence with Cecil, Northumberland and Henry Howard in the two years before Elizabeth's death corroborate Scaramelli's speculations about the Cecilian cabal, their frustration with a female monarch and the possibility of Catholic toleration. James concedes to the Earl of Mar and Edward Bruce that Cecil 'is king ... in effect'. He complains of Elizabeth's 'hen wiles' to Sir Michael Balfour, and thanks Cecil repeatedly for allaying her 'jealousies' and 'prejudices'. Presenting himself as pander in a delicate political courtship, Cecil cautions James against showing too open an interest in English affairs of state: to one of Elizabeth's 'sex and quality nothing is so improper as needless expostulations or over much curiosity in her own actions'. Cecil reassures James that 'his ship should be steered into the right harbour, without cross of wave or tide that shall be able to turn over a cockboat' if he will only trust to Cecil's guidance. Although James complains of 'popery' to Cecil, his letters to leading English Catholics support Scaramelli's hopes that he will suspend Elizabeth's anti-Catholic persecutions. When the Earl of Northumberland writes to James that 'it were pity to lose so good a kingdom for not tolerating a Mass in a corner', James replies that he would 'neither persecute any [Catholic] that will be quiet and give but an outward obedience to the law, neither will I spare to advance any of them that will by good service worthily deserve it.'[3]

Documentary evidence is too contradictory to pin down James's attitude toward Catholicism. His letters manifest two antithetical constructions of the English Catholic community, both as a religious minority potentially loyal to a tolerant Crown and as a fifth column inevitably allied with the Crown's foreign enemies. By following Elizabeth in treating Catholics as enemies, he could appease the powerful southern gentry and urban mercantile classes whose Protestantism was fiercely anti-papist. As Peter Lake has argued, popery 'became a unifying "other" in the presence of which all those not directly implicated in the problem (popery) became part of the solution (non-popery)'.[4] But demonizing Catholics bridged certain divisions at the expense of widening or creating others. By granting Catholics limited toleration in exchange for 'an outward obedience to the law', James could ensure the cooperation of the recusant gentry and nobles who still had power in the many sections of the country.[5] Toleration would diminish the threat of assassination, obviate the need for a large and potentially militant Catholic underground, and simplify diplomatic relationships with the Catholic Continent.

Once Elizabeth died, James had to transform his speculations into actual policy without alienating a population steeped for two generations in anti-Catholic propaganda. Since popular anti-Catholicism tended to increase during national crises, the period following Elizabeth's death was a bad time to broach toleration.[6] In order to foster loyalty to the new regime, the ruling elite needed to downplay James's foreign birth and descent from a Catholic woman popularly decried as Elizabeth's greatest enemy. Arguing that God ensured continuity between successive reigns, they stressed instead such credentials as his Tudor ancestry and tested experience as a ruler. Above all, they enlisted James's Protestantism as proof that God would continue to protect England against the Catholic forces that threatened its destruction.

Although little evidence suggests that the realm was ever really at risk, nothing figures more prominently in providentialist works about the Tudor–Stuart transition than the topos of an averted catastrophe.[7] The government's conspicuous security measures – closing the ports, patrolling the Channel and alerting the militia – were never used to fend off actual Spanish invaders, Catholic rebels or rival claimants.[8] But while James privately courted Catholic favor, the precautions allowed his panegyrists to familiarize him to his new subjects in Elizabeth's role as the defender of embattled Protestantism against Catholic insurgency. They may not have blinded anyone to his identity as a Scot whose gender, speech, personal manners and managerial style contrasted with the Queen who had ruled for almost half a century. But by insisting that England had barely escaped civil war or Spanish invasion, the panegyrists made such differences seem superficial.

Writers sealed this identification between the last Tudor Queen and the first Stuart King with metaphors of family relationship.[9] By diplomatic convention, early modern monarchs regularly addressed each other as siblings in formal correspondence. Elizabeth often presented herself as England's mother, and she sometimes used maternal rhetoric with James. James in turn openly addressed her as his 'loving mother'. This courtesy between an aging monarch and her unnamed, but apparent, heir established the terms through which panegyrists would celebrate continuity between their reigns. John King, Elizabeth's private chaplain and future Bishop of London, for example, argued from Scripture that James would preserve Elizabeth's 'clement, temperat and godly' government: 'It was no shame for Solomon to walke in the wayes of his father David; neither can it be a dishonour for our King to walke in the steps of his mother and predecessor.' King's compliment to Elizabeth as James's 'mother' glosses over the facts that Elizabeth never married, had no children and signed the death warrant of James's real mother. For King, James's commitment to the national Protestant Church proved his spiritual kinship with Elizabeth, which outweighed his biological descent from Mary and the hated Guises. Since Elizabeth's reign witnessed 'the exile of the divel out of our Country, his legendes, his false miracles, exorcismes, &c', the English people might hope that with her heir on the throne, the same Catholic devil 'shall never returne again'.[10]

Richard Mulcaster also envisaged a familial continuity between Elizabeth and James underwritten by God's commitment to the English people:

> How sore had mournfull death shaked th'english soyle,
> If God had not afforded present helpe?
> Who though he tooke our Queene, a King he gaue
> To play the fathers part in mothers lost.

Mulcaster broaches the trauma of dynastic rupture only to mitigate it by asserting God's abiding care for England. Just when Elizabeth's 'mournfull death' threatens national catastrophe, the same benevolent Providence that 'bred her up to be a Queene' gives her subjects

a King 'whose most royall vertues seed our hope / That he will
prooue so good the time he raignes'. Mulcaster downplays James's
foreignness and unfamiliarity by characterizing him as a father
comforting his children 'in mothers losse'.[11]

In an epigram on 'The Offspring of the Virgin Queen', John
Owen likewise claimed that the Stuart succession testified to
Elizabeth's fecundity rather than her barrenness:

> Scotia nobiscum gentem concrescit in unum;
>   Iste tuae *Partus virginitatis* erat.
> Est vnire magis, quam multiplicare, beatum:
> Tuque magis felix non pariendo Parens.
>
> England, and Scotland's, blessed unity:
> The issue was of your virginity.
> She is more glorious, who unites two states,
> Than she, who like the Vulgar generate.[12]

Epigrammatic paradox overcomes the embarrassing fact that
Elizabeth's childlessness led to a foreign succession. Whereas other
women generated according to the order of nature, Elizabeth
achieved the miracle of a virginal procreation in bequeathing her
throne to the King who united the English and Scottish crowns.

In dying, Elizabeth finally provided her admirers a way to complete their fifty-year identification of her with Mary, the Virgin
Mother. But perhaps because the implicit equation of James with
Jesus might seem blasphemous, most poets represented James's
miraculous virgin birth from Elizabeth through allusions to the
phoenix rather than to the Holy Family. References to James as a
phoenix rising from Elizabeth's ashes figure more frequently in
accession commemorations than any other topos:

> See how our *Phoenix* mounts aboue the skies,
> And from the neast another *Phoenix* flyes,
> How happily before the change did bring
> A mayden-*Queene*, and now a manly *King*.[13]
>
> The *Phoenix* that of late fled to the skies
> Hath left her ashes, from whence doth arise
> Another *Phoenix*, rare, vnmmatcht, vnpeered.[14]

Eliza's Memoriall. King Iames His Arriuall. and Romes Downefall
(London, 1603) enlists the topos against Catholic hopes that
Elizabeth's death will defeat the Reformation:

> O! But is not your hope frustrate and vaine?
> Succeedeth not King *Iames* our Soueraigne?
> A *Phoenix* from *Elizaes* ashes bred.

The phoenix trope asserted not just continuity but absolute identity
between the regimes. Since poets and painters had long associated
Elizabeth with the phoenix, the compliment's application to James
reinforced their claims that he was the deceased Queen reincar-
nate.[15] In Elizabeth's day, the iconography honored her uniqueness,
self-sufficiency and determination never to take a mate. The image
of the bird rising from the flames also associated her with a resur-
gent Protestantism that prevailed despite the burning of the Marian
martyrs. While the topos maintained many of these associations
when applied to James, it acquired new ones that mitigated dynastic rupture by giving Elizabeth mythic offspring and James a
Protestant English origin.

II

Government apologists found the iconography of the phoenix
rising from the flames particularly useful in characterizing the
Gunpowder Plot as a re-enactment of Catholic treachery against
Elizabeth. In order to appreciate their response to the Plot, I will
situate it in a debate over Catholic toleration that precipitated the
earliest crisis in the representation of James as Elizabeth's moral offspring.[16] Since panegyrists identified Elizabeth and James primarily
as champions of embattled Protestantism, the possibility that James
might suspend Elizabeth's anti-Catholic strictures raised a potentially unbridgeable point of discontinutity between them. Although
James's private assurance that he would not 'persecute any
[Catholic] that shall be quiet' hardly guaranteed religious liberty, it
did challenge the providentialists' representation of the relationship
between Protestants and Catholics as a war between good and evil.
A king willing to advance any Catholic that might 'by good service
worthily deserve it' was hardly imitating what Protestant apologists

like Spenser, King, and Mulcaster hailed as Elizabeth's apocalyptic struggle against the Whore of Babylon.

Even if James were willing to permit a 'Mass in a corner', he saw the risks of openly appeasing a community that his predecessor had treated as an enemy. To avoid outraging public opinion, James had to keep discussion about religious toleration discreet. But Catholic pamphleteers soon publicly pressured the King to grant open liberty of conscience, and Protestants countered by urging the King to uphold Elizabethan precedent. As the debate heightened, it centered on conflicting accounts of Elizabeth's character, governance and status as an example for her successors to follow. In order to influence the realm's religious future, Catholics and Protestants fought over the narration of its past.

The moment Elizabeth died, Catholic apologists cast her as a woman haunted by her crimes against her Catholic subjects. Only a week after her death, John Chamberlain complained that Dudley Carleton would soon 'heare her Majesties sicknes and manner of death diversly related: for even here the papists do tell strange storeis, as utterly voyde of truth, as of all civill honestie or humanitie'.[17] Elizabeth Southwell, a maid of honour who later eloped with Leicester's son, circulated a terrifying account of Elizabeth's final days. According to Southwell, Elizabeth had visions of herself 'in her bed her bodie exceeding leane and fearfull in a light of fire'.[18] When a courtier urged her to retire and rest, Elizabeth allegedly replied 'that yf he knew what she had sene in her bed, he would not perswade her as he did'.[19] Even after the Gunpowder Plot proved a decisive setback to hopes for toleration, Catholic apologists continued to protest against the realm's official anti-Catholicism by locating its roots in Elizabeth's hysteria, malice, paranoia and probable damnation. When the Jesuit Robert Persons obtained a copy of Southwell's manuscript, he incorporated its gothic details in a more comprehensive psychological portrait of a woman broken by decades of Reformation politics. In a widely circulated tract urging that English Catholics be exempted from the Oath of Allegiance, Persons claimed that Elizabeth suffered inward torment from the moment Parliament and her own father proclaimed that 'she was unlawfully borne'. Later in life, Elizabeth fell prey to corrupt advisers who drew her into 'continuall suspitions, feares, and frights of her mynd and spirit'. At last, 'this gryping passion of feare and iealousy did so vexe & consume her inwardly' that she 'made away ... his Maiesties noble renowned Mother, Queene of France & Scotland'.[20]

In pointing to Mary Queen of Scots' execution as Elizabeth's crowning atrocity, Persons and other Catholic writers countered the panegyrists' representation of James as Elizabeth's mythic progeny. Mobilizing filial piety against James's commitment to the Protestant establishment, Persons implies that James could not persist in Elizabeth's anti-Catholicism without violating his mother's memory. The argument trapped James within a narrative of associational matricide from which he could extricate himself only by excusing his mother's co-religionists from an oath that brought their private consciences into conflict with their duties as loyal subjects. Blaming James for ultimately upholding Elizabeth's anti-Catholic policies, Father John Gerard accused him of using 'far different speech of and against Catholics than was expected from the son of such a mother'.[21]

One primary factor prevented James from overturning Elizabeth's anti-Catholic precedent: the consensus of the ruling elite. From the moment he ascended the throne, the Protestant establishment encouraged him to reject toleration. If pragmatism argued for 'tolerating a mass in a corner', it also argued for maintaining the state's monopoly over religion and against offending the Puritan sympathies of the commercial classes and lower gentry. By 1603, the 'middling sort of men' wielded political and economic power rivalling and even exceeding that of remote Catholic aristocrats like Northumberland. At least as far as religion went, the same men who had longed to replace Elizabeth with a male sovereign now wanted him to honor her example of uniting Protestant Englishmen against a common Catholic menace. But the more individuals like Persons and Gerard characterized Elizabeth's reign as the greatest period of religious persecution since Diocletian, the harder it became to uphold Elizabeth's more extreme measures. The Catholic characterization of Elizabeth as paranoid and hysterical posed a particular challenge to Cecil and his associates, since they themselves had used this misogynistic characterization in their correspondence with James.

Mary Stuart's execution was the Protestant establishment's greatest challenge in refuting the Catholic case against Elizabeth. Scaramelli reported that the privy councillors were determined either to deny their role in Mary's death or to persuade James of its necessity by producing a secret letter proving that she not only murdered his father Darnley but also plotted to kill James himself: 'They hope to make it appear that Elizabeth, full of compassion for this innocent nephew of hers, resolved, under the impulse of this secret stimulus … to put Mary to death.'[22] Although other sources fail to corroborate Scaramelli's account of a forged, exonerating letter, they do suggest that the ruling elite worried about James's interpretation of his mother's death and about his rapport with Catholic aristocrats. The letter's portrayal of Elizabeth as a compassionate aunt saving her 'innocent nephew' from his murderous natural mother would certainly reinforce her portrayal as James's spiritual mother in the accession tributes. There too, Elizabeth takes the maternal place of the Catholic mother who is either condemned or consigned to oblivion.

To maintain their influence over the King, Cecil and his associates countered Catholic charges by disseminating a staunchly Protestant account of Elizabeth. They may not have gone so far as to charge Mary with attempted infanticide, but they tried to exonerate Elizabeth from charges of tyranny towards Catholics in general, of specific malice towards Mary, of an impious and embittered life, and of an unholy death. Shortly after Persons's tract appeared, Bishop William Barlowe of Lincoln responded to it in his massive *An Answer to a Catholike English-Man*. Dismissing Persons's charges as 'an impostume of venomous filth' and 'barbarously loathsome contumelies', Barlowe insists on Elizabeth's legitimacy: 'SHE was a *daughter* of the *blood roiall*, borne to the Crowne (In the Prophets words, *from the Birth, from the Wombe, from the Conception*:) a Princesse aduanced to the Crowne in apparant right, and by vncontroleable succession.' Denying Southwell's and Persons's stories about the misery of Elizabeth's final, guilt-ridden hours, Barlowe upholds them as a model of holy dying. Although he concedes that Mary's death was 'the most indelible blot that can be recorded of this country', he maintains that 'the wicked act was committed' without Elizabeth's knowledge. Significantly, Barlowe seals Elizabeth's exoneration by maintaining that James himself accepted her innocence: 'our now *Soueraigne* … was long agone satisfied by her Maiesties owne purgation'.[23]

About the same time, Francis Bacon composed a Latin tribute, *In Felicem Memoriam Elizabethae,* and sent a copy to Sir George Carew with a letter describing it as a response to 'a factious book that endeavoured to verify *Misera Foemina* (the addition of the Pope's Bull) upon Queen Elizabeth'.[24] Bacon's memorial engages Persons's arguments, or those of a similar Catholic apologist, in a point-by-point debate that transforms Elizabeth's alleged demerits into advantages. In contrast to princes assured of the succession from birth, for instance, Bacon maintains that Elizabeth was not 'corrupted by the indulgence and liberty of [her] education'.[25] While her mother's disgrace and sister Mary's later hostility were miserable for her, they disciplined her character so that she was a better ruler. In tackling the question of her illegitimation, Bacon dismisses the charges against Anne Boleyn as slanders fabricated by Henry VIII.[26] Whereas Barlow evoked the Protestant cult of holy dying against papist suspicions about Elizabeth's death, Bacon appeals characteristically to science: 'for a few days before her death, by excessive dryness of her body – weakened by the cares which follow the height of royal power, nor ever irrigated with wine or rich food, she was stricken with a numbness of the nerves. Nevertheless, she retained her voice (which does not usually happen in this kind of illness) and mind and motion, albeit slower and more sluggish'.[27] Instead of replacing Catholic intimations of Hell with Protestants ones of Heaven, Bacon adopts a secular discourse honoring Elizabeth's stoical acceptance of 'that *euthanasia* which Augustus Caesar was accustomed to invoke for himself so earnestly with votive offerings'.[28] What matters in Bacon's account is the sheer unremarkableness of Elizabeth's last illness, in which there 'was nothing miserable, nothing foreboding, nothing foreign to human nature'.[29] In short, it was entirely comprehensible without appeal to the supernatural.

The shift from religious to secular discussion in Bacon's treatment of Elizabeth's death underlies his overall polemic strategy in refuting charges that Elizabeth was hysterically suspicious of Roman Catholics. Realizing that portraying her as a Protestant saint might reinforce portrayals of her as a fanatic, Bacon stresses the moderation of her religious belief and practice: 'In religion Elizabeth was pious and moderate, and constant, and adverse to novelty.'[30] 'Not troubling' either clergy or laity 'with any sharp inquisition, she proved a shelter to them by benignly overlooking [their religion]'[31] until Spain began to transform the English Catholic community into 'a party alienated from the state and eager for new things, which would join with the invading enemy'.[32]

Instead of joining Barlowe and other apologists in trying to explain away Elizabeth's complicity in Mary Stuart's death, Bacon avoids specific references to Mary or the Babington conspiracy. Like the 1603 encomiasts, he attributes a figurative kinship to Elizabeth and James that diminishes the dynastic consequences of Elizabeth's failure to bear offspring and glosses over James's descent from her most celebrated enemy. By comparing the succession to a son's inheritance of his father's estate, Bacon even dampens the challenge posed to a patriarchy by Elizabeth's gender:

> She was healthily childless, and left no offspring of her own .... For successor she obtained one by lots who might favor her name and honors, and will give her acts a kind of perpetuity: when he has not much altered anything respecting either [her] choice of persons or [her] order of arrangements: so far that a son has rarely succeeded a father with such silence and so meagre change and perturbation.[33]

Although Bacon does not attribute James's 'sudden and peaceable succession' to Providence, he follows the encomiasts in raising the threat of dynastic rupture only to deny it. Elizabeth achieves secular immortality in James, who 'will give her acts a kind of perpetuity' by retaining her policies. Within the immediate polemic context of Bacon's memorial, this 'perpetuity' means a perpetuation of the goverment's official anti-Catholicism. Bacon rejects toleration because the English are too uncivil to permit it: Elizabeth 'judged the toleration and privilege of two religions by public authority a most certain destruction in a spirited and warlike people easily passing from the contention of minds to hands and arms'.[34]

The fact that Barlowe and Bacon come to the same conclusions despite their opposing perspectives on the supernatural suggests the breadth of the consensus against modifying Elizabeth's anti-Catholicism. Barlowe writes as a believing churchman who surveys recent history in Providentialist terms as struggle between a saintly Elizabeth and her diabolical Catholic detractors. Bacon writes as a pragmatist who values Elizabeth's practical wisdom more than her godliness. From a secular, twentieth-century standpoint, Barlowe may seem to have more in common with his opponent Persons, who shares his sense of history as a war between good and evil, than with his ally Bacon, who treats it as a competition between divergent human interests. But regardless of their theoretical differences, Barlowe and Bacon agreed in policy: from both of their perspectives, James ought to preserve Elizabeth's anti-Catholic strictures lest 'the privilege and toleration of two religions by public authority' would bring the realm to 'most certain destruction'.

III

One event, the 1605 Gunpowder Plot, united the Protestant elite so effectively against the recusant pleas for toleration that English Catholics continued to suffer legal discrimination until the nineteenth century. Historians still debate how much the government, under Cecil's guidance, stage-managed the plot.[35] But regardless of whether the conspirators were set up, entrapped or acted on their own, the goverment controlled the plot's transformation into the reign's greatest propaganda event. Cecil worked with Coke and the other prosecutors to characterize the Plot not as an isolated incident but as a continuation of papist challenges to England's sovereignty that dated to Henry VIII's break with Rome.

Above all, the governing elite used the plot to seal James's identity as a second Elizabeth protected by God against papist intrigue. Within the historical myth that they perpetuated, the defeat of the Gunpowder conspirators repeated Elizabeth's 1588 triumph over the Armada. When Cecil ordered that the first batch of conspirators be executed in St Paul's Churchyard, Arthur Gorges asked him to reconsider the venue: 'I well remember that that was the place of happy memory ... where our late dread and dear Sovereign offered up in all humility upon her knees her thanksgiving to God for the great victory upon the Spaniards and therefore too worthy now to be polluted with gibbets, hangmen, or the blood of traitors.'[36] Gorges missed the obvious point: the executions at St Paul's underscored the Plot's mythic association with the Armada. Once more, the Protestant God had empowered Englishmen to triumph over their Catholic enemies. Sir Edward Coke presented the Plot as the climax of a series of Catholic outrages that began with the 1570 Bull of Excommunication, continued through the assassination attempts against Elizabeth, and reached a highpoint in the Armada expedition. Revising the phoenix topos that linked James and Elizabeth in the 1603 encomia, Coke characterized the attempt to assassinate James as a 'Treason ... in the conception and birth most monstrous, as arising out of the dead ashes of former Treasons' against Elizabeth and her subjects. He upheld one particular conspirator, Henry Garnet, as a direct link to the Armada crisis. As Coke stressed to the judges, Garnet had first arrived 'when the great *Armado* of *Spain* ... was by the instigation of that High Priest of *Rome*, preparing and collecting together'. According to Coke, 'the Purveyors and Forerunners of this Navy and Invasion were the Jesuits, and Garnet among them, being a Traitor even in his very entrance and footing in the Land'. Fortunately, the same God who fought against Spaniards and Jesuits alike 'by Fire, and Sea, and Winds, and Rocks, and Tempests' had once more defeated an intended treason.[37]

Preachers, dramatists, chroniclers and engravers amplified Coke's connections between the plot and the Armada. In 1606, Prince Henry's Men staged Thomas Dekker's *The Whore of Babylon*, an apocalyptic retelling of Elizabeth's struggles against Rome. The play, which rehearses almost all the major plots against Elizabeth, concludes with a two-act re-creation of the Armada as a foreshadowing of James's triumph over the Gunpowder conspirators. Dekker reinforces the association with references to 'sacramental oaths' (1.2.284), 'devils in vaults' (1.2.304), conspirators forging 'three-forked thunderbolts' and melting 'sulphur' (1.2.307–8), and traitors who 'turn [themselves] to moles, / Work underground and undermine [their] country' (3.1.165–6).[38] When the Empress of Babylon commissions the Armada to invade England, her language echoes popular exaggeration of the intended Gunpowder treason into a universal holocaust: 'Burn, batter, kill, / Blow up, pull down, ruin all' (4.4.128–9).

This double evocation of the Armada as a triumph over Antichrist and as a prototype of the more recent Gunpowder Plot complicates the play's apocalypticism. Although the Empress of Babylon concludes the play by lamenting that 'Great Babylon thus low did never fall' (6.6.160), other voices hint that she is about to suffer even greater indignities under Elizabeth's successor. Warning that even Elizabeth's death might not thwart the Reformation, a Babylonian Cardinal predicts that 'a second Phoenix will arise' from her ashes who will prove 'of larger wing, / Of stronger talon, of more dreadful beak' (3.1.253–4). His talon promises to 'be so bony and so large of grip / That it may shake all Babylon' in a conclusive, fully apocalyptic confrontation (261–2).

By hailing James as a Phoenix risen from Elizabeth's ashes and his triumph over the Gunpowder conspirators as a re-enactment of Elizabeth's victory over the Armada, Dekker mobilizes a providentialist account of the Tudor–Stuart transition against alternative interpretations that might support the recusants. The phoenix topos glosses over the weakest point in the his apocalyptic argument: the fact of James's descent from Mary Stuart. The play's Spenserian coupling of historical allegory and eschatological fantasy locates its characters' prototypes not only in the Book of Revelation but also events at Elizabeth's court. But if Titania is clearly Elizabeth;

Florimell, Leicester; Parthenophil, Burghley; and Paridell, Dr Parry, the Empress of Babylon has no definitive historical counterpart. Unlike Spenser, who enraged James by equating Duessa with his mother, Dekker avoids explicitly identifying Mary with the Whore of Babylon. Consequently, while the play recalls most assassination plots against Elizabeth, it avoids the most notorious one of all, the Babington conspiracy, because that one directly implicated Mary.

Honoring Elizabeth as an agent of providential victory and as James's metaphorical mother, Dekker joins Barlowe and Bacon in refuting recusant charges that she was paranoid, treacherous, cruel and generally immoral. He takes particular pains to refute the argument that Elizabeth's paranoia turned her into a tyrant. When Paridell discovers Titania in her garden, she is reading a *Furstenspiegel* on the bitter ends awaiting despotism. The contrast between her and the actual tyrants in her book temporarily disarms Paridell, who can only steel himself to kill her by believing that she has betrayed her people. When pressured to condemn a conspirator in Act IV, she protests that on 'impartial beam' between justice and mercy, she 'would incline / To that where mercy lies' (4.2.28, 29–30). Only after considerable prompting from Fideli does she concede to justice less for her 'own breast' than for 'our people's; for their own good / We much the surgeon play and let our blood' (4.2. 32–3).

Unlike the Whore who prostitutes herself to the men of all nations, Titania preserves her body's wholeness and her realm's independence. Even if her impregnability leaves her without a biological heir, it does not threaten England's future. After the Spaniards' defeat, Dekker looks to the post-Armada generation to complete their predecessors' struggle against Babylon. In the play's final moments, a child is born to an unnamed English mother. Cradled in 'the hollow back-piece of a rusty armor' and carried to the font by a captain rather than a midwife, he will serve Titania's successor in routing the last vestiges of papistry from the land. Christened 'Beria' after the Latin name for Tilbury, he embodies a lasting continuity between the Armada's destruction and James's future victory over his Catholic enemies.

Throughout the rest of James's reign, poets, preachers and engravers developed analogies between the conspiracies against Elizabeth, the Armada and the Gunpowder Plot that linked Elizabeth and James as threatened defenders of the Protestant establishment. Probably between 1615 and 1618, Thomas Campion drafted a neo-Latin brief epic on the Gunpowder Plot to clear himself of suspicions of crypto-Catholicism. *De Puluerea Coniuratione* opens with a description of Satan's disappointment that Elizabeth's death has failed to weaken her bonds with the English people. Determined to regain his influence over England, he inspires the Gunpowder conspirators, but is finally thwarted by Sancta Religio, who pleads for God's protection during her nightly visits to Elizabeth's tomb. Associating the plot to blow up Parliament with a plot to exhume and burn Elizabeth's remains, Sancta Religio begs God not to abandon the King 'who possesses and splendidly carries Eliza's scepter' (1. 485–6).[39] God hears her prayers and protects James even as He saved Elizabeth when 'she saw the Iberians' floating towers and ultimately conquered the seas with pious prayers'.[40]

Campion's opening finds a prototype for England's triumph over its Catholic enemies in the Exodus account of Pharoah's armies drowned in the Red Sea: 'I sing the great, wondrous, sweetly saving work of the omnipotent defender, who did not so distinguish himself when formerly he entrusted the exiles to the sea and over-whelmed the surging enemies.'[41] In 1624, George Carleton reinforced this typological association among the Gunpowder Plot, the Armada and the biblical Exodus in *A Thankfull Remembrance of God's Mercy*, a parallel account of the crises of 1588 and 1605. Across the top of the frontispiece appears a verse from the Israelites' song of thanksgiving for the Egyptians' destruction: '*Quis sicvt tv domine in fortibvs?*' [who is like you O Lord in might?]. On the left of the title, Elizabeth carries a banner with the menacing Armada; on the right, James carries one with Guy Fawkes approaching the Parliament House. At the bottom of the page, the respective Latin captions *per aquas* and *per ignem* suggest that the thwarted invasion by water and the destruction by fire are two phases of the same apocalyptic struggle against the Pope, whose tiara tumbles at the bottom of the page from a personified *Ecclesia Malignantium*.[42] Coupled with inset depictions of Noah's Ark and Moses' burning bush, the captions reinforce the Old Testament foundations of watery and fiery struggles. Elizabeth and James, further paired and identified as England's Deborah and Solomon, continue their biblical predecessors' work of protecting the godly against their murderous and idolatrous enemies.[43]

For a generation of Stuart panegyrists, the Gunpowder Plot became the averted catastrophe that sealed James's identity as a phoenix risen from Elizabeth's ashes. But in stressing the plot as a re-enactment of the Armada, the panegyrists downplayed a stronger parallel between the events of 1605 and a different incident in

Elizabeth's reign, the Babington Plot of 1585. After all, the Armada – an attempted foreign invasion – and the Gunpowder Plot – an instance of domestic terrorism – were not particularly analogous. By 1605, England was at peace with Spain. Coke insisted throughout the Gunpowder prosecutions that no foreign king was on trial, even if Philip III had listened to the conspirators. The foes were the enemy within, the native English Catholics. They were the same foes that Elizabeth's government prosecuted in the 1585 trials that finally implicated and destroyed Mary Stuart. As several historians have commented, Coke based his forensic proceedings, investigations and the conspirators' trial on the earlier Babington Plot to murder Elizabeth and set Mary on her throne.[44] If the Gunpowder Plot established James as a second Elizabeth in vanquishing the Armada, it also established him as a second Elizabeth in prosecuting Catholic conspirators, a group that in 1585 had included his own mother.

We can only speculate about the extent to which James recognized these darker connections with the Elizabethan past. The Venetian ambassador noted that the King seemed unusually silent and melancholy during the Gunpowder trial. One night after dinner, he erupted in an anti-Catholic tirade: 'I shall certainly be obliged to stain my hands with their blood, though sorely against my will. But they shall not think they can frighten me, for they shall taste of the agony first.'[45] In a letter possibly written in January 1606, the first month of the conspirators' trial, John Harington recounts how James summoned him for a private conference during which 'the Queene his mother was not forgotten'. James told Harington that Mary's 'deathe was visible in Scotlande before it did really happen being … spoken of in secrete by those whose power of sighte presented to them a bloodie heade dancing in the air'.[46] We will never know whether James consciously associated the Gunpowder conspirators' blood that he imagines on his hands with the Catholic blood dripping from Mary's head. But just when the broadsides, ballads, commemorative poems, engravings and plays proclaimed with greater assurance than ever that Elizabeth lived again in her 'son' and successor, James remembered the other mother whose death secured his throne.

After the Gunpowder Plot, James adopted a conspicuously anti-recusant domestic policy. He encouraged leading English churchmen and intellectuals to write anti-Catholic tracts, authored several himself and even chartered King James's College in Chelsea as a center for anti-Catholic propaganda.[47] At least publicly, he played his part as a phoenix risen from Elizabeth's Protestant ashes. Yet in private, he advanced a few Catholics who gave 'but an outward obedience to the law'. He created Edward Wotton a baron and appointed the Earl of Northampton, whose attachment to Mary Stuart had often provoked Elizabeth and her councillors, to several important offices. With his obedience to the Pope held in check by his loyalty to the King, Northampton practiced a Catholicism so relegated to the private sphere that it obviated the justification for Elizabeth's repressions.

In 1612, Northampton cooperated with James in an act that symbolized the possible compatibility of Catholicism and English national identity, the translation of Mary Stuart's remains from Peterborough Cathedral to Westminster Abbey. When James broached the subject to the Dean and Chapter at Peterborough, he stated that 'it appertains to the duty we owe to our dearest mother that like honour should be done to her body … [as] ourselves have already performed to our dear sister, the late Queen Elizabeth.'[48] Northampton composed the Latin elegy for the new monument, and commemorated Mary's interment more candidly in a private letter to Rochester:

> We in this place acordinge to direction have laied vp the body of the most worthy quene that manie ages have beheld …. Though we brought her in verie late to shunne concurse yet the people in the streetes and out of the windowes caste their eies upon the passsage manie noting and with admiration that iustice of god and the piety of a motherlesse son that brought her into that place with honor from which she had been in former times repulsed with tiranny.[49]

In recounting the tyranny of former times, Northampton adopts Persons's and Gerard's oppositional historiography. Like Persons, he indicts Elizabeth's paranoia as cause of Mary's tragedy, even though he vents his anger primarily on William and Robert Cecil, 'the father of the littell one as the grand director and the littell one itself … as his fatheres instrument in her eare'. As the 'chefe artificeres', the Cecils enflamed 'the queenes feares and ielousies' and exploited them to engineer Mary's downfall.[50]

While espousing Persons's view of the past, Northampton rejected his oppositional politics. Unlike his infamous co-religionist, he did not live in exile, openly profess his Catholicism or express his subversive views about Elizabeth and her government in print. Accepting the lawfulness of an officially Protestant regime, he consoled himself with the belief that Elizabeth's successor and a sizeable number of her former subjects revered the memory of his Catholic mother. As a model collaborationist, Northampton embraced the terms of his conditional acceptance into the realm's ruling elite. Like Mary Stuart's evening interment, his Catholicism remained a semi-clandestine affair. Just as the placement of Mary's tomb opposite Elizabeth's in the Protestant sanctity of Westminster Abbey neutralized its potential as a shrine to a Catholic martyr, Northampton's acceptance as a crypto-Catholic within the royal establishment neutralized his potential as a leader of recusant resistance.

Mary's interment and Northampton's career typify the uneasy balance that James maintained between conflicting interpretations of his identity as Elizabeth's Protestant successor. In upholding her penalties against Catholics who openly professed their dissent, and in waging his polemic war against Catholic pamphleteers, James fulfilled his Providentialist role as a phoenix risen from her ashes. But he also resisted that role in elevating crypto-Catholics like Northampton, who proved their loyalty not only to his mother but to also his own Protestant government. James's pragmatic policy of 'tolerating a mass in a corner' paid off in Northampton's case. Although Northampton may have toyed with treason against Elizabeth, he never tired in his support of James's royal prerogative against both Protestant and Catholic detractors. But since early seventeenth-century England was far from embracing a notion of national identity that transcended and effectively neutralized confessional loyalty, his case remained exceptional. James's enemies already pointed to Northampton's loyalty to the King as evidence that Stuart absolutism was leagued with crypto-Catholicism. As the elements of a future Whig historiography began to coalesce, England attributed to Elizabeth not only an ardent Protestantism but also a respect for Parliamentary government that James and his descendants allegedly betrayed.

NOTES

1. *Calender of State Papers Venetian*, 38 vols. (London: Longman Green, 1864–1947), 9: 540.
2. Ibid., 9: 540, 9: 542, 9: 564.

3. G. P. V. Akrigg, ed., *Letters of King James VI & I* (Berkeley: University of California Press, 1984), 172, 175, 182, 193, 200–2, 204–5, 207.
4. 'Anti-Popery: The Structure of a Prejudice', in *Conflict in Early Stuart England: Studies in Religion and Politics 1603–1642*, ed. Richard Cust and Ann Hughes (London: Longman, 1989), 82.
5. See John Bossy, *The English Catholic Community 1570–1850* (Oxford: Oxford University Press, 1976), 77–107.
6. See Robin Clifton, 'Fear of Popery', in *The Origins of the English Civil War*, ed. Conrad Russell (New York: Harper and Row, 1973), 144–67; 'The Popular Fear of Catholics during the English Revolution', *Past and Present* 51 (1971): 23–55.
7. See Wallace MacCaffrey, *Elizabeth I: War and Politics 1588–1603* (Princeton: Princeton University Press, 1992), 439–41; Clifton, 'Fear of Popery', 166.
8. See *CSP Venetian*, 9. 558, 561–2.
9. See Christine Coch, '"Mother of my Contreye": Elizabeth I and Tudor Constructions of Motherhood', *English Literary Renaissance* 26 (1996): 429–50.
10. Quotations are from John Manningham's notes in *The Diary of John Manningham of the Middle Temple, 1602–1603*, ed. Robert Parker Sorlien (Hanover, NH: University Press of New England, 1976), 214–17.
11. Richard Mulcaster, *The Translation of certaine latine verses written vppon her Maiesties death, called A Comforting Complaint* (London, 1603), A2, A3, B2.
12. *Epigrammatum Ioannis Owen Cambro-Britanni Libri Tres* (London, 1607), III.4. I have included Thomas Pecke's translation from *Parnassi Puerperium; or some well-wishes to ingenuity* (London, 1659).
13. John Lane, *An Elegie vpon the death of the high and renowned Princessse, our late Souerayne Elizabeth* (London, 1603).
14. I. F., *King Iames His Welcome to London. With Elizaes Tombe and Epitaph / And our Kings triumph and epitimie* (London, 1603).
15. See Roy Strong, *Gloriana: The Portraits of Queen Elizabeth I* (London: Thames and Hudson, 1987), 80–83.
16. See Thomas Clancy, *Papist Pamphleteers: The Allen-Persons Party and the Political Thought of the Counter-Reformation in England, 1572–1615* (Chicago: Loyola University Press, 1969), 125–58; Francis Edwards, *Robert Persons: The Biography of an Elizabethan Jesuit 1546–1610* (St. Louis, MO: The Institute of Jesuit Sources, 1995), 321–5, 380–3.
17. *The Letters of John Chamberlain*, ed. Norman Egbert McClure, 2 vols. (Philadelphia: The American Philosophical Society), 1: 188.
18. 'A True Relation of what succeeded at the sickness and death of Queen Elizabeth', transcribed by Catherine Loomis, 'Elizabeth Southwell's Manuscript Account of the Death of Queen Elizabeth [with text]', *English Literary Renaissance* 26 (1996): 485. Loomis's article provides a valuable account of Southwell's manuscript, its polemic context, and its later reception.
19. Loomis, 485.
20. Robert Persons, *The Judgment of a Catholicke English-man, Living in Banishment for his Religion* (1608), 32, 33, 34.

21. *The Conditions of Catholics Under James I: Father Gerard's Narrative of the Gunpowder Plot*, ed. John Morris, S. J. (London, 1871), 25.
22. *CSP, Venetian*, 10. 25
23. Barlowe, *An Answer to A Catholike English-Man (So By Him-Selfe Entituled)* ... (London, 1609), 64, 85, 95–6.
24. *The Works of Francis Bacon*, ed. James Spedding et al., 15 vols. (Boston: Houghton, Mifflin, 1864), 11: 109.
25. Ibid. 6: 30. I have provided my own translation of Bacon's original Latin.
26. Ibid., 6: 292.
27. Ibid., 6: 296.
28. Idem.
29. Idem.
30. Ibid., 6: 297.
31. Ibid., 6: 298.
32. Ibid., 6: 299.
33. Ibid., 6: 296, 297.
34. Ibid., 6: 298.
35. See especially Mark Nicholls's discussion of the historiographical controversy in *Investigating Gunpowder Plot* (Manchester: Manchester University Press, 1991), 213–21.
36. Hatfield MSS, xviii, 36 quoted in Hugh Ross Williamson, *The Gunpowder Plot* (London: Faber, 1951), 224.
37. *A True and Perfect Relation of the Whole Proceedings against the late most barbarous Traitors, Garnet a Iesuite, and his Confederats* ... (London, 1606), E1, P2.
38. *The Whore of Babylon: a Critical Edition*, ed. Marianne Gateson Riely (New York: Garland, 1980). All references are to this edition.
39. *De Puluerea Coniuratione*, ed. David Lindley, Leeds Texts and Monographs New Series, 10 (Leeds: Leeds Studies in English, 1987), 1: 485–6. I have provided my own translation of Campion's Latin.
40. Campion, 1: 335–47.
41. Ibid., 1: 1–3.
42. Throughout the rest of the century, broadsides and commemorative paintings appeared that linked the two events. A 1623 engraving entitled '*Deo trin-vni Britanniae bis ultori*', for instance, showed a Hell council with the Pope and Satan presiding. The Armada appears on the left and the Parliament House on the right. An overarching caption dedicates the whole 'to God, in memorye of his double deliveraunce from the invincible navie and the unmatcheable powder'. Alan Haynes reproduces the engraving in *The Gunpowder Plot: Faith in Rebellion* (Dover, NH: Alan Sutton, 1994), 99.
43. English writers and engravers reinforced the parallels between the Armada and the Gunpowder Plot long after James's death. In 1671, Samuel Clarke issued a joint commemoration entitled *A True & Full Narrative of Those Two Never to Be Forgotten Deliverances*.
44. See Williamson, 47–8.
45. *CSP Venetian*, 10. 293–7, 308.

46. *Nugae Antiquae: Being a Miscellaneous Collection of Original Papers ... By Sir John Harington*, ed. Thomas Park, 2 vols. (London, 1804), 1: 369. For discussion of the letter's date, see Park 1: 366 n. 2.
47. See David Harris Willson, *James VI and I* (New York: Holt, 1956), 217–42.
48. Akrigg, *Letters of James VI & I*, 326.
49. Fragment of a letter signed by Northampton, PRO SP 14/71/24 . See Julia Walker's discussion of the dynastic politics involved in Mary's internment near the tomb that James erected for Elizabeth (*English Literary Renaissance*, 26 [1996], 523–5).
50. PRO State Papers 14/17/25.

6

'What's in a Name?': A Papist's Perception of Puritanism and Conformity in the Early Seventeenth Century

Michael Questier and Simon Healy

The existence in early modern England of large numbers of people who did not share the zealotry of Romish recusants and Protestant Puritans has recently become important for explaining what happened in the later English Reformation. In particular we have had our attention drawn to the 'occasional conformists' whose opinions were more or less Catholic. In the words of Christopher Haigh,

> those (or the children of those) who had reluctantly surrendered Catholic ritual in the 1560s now expected from their ministers as much ceremony as the Church of England would sanction. Although theirs was a residual religion, and they were the spiritual leftovers of Elizabethan England, they should not be dismissed as 'mere conformists', for in their defence of ceremonies and festivities they formed a factor to be reckoned with.[1]

They consciously rejected the interfering ministrations of Puritan evangelicals, though, we are told, the new seminarist clergy never ministered to more than a minority of them.[2] But what did these conformists actually think about religion and religious conflict? Have we said all there is to say about them when we describe their staid attachment to pre-Reformation norms of sacramental practice, liturgy and church furnishing? There is the

difficulty. These people, it seems, rarely if ever spoke. Their alienation from the new order of things and longing for ancient time,
essentially non-political, certainly unevangelical, estranged from
virtually every active element of Reformation thought and practice,
is constructed on their own almost absolute silence.

    John Bossy, however, has suggested that the way forward in this
area *is* the investigation of attitudes among individual church
papists.[3] This is the purpose of this chapter – to test some of the
current arguments about Catholicism and conformity, by talking
about one (outwardly ordinary) conformist who did think. His
thoughts do not accord well with some prevailing historiographical
paradigms, but they tell us much about the nature of conformity
and even the processes of religious change in the later English
Reformation.

I

On 25 April 1604, John Good, MP for Camelford, stood up in the
House of Commons and made an extraordinary and impassioned
speech at the second reading of a 'bill intituled, An acte against
Puritans' brought in 'by a knight of honorable birthe and greate
experience'. As Good saw it, the problem with the bill (presented by
Sir Francis Hastings)[4] was that it was 'soe framed as it never so
much as leviled, much lesse intended to strike them, against whom
it semed to be preferred'.[5] In other words, it defined Puritanism as
out-and-out separatism. (It was the classic Puritan maneuver,
described so well by Peter Lake. Moderate Puritans would invoke
'the threat of extremism in order to create as large an area as possible in the "middle ground"'.)[6] This was what the bill's author
intended, but Good was not having any of it. It made him 'out of
zeale for the preservation of unitye against these novelists, to
breake silence, and to deliver, what I conceived of the bill, of them,
and the religion which I then professed'. Good told his fellow
members that 'this bill serves but as a bridg, to passe over the
knowen Puritans indeede, to certaine obscure and imaginary sec-
taries'. He thought it was better to define Puritans rather more com-
prehensively as those 'who contest and impugne the orders and
Cerimonies of the Church, the callinge of the Reverend Bishops and
the lawes of ecclesiastical policie here established'. For good
measure he complained also of the 'seditious libeles, bitter invec-

tives and unlawfull petitions' presented to the Commons at the beginning of the session, particularly an anti-episcopal petition by 'brainsicke [Brian] Bridger',[7] and the petition of the Northamptonshire clergy tabled by Sir Edward Montagu

> which although at the first sight, it carrie a show of milder temper, yet upon deeper insight, will prove of dangerous sequel, for … what eles do those ministers crave, who complaine against suspension from their functions because the[y] dislike some cere-monies, and doctrine here publikly allowed and taught; but liberty to impugn the lawes, orders, and government of the Church …?

He moved therefore

> to have it inserted into this bill, That whosoever shall in publike preachinge or private Conventicle teach or inveigh against the orderse and ceremonies of the Churche heare established or against the callinge or iurisdiction spirituall or temporall or the reverend fathers the LL. Bishops. That every such person so of-fendinge should by this Acte be adiudged a Puritan and suffer the penalties as is therin ordained.[8]

His speech was not well received. He claimed that his opponents had 'cried me down for a papist and called me to the barre', though there is no record of any such censure taking place. It certainly achieved instant notoriety. The author of the 'Censure' poem upon the breaking of wind in the House parodied his views thus: 'Naye quothe Mr Good and also som other / this farte came forthe from some reformed brother.'[9] He remained obsessed with the behavior of the Puritans. He returned to the subject in parliament in 1610 when he opposed the inclusion of the issue of the silencing of Puritan ministers in the ecclesiastical grievances petition.[10] What do we make of Good's ill-judged intervention, and particu-larly the opprobrious label of papist which his opponents attached to him? Was he, in fact, a person who was in some sense popishly or Romishly affected and who was using this opportunity to attack what he saw as the cause of the Church of England's continuing sep-aration from Rome? His tactics were remarkably similar to the cam-paign for toleration then being conducted by Romish polemicists. (They argued like Good that the Church of England was disfigured, and, indeed, the established political order threatened, by the existence of Puritans who, *unlike* Roman Catholics, were tainted by disloyalty as well as unorthodox beliefs.)[11] Towards the end of his life, Good wrote a long discourse about his religious opinions. It records his feelings of insecurity in religion, and it relates in some detail all the influences which had acted upon him in this regard, everything from illness to books of patristic theology. In his discourse he says that his upbringing was entirely Catholic in the full Romish sense. He was 'borne of Catholike parentes' who took care that their religion 'should be delivered to me puer and intire'. But at an early age he was sent to Oxford, 'where according to the time and place ... [he] was drawn from ... [his] former Catholike instruction, to the nowe protestant institution', but ineffectually and he reverted to Romishness when he returned home.[12] Subsequently he wavers on the margins of the Catholic religion, wondering why he cannot summon up sufficient resolution and courage to take the plunge and reject Protestant schism. His account of his religious experiences might be styled the 'diary of a church papist'. People like Good conformed to the religion established by law, but could still find attractive the ritual of Catholic sacramental practice if the opportunity presented itself (as it appears it did when he returned home from Oxford during the 1580s).[13]

While Good was technically a 'mere' church papist, his speech to the Commons in 1604 reveals that his religious beliefs were anything but passionless and passive. The extraordinary tergiversations which he experienced within religion (while remaining technically a conformist) do not allow us to cast him as part of a quiescent majority whose preferences were tempered according to the fashion of the time and characterized mainly by a determination to ignore the period's religious zealots. Furthermore, we argue, his experience of religion and politics tells us things about the nature of Catholicism and conformity and their opposites which modify the model of church papistry devised by those who have charted the gradual transfer of the mass of the population from the 'old religion' to 'parish anglicanism'.

II

Let us examine John Good's sense of ecclesiastical allegiance in more depth. First, what of his political milieu? It was a contemporary commonplace that papists were an unstable fifth column. Protestant fear of popery was focused heavily on Romish plots. Of course, some modern accounts of post-Reformation English Catholicism, styling it as a sacramental conservative impulse, have largely dissociated church papistry from this element of Romanism. But Good's background was politically extreme. His father, James Good (fellow of Magdalen College, Oxford, and, after moving to Chancery Lane in 1556, fellow of the Royal College of Physicians), was one of the doctors chosen to attend Mary Stuart during her detention in England. He was accused of helping her to maintain a secret correspondence with her supporters, and he was imprisoned in the Tower between 1573 and 1575. The Privy Council kept him under surveillance after his release. His colleague in providing medical services to the Scottish Queen was the infamous Edward Atslowe, a political subversive who, with James Good, prevented Protestant reforms in the Royal College of Physicians, was regularly arrested and even tortured by the regime for his conspiratorial activities, and was a life-long recusant.[14]

Good's mother remained an object of suspicion after his father's death. In August 1586 she was dragged in to be examined together with the lunatic priest John Ballard, the moving spirit behind the Babington Plot. It was alleged that one of the conspirators, Henry Donne, had brought Ballard to her house.[15] In addition there seems to have been a connection between the family and the politically active Henry, Earl of Arundel and his son-in-law John, Lord Lumley, from whom Good's mother acquired a lease of the manor of Malden in Surrey. Both men were Catholics and supporters of a fast-track Stuart succession. They had been imprisoned for involvement in the Ridolfi Plot, and that disaster had not sufficiently educated Lumley to keep him out of the conspiracies around Mary Stuart in the mid-1580s.[16] One of Good's uncles, Lodowick Bruskett, was a spy who moved in Catholic circles.[17]

Of course, John Good was never involved in any political conspiracy against the Elizabethan State. But from what we know of his politics, his opinions were closely connected with the Catholicism he had experienced at an early age. And in this, we argue, Good's attitudes to State and Church, the monarchy and the succession, were probably far from unique. They may be a pointer to the political activism possible within the church papist's (supposedly sluggish) conformist mentality. It was no great secret that many Elizabethans with Catholic associations thought it was a

waste of time experimenting with the possibility of a Spanish succession. Their candidate was James VI, whether his own beliefs
(about which there was perennial doubt) were Catholic or Calvinist.
It appears that for some of these people, their enthusiasm for the
Scottish interest and, later, virtually unconditional allegiance to
James took precedence over quibbles about recusancy, for example.
They had always supported James and would continue to do so,
even at the price of conflict with co-religionists who were less
enthusiastic about him. Some of them were prepared to compromise over conformity to the Church of England during the 1590s
and after 1603, principally because the issue of strict recusancy was
less important to them than demonstrating the potential extent of
their loyalty to the Crown and doing away with Catholicism's
pariah status. Good was one of these people. Admittedly we do not
know for certain of any direct link between him and the Catholic
politicians and clergy who in the 1590s were working so hard to
assure James VI of their goodwill and thwart their enemies in Rome
who opposed him.[18] But Good did stress very strongly his loyalty to
James, not just in his speech in 1604 but also in June 1607 when
Sir William Bulstrode moved to read the Commons petition for
enforcement of the recusancy laws and Speaker Phelips advised the
House that the King wished to deal with the matter himself. In a
carefully judged speech, Good attempted to prevent the predictable
outcry over the breach of the privilege of freedom of speech:

> If the arrest of one Member be held with us an impeachement of
> our liberties, what shall an arrest of the whole howse be? But … I
> do not interpret his Majesties message as a stoppe by displeas-
> ure, but rather he doth as a kind father that doth not hide from us
> what will displease him, and what he would have us do.[19]

Catholic loyalists such as Good were also the ones who showed
most enthusiasm for the Jacobean Oath of Allegiance of 1606 when
it was used to establish a dividing line between the Catholics who
would support the Stuart regime and those who would not.[20] At the
same time that he was struggling intellectually to assure himself of
the rightness of communion with Rome he was also composing a
tract in defence of the Oath which he sent to Lord Chancellor
Ellesmere. Good's tract is written exclusively from a Catholic view-
point (in order, he said, to make it more convincing to Romanists).[21]
The government's propaganda presented the Oath as a moderate

measure to contain potential violence after the Gunpowder Plot by allowing moderate Catholics to swear their loyalty to the regime. Many Catholic polemicists, however, said it was nothing but a restatement of the Oath of Supremacy. But this did not prevent other Catholics from defending it, even in print.[22] And some of the Oath's defenders, particularly laymen like the northerner Roger Widdrington, and priests like Anthony Hebburn, shared Good's political roots among the papists who had advocated a Stuart succession in the 1590s.[23] For such people, the taking of the Oath was more than a concession to the demands of the regime. It was an enthusiastic affirmation of the legitimate place of a certain style of Catholicism within the State. Moreover there was a clear connection between the thinking which justified the Oath of Allegiance and that which allowed attendance at Protestant service in obedience to the legitimate command of the supreme governor.[24]

III

One may, therefore, trace Good's conformist tendencies to a Romanism that was far more than an aesthetic preoccupation with pre-Reformation Church interiors and conservative sacramental thought. But how Roman was Good's Catholicism? Did he think that the Elizabethan settlement of religion was so repellent that nothing but a thorough purging of it, along the lines set down in the violent Catholic polemical books (which Good obtained and read), would do? Let us turn from his political associations to the opinions which he expressed about doctrine. After he returned from Oxford in the mid–1580s he says he initially renounced his conformity to the English Church, but soon fell under the influence of 'an unhappy guide ... false to god and himselfe' who exploited a thoroughly un-church-papistical horror which Good experienced of auricular confession.[25] Decoded, this probably means that his conformity in practice was more than technical or occasional. Not only is there no evidence that he was ever indicted in any court for recusancy. As late as 1610 he was spending large sums on the refurbishment of his local church at Malden, Surrey.[26] And in his conversion tract he hinted at positive elements in his conformity when he said that he assumed that people on both sides were 'members of the same misticall body and diffred more in form and Ceremonies then in matter and substance'.[27]

Good's obsessive preoccupation with Puritanism was probably not just a residual Romanist disapproval of the hotter sort of Protestants. In his 1604 intervention over the bill 'against Puritans' he referred 'all men that are desirouse to be satisfied herein to those absolute and unanswerable workes of reverend Mr Hooker wherin are discovered sundrie degrees of Puritans'.[28] We may surmise that Good's reference to Hooker conceals a more solid, even active, attachment to the Church of England than is revealed by the polemic of his spiritual autobiography. Although there is no direct evidence, Good may have first encountered Hooker when the latter expounded his ideas in controversy with the puritan Walter Travers at the Temple Church, a few hundred yards from Good's house in Chancery Lane.[29] Controversy surrounds the modern interpretation of Hooker and the polemical agenda which he was following. But it is possible that Good was deliberately drawing on Hooker's infusion of conformity with a positive religious content (utterly different from the minimalist position of people like Whitgift). Hooker is not really a natural starting point for conversion to Rome. He erects barriers against it by exalting the role of the sacraments, establishing apostolic succession of ecclesiastical orders and discipline, and magnifying the status of the visible Church (all perceived through and in the structures of the English Church). Hooker's English Church may in some sense be halfway between Rome and Geneva, but this 'moderate' polemical position is adopted without even a moderate goodwill towards either.[30] In Good's account of his polemical reading he makes a clear distinction between his initial and speedy rejection of the arguments of the continental reformers (and fellow travellers in England, including John Jewel and John Foxe) and his much more measured doubts about the Church of England as a true Church.[31] His defense of papal primacy is not straightforward. Initially the attack is directed straight at Jewel's *Apology*, but when Good moves on to Richard Field's citations of Augustine, and particularly the standard polemical text employed by so many Roman controversialists of the period, *Retractationes*, book 1, chapter 21, concerning the primacy which the Roman bishop enjoys, whether of power or of order, he turns this (and other places from the Fathers) to a discussion of the difference between ministerial and episcopal authority, rather than focus just on the papal variety, and so gives the text a peculiarly conformist concern.[32]

Although Good's exposition of an ecclesiology which bore a recognizable resemblance to Hooker's was quite remarkable in a tract in which he proclaimed his conversion to Rome, it does much to explain his decision to secure a seat in the Commons as burgess for Camelford in 1604.[33] James's accession in 1603 brought forth a flurry of petitions from Puritan ministers, and, while this crisis was defused by the Hampton Court Conference in January 1604, it must have been obvious that Puritan sympathizers would attempt to raise the issue of ecclesiastical reform in the Commons as they had done during the presbyterian controversies in the 1580s.

IV

These two aspects of John Good, his political affiliations and his ecclesiastical preferences, raise several questions about our labelling him as a church papist or occasional conformist. We might say simply that he was one of a number we can find who thought that it was possible to be a member of the true Church while still part of what he perceived as (in some sense) the admittedly schismatical Church of England. People like James I's chaplain Benjamin Carier thought in precisely this way before circumstances combined to force them into the Roman Church.[34] But Good's background was different from Carier's, and his experience of conformity had very different origins and premises. Perhaps, then, he was simply a waverer who failed to make up his mind until the very last moment? But the problem with such a literal reading of his conversion tract is the one experienced with many examples of that genre – doubt and wavering are magnified with hindsight and then set against a newly grasped certainty. In fact, it is arguable that while the tract plays down Good's adherence to the Church of England and also disguises his former Catholic political associations, both were very much part of his mental world. So he seems to have held in tandem two completely contradictory sets of opinions. One possible explanation is that this was because he lacked the mental equipment to understand that they could not, as all polemical books made clear, in any circumstances be reconciled, and he was therefore so completely cut off from polemical and political reality that he is interesting only for the fact that the first Jacobean parliament should have contained someone so supremely dim. But his public and private utterances are framed quite astutely in such a way as to echo recognized forms of polemical and political thought. He may not have integrated particularly well into the establishment, and after 1610 was clearly very much outside it,[35] but until the last years of his life, when, for example, he refused to contribute in 1622 to the Palatine benevolence and was summoned before the Privy Council, and then in 1625 had his house searched for arms (showing that he was now definitely suspected of dangerous papistical inclinations),[36] he does not seem to have been cut off from mainstream patterns of religious thought and practice.

Let us return briefly to Good's conversion tract, where he describes his embrace finally of true religion. Extensive sections of it are polemical, notably the detailed assault on Protestant polemicists. But look beyond these passages and what emerges clearly is a classic statement about evangelical conversion, a narrative of his experience of grace, his probing of the inner self under the providential prodding of misfortune. As with so many converts who gave an account of their reading habits, it is not his intellect which is the problem. His conversion tract suggests he never really had any trouble sorting out which writers were orthodox. It is his own corrupt nature with which he struggles, though analyzed partly in terms of the current ecclesiastical division between the Churches of England and Rome. His lapse into Protestant profession in the 1580s and his horror of auricular confession were a defect not of his understanding but of his will, 'and what with the motives of my depraved will, prone to sensuality, suggestinge the facility of the solifidian way to salvation ... I quickly fell back againe to the doktrin and practise of the new Evangelicall libertie'. Later he lets 'loose the reines to ... [his] affections and pleasures' which carry him into 'many precipices', 'there being noe way so forceable to extinguish true faith as a loose and disolute life'.[37]

A great deal of the clerical conversion literature of this period which sets up a tension between the Roman and the Protestant Churches (that is, as an ecclesiastical conflict which may be resolved by determining which of them has institutional integrity) is informed by another tension, namely in the individual's experience of grace – how he will feel vocation, regeneration and assurance, and how he will persevere in faith more broadly understood than the dull polemical indices of truth delivered by the controversialists.[38] Good's conversion tract takes up evangelical themes. Disillusion with the world is ubiquitous in all conversion literature and Good relates such a sense to the problems he experienced when trying to retain control over his landed estate at Malden (though, like all converts describing the providential preparation of the heart through affliction, he denies that he converted merely through frustration at his difficulties).[39] Like so many evangelicals, he cites his constant illnesses to explain how he was incited to return to true faith and religion. God visited him with a dangerous sickness which raised his mind to heaven and the principles of the 'Catholike faith' and stirred up his will 'to desier some fuller and more perfect information of my understandinge for the truth of the Catholike Church which in the Creede I dayly professed'.[40] He abused this temporary recovery of his health 'in servinge the vanities of the worlde, the concupiscence of the fleshe and the suggestions of the devill'. Like almost all converts he made sense of perceived instability in institutional religion by correlating it with movement in grace. He said that

> the onely desier to continue my pleasures more freely and fully and feare to incurre those penalties which the rigour of the lawes imposed, not onely by losse of goodes landes and libertie, but alsoe of life, in many cases, where the Catholike profession was made treason; weare the true and onely motives, that kepte me in the practise of protestant religion.

Like other evangelicals he saw his capacity to drift aimlessly from one doctrinal profession to another as a clear sign that he had not converted effectually.[41] All movement between denominations (even to a true particular Church) not dictated by grace is likely to be the result of deception. Instability in grace leads to mere intellectual dabbling with religious theory. Good thought that his continuing as a Protestant was reinforced by an 'illution, under a coulourable pretence of more knowledge, to infect me with curiositye stirring up a continuall desier to be alwaies seekinge and serchinge more fully to informe my understandinge; when in verie truth the fault was not so much therin, as in my depraved and corrupted will, that could induce no reformation', even though he had 'found by ... readinge of som of our owne authours, such difference betweene the Catholike and protestant Church and Religion, as must of necessity convince the one of falshood'.[42]

Good's own polemic is ambiguous as a model of how he became a Catholic. Like other evangelicals, he uses polemical theory to determine which institutional Church is in the right over doctrine, and yet that polemical perception cannot itself be the basis for his decision to convert one way or the other. Though it reflects his own predilections for a particular type of ecclesiastical order, his doctrinal attraction towards the institutional Church of Rome is not coterminous with his search for the unity of the Catholic and Apostolic Church which he thinks may be grasped through conversion in grace. And Good did not take his quarrel against his Puritan opponents to a conclusion in the way that the period's famous anti-Puritan clerical converts to Rome did – people like Benjamin Carier and Humphrey Leech, who went abroad and announced noisily that they had changed religion.[43] Good remained consciously within the English Church almost to the end of his life, and may never have physically separated himself from it at all. Even the religious preamble of his will, drawn up in August 1626, is a model of studied ambiguity.[44] But Good's vigorous conformism was not pure laziness, in the way that church papistry is generally portrayed in conversion tracts. What we know of his background and his politics means he cannot be called a 'church papist' if by that we mean a *via media* resistance to the blandishments and rhetoric of the zealots who urged their audience towards explicitly Catholic or Protestant professions of faith. He was certainly not one of Christopher Haigh's church papists, the medium for the transition between Marian reaction and prayerbook Protestantism, the reservoir for a parish Anglican/prayerbook Protestantism.[45] An investigation of Good's mental world suggests that we should not ignore the possible appeal of Catholic or anti-Catholic schemes of thought to spiritual floating voters (like Good) in early modern England. But at the same time, the way in which he read and reacted to polemic warns us not to assume that people would act on what they read precisely in the way that polemical writers seem to envisage (that is, to reject one or other Church or theological tradition entirely).

V

So, finally, we think, Good's account of his conversion draws heavily upon contemporary polemical language to express his break with sinful life and heretical opinions, but his very eclectic mental adoption of several different religious positions (underpinned by loyalist political philosophy) was not merely a neutral incompetent failure to discern that certain beliefs and practices were irreconcilable. And the tensions and contradictions between his religious aspirations and allegiances were not hidden from him. Good's religious impulse expressed itself positively through both conformist *and* evangelical urges, though he could occasionally describe both negatively, as in his castigation of (Protestant) 'evangelical liberty' and of (Catholic) occasional conformity for fear of the law. And the tension between evangelical and conformist practice in religion could sometimes be characterized for Good by the oppositions set out in Catholic and Protestant accounts of true religion. It seems that various aspects of religious thought and practice which historians have seen as separating out (in practice as well as theory) quite neatly during and after the 1570s never separated out so clearly in the mind or behavior of people like John Good, the quintessential nonseparatist.

At the same time, some contemporary polemicists were also far more aware of this ambivalence than some modern historians have given them credit for. Protestant anti-papists knew very well that certain central aspects of grace and conversion could be assimilated (by conformists like Good) into a Roman as well as a Protestant scheme. Likewise, the Catholic polemical war over conformity was not simply about how far Catholics should associate themselves with the formal worship and liturgy of the Church of England. It was also about how evangelical impulses could be interwoven with separatist ones within the structure of a national Church which was not in communion with Rome. The fact that these polemicists addressed both sets of issues, often in terms of each other (conversion to the life of faith expressed through separation from a false Church and vice versa), perhaps demonstrates to us that they recognized how a pitch could be made for proselytes like Good, even if his conversion was not typical of the changes of religion which we find described in the printed polemical literature. Put another way, we argue that the obsessive historiographical concern with a specific type of outward behavior, church-going or the lack of it, has distorted the historical investigation of this topic. Undoubtedly, an individual like Good (who left such a vivid account of his religious experience) was unusual for that reason alone, but, it appears, such people who were subject to conflicting impulses in religion, instigated by evangelical *and* conformist, Catholic *and* Protestant, ideas, were receptive to a whole range of polemical and rhetorical strategies.

NOTES

1. C. Haigh, 'The Church of England, the Catholics and the People', in
    C. Haigh, ed., *The Reign of Elizabeth I* (London, 1984), 195–219, at 219,
    and *passim*. See also now A. Walsham, *Church Papists* (Woodbridge,
    Suffolk: Boydell Press, 1993).
2. C. Haigh, 'The Continuity of Catholicism in the English Reformation',
    Past and Present 93 (1981): 37–69; 'From Monopoly to Minority:
    Catholicism in Early Modern England', *Transactions of the Royal
    Historical Society*, fifth series, 31 (1981): 129–47; 'Puritan Evangelism
    in the Reign of Elizabeth I', *English Historical Review* 92 (1977): 30–58.
3. J. Bossy, 'Motives for Church Papistry' (unpublished paper delivered
    at the Neile Colloquium, University College, London, January 1996).
4. Hastings, with Sir Edward Montagu and Sir William Bulstrode (who
    opposed Good's parliamentary speech of 1607) were all related to
    Lord Harington and formed part of a group who tried to ease the lot
    of the deprived Puritan ministers of 1604.
5. BL Lansdowne MS 776, f. 14.
6. By constructing a 'false image of the radical and subversive Puritan'
    they attacked separatists and semi-separatists with the intention of
    favouring the 'mass of Puritan ministers' (P. Lake, 'Matthew Hutton –
    a Puritan Bishop?', *History* 64 [1979], 182–204, at 197).
7. In his petition of 29 March, Bridger, a poor curate who was under
    investigation by the court of High Commission, condemned the
    enforcement of clerical subscription, and claimed 'that the whole
    land is defiled by the means of the Bishops'. When examined by the
    Commons, he refused to reveal any accomplices, and was con-
    demned as 'a schismatick in the highest degree' (*Commons Journals*, 1,
    157–8, 161).
8. *Commons Journals*, 184b, 956b; BL, Lansdowne MS 776, ff. 14^v–16; BL,
    Lansdowne MS 849, f. 14; Huntington Library, MS EL 2077.
9. BL, Lansdowne MS 776, f. 16; BL, Additional MS 34218, f. 21^v.
10. *Commons Journals*, 420b.
11. Richard Broughton, *An Apologicall Epistle* (Antwerp [imprint false,
    printed secretly in England], 1601), 87–8; Christopher Muriell, *An
    Answer unto the Catholiques Supplication* (London, 1603), sigs D^v–D2;
    cf. Gabriel Powell, *The Catholikes Supplication unto the Kings Maiestie;
    for Toleration of the Catholike Religion in England* (London, 1603), 11; *A
    Petition Apologeticall* (Douai [imprint false, printed secretly in
    England], 1604), 11–12, 28; John Colleton, *A Supplication to the Kings
    most excellent Maiestie* (printed secretly in England, 1604), 4.
12. BL, Lansdowne MS 776, f. 11^v.
13. Ibid., ff. 11–12. Good's parents' house in Chancery Lane was ideally
    situated for clandestine Catholic worship, as the neighbouring Inns
    of Court were regularly visited by priests, and the entire area of the
    liberty of the Rolls was exempt from the jurisdiction of the local
    authorities.
14. J. Foster, *Alumni Oxonienses: The Members of the University of Oxford,
    1500–1714*, 4 vols. (Oxford and London: Parker & Co., 1891–2), *sub*

Good, James; P[ublic] R[ecord] O[ffice], PROB 11/38, f. 110ᵛ; Royal College of Physicians, Annals 1, f. 23, 26, 30–2, 34; *A[cts of the] P[rivy] C[ouncil] of England (1542–1628)]*, ed. J. R. Dasent *et al.*, 32 vols, (London: HM Stationery Office, 1890–1907), *1571–5*, 390; *APC 1575–7*, 23; *Calendar of the Manuscripts of the Most Honourable the Marquess of Salisbury*, ed. M. S. Giuseppi *et al.* (H[istorical] M[anuscripts] C[ommission], 1888–1976), 2: 110; *APC 1577–8*, 162, 174–5; *C[alendar of] S[tate] P[apers] D[omestic Series]*, 12 vols. (for 1547–1625), ed. R. Lemon and M. A. E. Green (London: Longman, Brown, Green, Longmans & Roberts, 1856–72), *Addenda 1566–79*, 550–1. James Good was said to be attending Mass at a Catholic conventicle in a house in Old Fish Street. There resorted there not only Good but also Dr Atslowe and the Catholic lawyer Edmund Plowden, another supporter of Mary Stuart (G. de C. Parmiter, *Edmund Plowden* [London: Catholic Record Soc., 1987], 143–4). Atslowe had served as physician to the eighth earl of Northumberland (L. J. Hicks, *An Elizabethan Problem* [New York: Fordham University Press, 1964], 26, 47, 99); see also M. O'Dwyer, 'Catholic Recusants in Essex *c*.1580 to *c*.1600' [unpublished MA thesis, London, 1960], 21–2, 130–5).

15. *CSPD 1581–90*, 343. In early 1584 Lord Hunsdon's notes of the papists operating in London included 'one Phillippes, dwelling at Dr. Goods' [*sic*], in Chancery Lane, a great dealer with priests, and a sender and director of them from place to place' (H. Foley, *Records of the English Province of the Society of Jesus* , 7 vols. [London: Burns and Oates, 1875–83], 6: 721). A government informant mentioned vaguely that 'divers of the seditious parties' would be found at Good's house in Chancery Lane over Easter 1594 (*CSPD 1591–4*, 471).

16. PRO, PROB 6/3, f. 21; PRO, C 78/474/6; R.B. Manning, *Religion and Society in Elizabethan Sussex* (Leicester: Leicester University Press, 1969), 226–8; *HMC Salisbury MSS* 3: 115, 136–7. Lumley had also founded a lectureship at the Royal College of Physicians.

17. PRO, PROB 11/56, ff. 250ᵛ–1; we are grateful to P. J. Hammer for this point about Lodowick Bruskett; *HMC Salisbury MSS* 11: 169–70.

18. Lord Lumley (the Goods' acquaintance and eventual neighbour at Malden) employed as a servant the brother of Cuthbert Trollop, one of the most vitriolic supporters of James against the pretensions of Spaniolized English Romanists (*CSPD 1601–3*, 211; G. Anstruther, *The Seminary Priests*, 4 vols. [London: Ware and Great Wakering, 1968–77], 1: 363–4).

19. D. H. Willson, ed., *The Parliamentary Diary of Robert Bowyer 1606–1607* (Minneapolis: University of Minnesota Press, 1971), 330–3; *Commons Journals*, 1053a records only the first point, and thus garbles the sense of the speech. Good's speech is an excellent example of how someone can shape a debate by highlighting the areas in which he agrees with the previous speakers (who were in this case attacking the violation of the Commons' privilege of free speech) but then effecting a U-turn, in Good's case, by interpreting James's intervention as a benevolent request rather than a peremptory command.

20. M. C. Questier, 'Loyalty, Religion and State Power in Early Modern England: English Romanism and the Jacobean Oath of Allegiance', *Historical Journal* 40 (1997): 311–29.
21. Huntington Library, MS EL 2187 (unpaginated).
22. P. Milward, *Religious Controversies of the Jacobean Age* (Lincoln: University of Nebraska Press, 1978), 99–119.
23. M. C. Questier, 'The Politics of Religious Conformity and the Accession of James I' (forthcoming in *Historical Research*).
24. Questier, 'Loyalty', 321–2.
25. BL, Lansdowne MS 776, ff. 12, 24–5, 32^v.
26. *CSPD 1603–10*, 486; K. N. Ross, *A History of Malden* (New Malden, 1947), 72–4; O. Manning and W. Bray, *History and Antiquities of the County of Surrey*, 3 vols. (London: J. Nichols & Son, 1804–14), 3: 8.
27. BL Lansdowne MS 776, f. 13.
28. Ibid., ff. 14^v–15.
29. *Dictionary of National Biography*, *sub* Richard Hooker, Walter Travers; cf. R. Bauckham, 'Hooker, Travers and the Church of Rome in the 1580s', *Journal of Ecclesiastical History* 29 (1978), 37–50.
30. P. Lake, *Anglicans and Puritans?* (London: Unwin Hyman, 1988), 146, 156, 173.
31. BL Lansdowne MS 776, ff. 29–37.
32. Ibid., ff. 20^v–3; cf. R. Dodaro, and M. C. Questier, 'Strategies in Jacobean Polemic: the Use and Abuse of St Augustine in English Theological Controversy', *Journal of Ecclesiastical History* 44 (1993): 432–49, at 439–41.
33. The nomination probably came via the Carnsew family. William Carnsew had sat for the borough in the two previous parliaments. He had been a fellow of All Souls in the 1580s (Foster, *Alumni Oxonienses*, *sub* Carnsew William) where Good may have met him. Carnsew contributed £8 17s 6d to the repair of Malden church in 1609–10 (Ross, *Malden*, 73). In 1613 a friend informed Carnsew that Good's mother-in-law Jane Brusket had 'dealt very well' with him prior to her death (PRO, SP 46/72, f. 110; PRO, PROB, 6/8, f. 117).
34. M. C. Questier, 'Crypto-Catholicism, Anti-Calvinism and Conversion at the Jacobean Court: the Enigma of Benjamin Carier', *Journal of Ecclesiastical History* 47 (1996): 45–64, at 54.
35. Apart from his sporadic attacks on Puritans, Good kept a relatively low profile in Parliament. He was named to the committee for John Arundel's estate bill on 27 April 1610, only six months before the latter's sister married Good's parliamentary patron William Carnsew (*Commons Journals*, 421b; *Visitation of Cornwall*, 76–7), the bill to attaint the Gunpowder Plotters, the sabbath bill (29 January 1606), the bill for suppression of idleness (19 April 1610), and the reformation of the West Country fishing trade (20 June 1604). The last of these bills may have been of some interest to his constituents. There is no evidence that he ever held public office of any kind except his seat in Parliament. Carnsew could probably have secured his re-election for Camelford in 1614 but Good evidently chose not to stand again.

36. PRO, SP 14/127/80; *CSPD 1625–6*, 168. Probably as a precaution against seizure he passed his Malden estate to his son Sebastian in May 1622, leasing back a life interest for an annual rent of £84, PRO, C 78/474/6.
37. BL Lansdowne MS 776, f. 12^{r-v}.
38. M. C. Questier, *Conversion, Politics and Religion in England, 1580–1625* (Cambridge: Cambridge University Press, 1996), chs. 2–4.
39. BL Lansdowne MS 776, f. 10^{r-v}. In June 1607 a bill came before the House of Commons to allow the Crown to add 22 acres of Good's estate at Malden to the neighbouring grounds of Queen Anne's estate at Nonsuch Park. Legislation was required to confirm the residue to Good, who had technically forfeited his title under the terms of Joan Good's will, which stipulated that any of her heirs who attempted to alienate the original lease should be deprived of their inheritance. The Earl of Worcester, who had arranged the deal, took care of the bill in the Lords, but it was delayed at the committee stage by a complaint from Merton College, which disputed the validity of the lease and attempted to insert a proviso allowing them to sue for their rights. The judges eventually ruled against the proviso, and the bill passed its final stages on the last day of the session (PRO, C 78/474/6; *CSPD 1603–10*, 340, 379; PRO, PROB 11/73, f. 374^v; *Lords' Journals*, 2: 521b, 538a; *Commons' Journals*, 398b; House of Lords' Record Office, 4 James I, O. A. 15). Merton College brought a suit to establish their title to the manor of Malden in King's Bench in 1623. Good replied with a bill in Chancery which both asserted the validity of his lease, and explained that he had sold many of his other lands and spent £2,700 on improving the estate and building a manor house. The college, which recruited the help of Archbishop George Abbot (born at nearby Guildford) claimed that the title belonged to them, as the original lease had been procured under duress, a claim which was ultimately upheld. However, the verdict was only pronounced six months after Good's death, and it was tempered by a grant of an eighty year lease of the manor to Good's heirs (PRO, PROB 11/80, f. 126, PROB 11/151, ff. 338–9; Manning and Bray, *History and Antiquities*, 3: 8).
40. BL Lansdowne MS 776, f. 12^v. Cf. Questier, *Conversion*, 192.
41. BL Lansdowne MS 776, f. 13.
42. Ibid., f. 13^{r-v}.
43. Questier, *Conversion*, ch. 4.
44. Good's will commenced 'First into Thy hands (O Lord) I commend my soul; Thou hast redeemed me, O Lord God of truth' (PRO, PROB 11/80, f. 126).
45. C. Haigh, *English Reformations: Religion, Politics, and Society under the Tudors* (Oxford: Clarendon Press, 1993), 267.

7

Multiple Conversion and the Menippean Self: the Case of Richard Carpenter

Alison Shell

Richard Carpenter is perhaps the only religious controversialist in seventeenth-century England who allowed himself to be illustrated vomiting. We know of him through some singular portrait-engravings, through the controversial writings which they preface, through a closet-drama, *The pragmatical Jesuit new-leaven'd*,[1] and from scattered references in mid-seventeenth-century ecclesiastical records, chronicling his erratic behaviour and multiple apostasies. Taking their bearings from Anthony Wood, who styles Carpenter a 'religious mountebank', most commentators on Carpenter have simply concluded that he was eccentric;[2] but this betrays some insensitivity to the specific intellectual crises posed to the religiously unstable during the period of the Civil Wars and Interregnum. This kind of historical judgement now looks very dated when applied to Ranters or female prophets, and there is every reason to assume that learned theological writing of an abnormal kind, written at the same period, is also a serious attempt to communicate religious exploration by the best generic means at the writer's disposal. To extend the analogy with Ranters and prophetesses, something similar is true of religiously inspired conduct abnormal in a given context; convention is to social behaviour what genre is to writing.

The affinities of religious controversy to dialogue and satire have long been recognized;[3] Nigel Smith has said of the literature of the English Revolution that 'genres, with their capacity for transformation as well as representation, define the parameters of public debate, the nature of change, and the means for comprehending that change'. Menippean satire has been called a super-genre which suborns all kinds of generic form to its attempt to discern truth from among diverse possibilities.[4] It should not, therefore, be any surprise that religious controversy during the Civil Wars and Interregnum should sometimes have taken on Menippean characteristics.[5] This has been discussed within studies of popular pamphleteering, and the unstoppable rise in the 1970s and 1980s of Mikhail Bakhtin's term 'carnivalesque' has increased awareness, among both historians and literary critics, of how both literary texts and popular movements may fall into generic patterns.[6]

But Carpenter's case is different again, showing how genres may be individuated; his life and works, placed together, display a connection between the genre of the Menippea and ascertainable autobiographical fact. This can be seen in both Carpenter's retrospective interpretation of his early life, and his writing and behavior in the 1640s and 1650s. His erudition, which aligns him with intellectual rather than popular Menippeanism, makes it clear that he knew what he was doing; and his uniqueness, even the eccentricity of which he has been so often convicted, is best analyzed through the very selective use he makes of the genre's possibilities.

This chapter describes how Carpenter used Menippean conventions in representing himself; why Menippean satire and religious flux went together at this date; and how Carpenter's Cynic integrity has the effect of overriding the usual distinction between life and works. Carpenter was a lifelong wanderer around Europe and an ideological nomad; Menippean satire often depicts the protagonist voyaging through many lands and many philosophical persuasions, encountering irredeemable satiric types on the way. The picture is complicated, though, by the fact that Carpenter takes pains to condemn manifestations of changeability other than his own; and so the following discussion will also pay attention to a central metaphor of his, the straight path versus the crooked. Every autobiographical narrative is a trajectory; the idea of right and wrong trajectories links the structural demands of autobiography with the personal quest for salvation and the known penalties of choosing wrongly. Carpenter's portraits and character-descriptions of Jesuits, monks, Anabaptists and other arch-enemies are also figured in terms of a potential for crooked behaviour, iconically conceived. If one moral message can be said to obsess Carpenter above all others, it is this: the compulsion to distinguish between his own religious quest, arising from disillusionment with one sect after another, and the iconographical representations of moral inconstancy which it is his aim to condemn.

I

Appropriately for a genre which aims more than any other to subvert genre, definitions of Menippean satire have proved divisive. The genre's bibliographer, Eugene Kirk, adopts a Wittgensteinian notion of family resemblances in his preface: Menippean satires, in his view, include unconventional diction, 'neologisms, portmanteau words, macaronics, preciosity, coarse vulgarity, catalogues, bombast, mixed languages, and protracted sentences', they are a medley, 'usually ... of alternating prose and verse, sometimes a jumble of flagrantly digressive narrative, or again a potpourri of tales, songs, dialogues, orations, letters, lists, and other brief forms', and they include outlandish fictions, 'fantastic voyages, dreams, visions, talking beasts', and, being concerned with right learning or right belief, they often call for 'ridicule or caricature of some sham-intellectual or theological fraud'.[7] In the most recent study of the genre Ingrid de Smet has taken a more exclusive approach to the problem, suggesting that writers about Menippean satire in the early modern period should take their bearings from contemporary humanists and other scholars who identified their own works in those terms; she gives a working definition of it as 'fictional (mostly first-person) narratives in prose interspersed with verse ... aimed at mockery and ridicule and often moralising'.[8] But even while arguing for an epicenter to the definition, de Smet recognizes that there are a number of related genres, 'the horizon of the Menippean satire', where Menippean characteristics are often present; and among these, pamphlet literature and controversy figure prominently.

Carpenter was a controversialist, who found – as many others did – that the datum of religious heterogeneity within one nation, or one continent, was constantly painful to comprehend. Yet as he travelled about Europe and about England, he himself kept shifting doctrinally. In the Menippean satire *Sesqueulixes* (Ulysses-and-a-half), written by Varro, the wandering protagonist visits many different places and converts to as many philosophical schools and persuasions.[9] A characteristic Menippean plot, according to Bakhtin, is indeed one in which the hero wanders through many lands; and a mixture of prose and verse became a feature of many travel accounts in the seventeenth century.[10] The linkage of travel with ideological flux is more characteristic still; the Menippean hero ascends into Heaven, descends into Hell and subjects truth to proof in extreme situations. Finally, Menippean satire is, Bakhtin contends, a device for the thorough provoking and testing of surpassingly important philosophical ideas that have a personal and practical relevance. Because Carpenter's quest was concerned with the question of salvation, it can certainly be termed surpassingly important; and because of his autobiographical presentation of the search for truth, everything he writes turns into a spiritual odyssey.

Carpenter's Menippean inheritance also had implications for his manner of self-presentation. Menippus was a Cynic, and proverbially, the Cynic philosopher Diogenes searched the world in a vain attempt to find an honest man; in 'The old men's chat', a dialogue from Erasmus's *Colloquies*, the protagonist engages on a similar quest, trying every sort of monastic order and coming to the conclusion that 'there's a lot of difference between wearing a cross on a cloak or tunic and wearing it in the heart'.[11] A parallel flux, and a similar perpetual dissatisfaction, characterized Carpenter's religious history from its beginnings, and governed his retrospective modelling of it. This is not a formal biographical account of him, but three episodes from his life will be narrated: two relate public disputes, but the first, and longest, is an account of how he turned against Laud because of a grievance over a benefice. If the second and third are dialogic, and even Menippean to some extent, the first, gleaned from depositions and minutes, seems simply to manifest Carpenter remodelling real life to improve its moral and polemical message.[12]

Born into the Church of England, Carpenter's initial conversion to Catholicism must have occurred around 1625, when he left King's College, Cambridge; and in 1627 he was admitted to the Jesuit seminary at Valladolid.[13] Leaving there, he joined the Benedictines in around 1630 and deserted them after a few months. He entered the English College, Rome, in 1633, was ordained priest in 1635, and sent to England the same year; but the next record we have of him is in 1637, as an apostate. He made a formal act of recantation at St Paul's Cross and, though various sermons preached not long afterwards were said by contemporaries to be Laudian in tenor, none survives.[14] Carpenter then petitioned Laud for a benefice and was eventually provided with one in Poling, Sussex.[15]

His living at Poling served only to exacerbate his anti-Catholic prejudice, since it was near one of the major Catholic centers of south-east England, Arundel Castle.[16] Complaining of the remoteness of his parish and the ignorance of the parishioners, Carpenter eventually turned against Laud and submitted evidence to the Committee of Religion, set up in 1640 to garner evidence on Laud in preparation for his trial.[17] The records that remain of his dealings with them are not easy to interpret. Writing in the 1650s, Thomas Gataker believed that Carpenter deliberately conceived his first sermons to ingratiate himself with Laud, who at first 'held him a loof off, and set light by him'; to counter this, Carpenter designed 'a publick profession of his approbation and wel-liking of those Imnovations [*sic*] that [Laud] here brought in ... that he found our Church at his return in a far better condition then when he left it; and that no man religiouslie affected would refuse to bow to the Alter.'[18] But Carpenter himself, not long after these sermons, claimed that his expressed preferences were the result of coercion.

Writing to Sir Edward Dering in 1640, he proffered testimony to the Committee of Religion. A 'Bishops Chaplyn' – probably Samuel Baker, chaplain to the Bishop of London – had asked him to include in his recantation sermon

> two pretty Items ... first, that I must not speake revengefully and ungratefully against the church of Rome, as having had my breeding from them: secondly, that I must insert in my sermon as a great reason of my conversion, the sight and love of the orders and ceremonies, newly begun in the Church of England; a thing, which (the Lord knowes) had not entred into my thoughts, before this admonishment.[19]

But in later sermons, on the encouragement of some friendly 'persons of quality', Carpenter claimed to have inserted some reasons for turning against Catholicism 'which (they sayd) would settle peoples mindes, first in religion, secondly, in their good opinion of my truth, and sincerity'.

If true – and there seems no reason to doubt Carpenter's story so far – this betrays something of how an apostate could be used as a pawn in public relations maneuvers between differing factions within the Church of England. On the one hand, Laudian clergy encouraged him to stress the beauty of holiness as a prime factor in his conversion, and to minimize his disaffection with Rome, perhaps with the idea of securing further converts from Catholicism or from among those popishly affected. But Carpenter's other friends wished Carpenter to place a heavy – and much more traditional – emphasis on the Church of England's opposition to

Catholicism; given the conspicuousness of an apostate, they must have felt that it was important to try to co-opt him for their own side rather than Laud's. Though the audience of any London sermon would have been extremely familar with the polemical differences between Catholics and Protestants, this second faction wished to capitalize on the added authority that objections to Catholicism would have, when given voice by one who had been there. In their second objection, the buried threat is that without explicit inveighing against Catholicism, Carpenter might well be thought still to be popishly affected himself, and to have converted only to gain preferment. The implication is plain: notwithstanding his usefulness to the Church of England, an apostate was still on trial after his recantation.

But in his letter to Dering, Carpenter goes on in a much more startling manner. Having attacked the Church of Rome in subsequent sermons as demanded, he claimed that in a second interview Laud

> was pleased to be wondrous angry with me for my Sermons, and amongst other words to tell me, that I made professions of my true conversion in my Sermons; but (sayd he) Mr Carpenter, I tell you, you had better have stayd where you were, then to have done as you have done.

The phraseology implies how Carpenter has revealed himself to be a convert to the wrong kind of Protestantism, and the pay-off line seems designed to reveal a genuine pro-Catholic bias through an overstated and bad-tempered rebuke. Its shocking effect is enhanced by Carpenter's subsequent comment, how a friend on hearing the story desired him 'for Gods sake, never to speake of the words; adding, that if I did, I was an undone man for ever'. This remarkable story, which would have been extremely effective as a condemnation of Laud, does not figure as part of Carpenter's testimony in the minute-books of the Committee of Religion. It is possible, of course, that it may have been recorded elsewhere and failed to survive; Dering was soon to fall from power, and his efforts had little effect on the eventual trial of Laud. But two pieces of evidence suggest a further possibility, which I believe to be correct: that Carpenter was misattributing and rewriting the reproof he received, and thus that the Committee had to discount Carpenter's first version simply because it was not reliable enough.[20]

The deposition of William Lowe, surviving amongst the papers of Laud, testifies how opposition was mounted to Carpenter's testimony, and throws some doubt on whether Carpenter was telling the truth. According to this document, Lowe accompanied Carpenter on a visit to Laud on three occasions. On the first, Carpenter was referred to the Bishop of London to arrange for making his recantation at Paul's Cross; and on the second occasion, after his sermon, Carpenter petitioned Laud for a benefice and was told that he would be provided with one in six months or less. The first possible benefice in Lancashire proving litigious, Lowe and Carpenter waited on Laud for a third time, and Carpenter was eventually provided with the one in Poling. Lowe concludes by saying, 'I nev[e]r heard one syllable that ev[e]r his Grace dishartened the said Mr. Carpentor or spake any ιωτα tending to wishe him to staie where he was; but aduised him to carrie himselfe discreetly, & prudently & words to that purpose.'[21]

The second piece of evidence is, in fact, Carpenter's testimony as recorded in the Committee of Religion's Minute Books. In December 1640, Carpenter appeared to give evidence on how Samuel Baker forbade his recantation sermon to go to print, giving as his reason that 'the Church of Rome and we are in a peaceable way, and therefore not fitt to augment controversys', and advising Carpenter, 'Be patient, the time may come that you may be heartily glad that your sermon is not printed.' Carpenter objecting, Baker asked 'What, will you turne to Rome againe? If you will, you may, the Church of England hath no need of you.'[22] Carpenter's original story was probably a reattributed, heavily embroidered version of this exchange. If so, the disjunction between Carpenter's two accounts suggests a factual unreliability characteristic of him; this became more pronounced as his career progressed, and the various autobiographical elements in his writing diverged further and further from early accounts.[23]

Obliquely glimpsed through the pattern of his early career and the depositions quoted above, Carpenter appears untrustworthy: but not with a simple untrustworthiness. The difference between the accounts very probably occurred because Carpenter was lying; but one can also see this as fictional improvement of a real-life incident, to improve the moral point contained therein. As he said later, in one of his quasi-autobiographical accounts of his early life, 'I may have misplaced and miscenter'd an Action, but in the substance I have been quadrate with Truth.'[24]

It is an untrustworthiness that arises, paradoxically, through a Cynic-inspired truth to personal emotion which is visible everywhere in his autobiographical writing: he pursues vindictive disavowals of past allegiance, and maintains an experiential view of how to judge dishonesty. But his search for truth demanded two things: an ability to detach oneself from the false, and, necessarily, as great a willingness to experiment with new truth-claims or authority-claims. Roaming from the Jesuits to the Benedictines to the secular priesthood, then converting and capitulating in turn to the demands of Laudians and anti-Laudians, Carpenter alternates between defiant assertions of his capacity to judge for himself, and a respect for his new superiors which is obsequious even by the standards of the seventeenth century. In his letter to Dering, he says of his reaction to Laud's supposed advice, 'I was young, and ... my Lord was throughly wise, and exquisitely knowing; and had I not been truly grounded, these words, in which my continuing Priest in the Church of Rome, was preferred before my preaching in the Church of England, against the Church of Rome; had overturned me.' Whatever the general reliability of his evidence, Carpenter witnesses accurately here to his own capacity for vacillation; it is a moment (fictional or factual) where truth is brought into collision with authority.[25]

According to his eighteenth-century biographer Charles Dodd, Carpenter became an itinerant preacher on the outbreak of the Civil War – 'His chief aim seem'd to be, to add fewel to the fire, that was then kindling, and widen the breach between the king and parliament'[26] – and, meeting with less success than he had hoped, he then repaired to Paris.[27] Returning to England, he joined the Independents, and according to Dodd again, 'play'd his pulpit-pranks according to the humour of the times, and became a mere mountebank of religion', then took a wife, resided at Aylesbury, and preached there until the Restoration: 'those that were merrily disposed, were much diverted by his spiritual anticks, and buffoonery' (310).[28]

Among the many accounts of public disputations in the 1640s and 1650s, there survives an independent account of Carpenter's 'pulpit-pranks'.[29] In a pamphlet of 1641, *A true relation of a combustion, hapning, at St. Anne's Church by Aldersgate*, an account is given of a polemical encounter between (to quote the pamphlet-title again) *a stranger, sometimes a Jesuite, but now, thankes be to God, reformed to our church, and one Marler a buttonmaker, contending which should first preach, the minister being absent that Sabbath day.* This absence provoked

a distracted Mutinie among the People, being somewhat
exasperated; many desiring their friends to goe up into the
Pulpit; others would not assent therto: some gave their assertion to one, some their astipulation to another, which did cause
a great confusion among them. Till at length among the rest in
this distraction, a Stranger and one Marler a Button-maker did
ardently contend which of them should first step into the
Pulpit.... (A2)

There follows an altercation between the button-maker and the
'Stranger' – who is, of course, Carpenter. The anonymous author,
saying that the two contended 'in these and the like words which
follow in this subsequent Tenour' (A2), seems concerned to stress
that reportage of an unpredicted event is necessarily inexact; nevertheless, the speeches given to Carpenter are strikingly similar to his
published writing.

Str.   Thou dost in a prodigious Apostacie degenerate from the
truth: for doest thou think thy selfe more worthy then I? alas! I
scorne such indignitie! Have I encompassed the spacious Orbe
with a girdle of my travels, and have tasted the Religion of each
Country, and dost thou goodman Button-maker Block-head,
thinke thy selfe more worthy then I? alas! I scorne such indignitie! Have I with a mutuall altercation, and vicissitude of fortune,
saluted every aire, and knowne every mans opinion in their
Religion, and dost thou thinke thy selfe more worthy then I? I
detest and abhor the nomination thereof, much more the realty
[*sic*] and mentall supposition. Honest Tom Coriate[30] get thee gone
quickly, or I shall abuse thee most abominably.

Marl.   Abuse me? how? or in what? Ide faine see that indeed.

Str.   Why, Ile tell thee, I can speake *Latinorum more*, so that you
shall not understand one word: which will be a sufficient abuse
(I hope;) therefore trouble me not any longer.

Marl.   Doe not you trouble me any longer, but let me come up.

Stra.   I scorn to give thee the preheminence, neither will I,
therfore get thee gone incontinently.

The pamphleteer concludes:

> These words being ended, he did resolutly step up into the Pulpit,
> and notwithstanding Marlers pulling him backe, he did with some
> difficultie get into the Pulpit, and would have questionlesse
> desseminated some of his doctrine in the Church, which
> (I suppose) he did intend to introduce: But the people being in a
> clamorous and confusive distraction, (he being heretofore knowne
> to have embraced a Jesuiticall Religion, it being ambiguous to some
> whether he was reformed as yet or noe) the Church-wardens pre-
> supposing his intent, did by the general assent and consent of the
> Parish, desire him to come out of the Pulpit into the Vestrie. (A3ᵛ)³¹

The incident dates from around Carpenter's time as an itinerant
preacher, and the pamphlet is referred to scoffingly in Carpenter's
first published work, *Experience, historie, and divinitie.*³²

> And the man that hath but sipped of outlandish experience, will
> easily beleeve, that a Papist was the malignant contriver of that
> swelling and wordy, but chaffie, senselesse, and empty Pamphlet;
> ballassed with the name of, *A true Relation of a combustion* ....
> Wherein the Author of the *true Relation*, hath scarce a true word,
> to beare witnesse, that he knowes what is truth. And if there be a
> true word in all the Pamphlet; it is that onely, *reformed to the
> Church of England*. For, neither was the Preacher a Button-maker,
> but a Divine; neither did we joyne any kinde of discourse; neither
> came I neere the Pulpit, though invited by the Minister, and
> Vestry-men. (Xx6)

Other evidence being lacking, one is, I believe, entitled to think that
Carpenter is improving the truth again, and that the anonymous
account is the more accurate; this time Carpenter is de-anecdotaliz-
ing it, narrating the episode as a much more mundane affair than it
was. He does not show to advantage in the published version, and
(as importantly, in view of the arguments advanced earlier) he is
not the narrator, but a satirical construct in someone else's narration.
But the discrepancy between first- and third-person account, however
characteristic of episodes involving Carpenter, is not the main point
here: the scandal is. As Bakhtin said: 'Very characteristic for the
menippea are scandal scenes, eccentric behaviour, inappropriate

speeches and performances, that is, all sorts of violations of the generally accepted and customary course of events and the established norms of behaviour and etiquette, including manners of speech' (117). This pamphlet, with much else, is testimony that Carpenter was happy to create a stir in real life; and given the manner in which it was reported, it is not particularly inconsistent that he should later have denied his actions.

Like so many in the early 1640s, Carpenter was questioning authority in a consciously transgressive manner; yet his experientialism did not extend to allowing platform-time to those without conventional learning. He stresses that he is better able to preach than his opponent, simply because he is more learned; in his later pamphlet, *The perfect-law of God* (1652), he writes portions of the text in Latin with the aim of excluding a non-scholarly audience, and even includes an appendix asking that any answer be written in Latin, as he has no wish to engage with anyone who is not a scholar. In its more erudite manifestations, Menippean satire is heteroglossic, allusive and very much demands a learned reader; and Carpenter uses familiar phrases from its popular manifestations to mock those who pretend to learning and fail. As already noted, news from Heaven or Hell was a trope of popular Lucianism; and Carpenter recounts an anecdote, again in *The perfect-law of God*, of

the person in a pure-white Dress at the Spittle: Whose mouth was big with strange News; and the grand Matter, to the which all the rest did offer, was, That he came lately from Heaven ... as a Legate sent from the presence of God; and had brought with him the perfect knowledge of Hebrew, the Language of Heaven. And when I address'd my poor skill, to the triall of him; I found, that his Language was a Wild-Irish-Welch-Scotch-Dutch-Hungarian Hebrew, a very Defluxion from his over-flown Brain. (61–2)[33]

False learning is mocked as a cerebral defluxion, but true learning is equated with the experience of travel; in both the reported speech and the autobiographical narrative of the 1641 incident, Carpenter is keen to stress his own broad experience acquired across Europe. As noted above, Menippean satire is often characterized by changing locales – indeed, the ability to read or write within the genre is itself an indication of worldly experience – and Carpenter takes care to link his bid for the pulpit, the site of authority, to his wide experience of different lands and different sects. 'Have I ... saluted every aire, and knowne every mans opinion in their Religion, and dost thou thinke thy selfe more worthy than I?'

This finds an echo in Carpenter's record of another public disputation, where he avers, 'I have lived beyond the Seas … and therefore, I have reason from Heaven, to be more prying into the matters of my Faith than every home-spun man …'[34] The occasion was a disputation on the efficacy of baptism between Carpenter and the Puritan John Gibbs, which took place some time between 1648 and 1653.[35] Carpenter, while an itinerant preacher, had come to Newport Pagnell to preach and had also baptized a child; when this action was challenged by Gibbs, a public disputation was fixed for twelve days later. Carpenter's immortally named pamphlet, *The Anabaptist washt and washt, and shrunk in the washing* (1653), gives a pro-Carpenter version of the event, both in the text and in an engraved frontispiece. On the latter (see Fig. 7.1) various activities of the Anabaptists are depicted around the top and sides;[36] but at the base, the disputation itself is pictured. The small but triumphant figure in the pulpit is probably intended as Carpenter, while Gibbs is shown heckling from the congregation – challenging, but not overturning, Carpenter's elevated position.

This is a rare glimpse of what Carpenter was doing during the English Revolution. We have a number of versions of Carpenter's early life, mostly, of course, Carpenter's own; but evidence of his later career is more difficult to track down. Dodd believed that Carpenter was alive in Aylesbury in 1670 and returned to Catholicism in later years; and his summing-up of Carpenter has been quoted by nearly all of Carpenter's few subsequent biographers: 'He wanted neither wit nor learning: which, notwithstanding, lay under a frightful management through the iniquity of the times, and his own inconstant temper' (310). One needs to pause on the idea of inconstancy, which here denotes what the twentieth century would call eccentricity. The judgement has to do, most of all, with his frequent confessional shifts. A capacity for change was the whole usefulness of an apostate, but if he was to prosper, change had to happen only once; the history of Carpenter as witness shows that he grew less useful to his superiors in proportion to the number of times he mutated. Even if self-interested motives had no part to play in his initial decision to convert from Catholicism, they were soon to manifest themselves, as demonstrated in his lobbying of Laud for a benefice; yet, in the seventeenth century, it would have been impossible consciously to

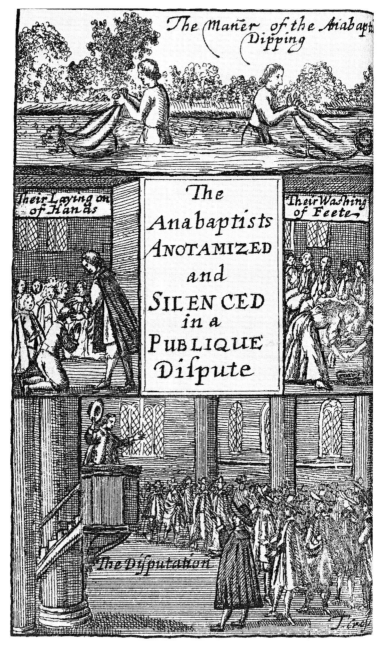

Figure 7.1   *The Anabaptist washt and washt, and shrunk in the washing* (1653).

convert for motives of self-advancement alone. Similarly, there must have been a variety of reasons for his perpetual restlessness; yet his defiant signing-off of *The perfect-law of God*, half-epitaph and half-colophon, illustrates the centrality of doctrinal allegiance to his self-definition:

> By Me
> *Richard Carpenter,*
> Not a Papist, but a
> PROTESTANT:
> As *Protesting* against all Corrupti-
> ons, both in *Faith* and *Manners,*
> Whatsoever, and wheresoever:
> But not, as *protesting* against ought
> that is *excellent,* and
> ιεροϖ η ιεραρχικον,
> Holy in point of Doctrine or *Go-*
> *vernment,* in any *Christian*
> Church,
> Wheresoever, or Whatsoever.
> Who likewise utterly disclame,
> That I am, or was, or will be,
> (*Aspirante Deo*)
> A *Iesuit,*
> From *Rome,* or from *Geneva.*

II

There is a lavish indictment of Carpenter in Thomas Gataker's tract *Discourse apologeticall* (1654).[37] In the course of it, Gataker comments that two tracts of Carpenter's, *The perfect-law of God,* and *The Anabaptist washt and washt,* are

> no other then as Satyrae Menippeae, or some of Aristophanes his Comoedies ... full of girds, and squibs, and scoffes, and jeers, and scurrilous expressions, and Satyrical excursions, as of one rather acting a part or varietie of parts and persons ... upon a Stage, then seriouslie and religiouslie delivering Gods Oracles, and soberlie debating Matters of Faith, and such as concern Mans eternal welfare. (89)

Quoting from *The Anabaptist washt and washt*, he complains of
Carpenter's 'Lucian-like Dream, how one in his sleep thought he
saw the Presbyterian come dancing in a Mask, with his Pue-dish[38]
in his hands, and our ... Anabaptist as round as a hoop dancing to
him, grapling with him, pulling it from him, and furiouslie dashing
it against the ground' (86). As suggested above, this article is written
in the belief that Gataker was right: that several of Carpenter's religious tracts, and his one drama, *The pragmatical Jesuit new leaven'd*,
represent an attempt to recast religious controversy as satire,
specifically Menippean satire.

Carpenter does not announce himself as writing classical
Menippean satire; indeed, part of Gataker's outrage is at
Carpenter's indecorousness in promising one genre, religious controversy, and tending towards another. Of Carpenter's writings,
only *The pragmatical Jesuit* displays Menippean *prosimetrum*, the
characteristic mixture of prose and verse; and his outlandish narratives have less to do with trips to the moon than with the religious
grotesques he encounters all over Europe – admittedly, sometimes
portrayed as talking beasts. But he is authentically evasive when it
comes to resisting categorization: his pamphlet *The perfect-law of
God*, one of those which Gataker specifically mentions as similar to a
Menippean satire, has the subtitle *a Sermon, and no Sermon; –
Preach'd, – , and yet not Preach'd; – In a Church, but not in a – Church;
To a People, that are not a People –*.[39] From the point of view of diction,
Carpenter's works are a salmagundi;[40] numerous sub-genres contribute to those genres in which he ostensibly writes, autobiography, controversy and quasi-drama; and the accusations of
eccentricity that have surrounded him refer, most of all, to the fact
that he indulges in constant autobiographical digression. He is
plainly inspired by Menippeanism, and his frontispieces propel the
genre somewhere new.

While approving de Smet's warning that many critics 'dwell too
much on proving at all costs that a certain work by a certain author
is a Menippean satire, even if the author was not aware of this ....
too often generic criticism has been seen as an end in itself' (28), one
must, in the case of Carpenter, be aware that generic criticism is a
way of understanding not only the works, but the man. Here, the
most important point is the historical association of Menippean
satire with moralism. Menippus himself was a Cynic philosopher,
and the genre's startling changes of scene are heavy with ethical
implication; the tradition begun in Lucian's *Dialogues of the dead*, of

hurling the protagonists up to heaven or down to hell, is particularly pervasive in Renaissance examples. But in what might appear to be contrast, recent critics have drawn on the definitions of Menippean satire in Northrop Frye's *Anatomy of Criticism* and Mikhail Bakhtin's *Problems of Dostoevsky's Poetics*, adopting their modifications. Bakhtin, in particular, has argued that the genre is especially concerned with the relativity of truth: that with its origins in the classical dialogue, it presents human thought as essentially dialogic, shifting and subversive, in contrast to the dogmatic monologic text.[41]

Even so, several points of similarity can already be discerned between Menippean satire and any piece of learned religious controversy within the Christian tradition. Heaven and Hell are exactly what is at stake; quotations in a number of languages are a commonplace; and controversy juxtaposes discussion of seraphic matters with elaborate abuse of those who think differently.[42] Controversy is dogmatic; but in order to condemn alternative ideologies it is obliged to invoke them, and the dialogic effect of this presents the reader with the option of turning the other way. Northrop Frye has commented that the characters of Menippean satire are conceived primarily as spokesmen for ideologies;[43] and, conversely, dialogue has the effect of gesturing towards characterization even in a non-fictional work.[44]

Long before Carpenter's time, during it and for a period after it, other sixteenth- and seventeenth-century writers exploited the similarity between the two genres. In England, Menippean satire tended to be especially prominent at times of controversial mayhem and copious, feverish print publication; in the 1670s and 1680s there appeared a number of anti-Catholic and anti-Jesuit 'News-from-hell' pamphlets, and during the Civil Wars, Menippean tropes were commonplace in controversial pamphlets, popular and otherwise.[45] Whether one believes in autonomous, perennial imaginative motifs within popular culture or not, these cannot simply be explained as deriving straight from classical texts; similarly, Carpenter's use of the Menippean genre, however well-informed, cannot be isolated from popular matter.

Many of the tropes of popular Menippeanism are recognizable within Menippus's later imitators, Lucian, Varro and Seneca, and in some cases, at least, must have been derived directly from them.[46] Lucian, the most popular of them, was a common classroom text in the Renaissance, and More's and Erasmus's influential rediscovery of him was accompanied by an assertion of his moral worth. But there were two factors that made the picture less straightforward. As already indicated, the dialogic tradition exploited by Menippean satire can throw up a multiplicity of moral interpretations, while for the more literal-minded, the Menippean tradition was also associated with profane and atheistical scoffing – a link which was only reinforced by Lucian's own anti-Christian gibes. It allowed irony at the expense of the gods,[47] and the questioning of religious premises: Lucian's 'Zeus catechised', for instance, mounts a scornful debate on predestination and free will centuries before the Reformation.[48] Christopher Robinson asserts that, as the sixteenth century progressed, conservative opinion hardened against Lucian from both Catholic and Protestant sides; yet the view of him as humanist and constructive satirist persisted, side-by-side with accusations of irreligion.[49]

It was part of a larger early modern debate about the legitimacy of juxtaposing religious matter and humor. Francis Bacon criticized the propensity 'to turne religion into a Comedy or Satyr, to search and rip up wounds with a laughing countenance, to intermix Scripture and Scurrility sometime in one sentence ... a thing farre from the devout reverence of a Christian ... *Non est maior confusio quam serii & joci*: there is no greater confucion than the confounding of jest and earnest'.[50] In Donne's Lucianic *Ignatius his conclave* (1611) a letter is quoted, claiming to be from the person who delivered the letter to the printer; it says that Donne himself was unwilling to let the work be printed because he felt the matter deserved graver treatment, but that the letter-writer disagrees, citing Erasmus's 'bitter jestings and skirmishings' and the fact that the papists themselves have written a number of similar works (A3–5). Whether the letter is part of the fiction or not, its apologetic character is significant.

The uncertainty about Lucian's moral status is illustrated by the packaging of the two main seventeenth-century English translations of his works; with one published in the 1630s and one in the 1660s, they coincide chronologically with the beginning and end of Carpenter's public career. The introduction to the dialogues translated by Francis Hickes and published in 1634 is apologetic about the immorality and blasphemous habits of their author,[51] but points out that he was imitated by St John Chrysostom (B2ᵛ–4), and concludes that 'it is no such impious thing, as some of the rigid censures of these times would persuade us, to make a good use even of the worst Writers, yea and that if occasion serve, in matter of divinity' (B3^v).[52] In his translations of Lucian published in 1663,[53] Jasper Mayne continued to assert Lucian's status as moralist, teacher and persecutor of idolatry, and so gives evidence of the debate which prompted Gataker's classification of Carpenter as indecorous, in his use of the language and genres of satire to discuss sacred matters.

There are differences between conscious Menippean rhetoric, like Carpenter's, a less self-aware use of Menippean tropes, and behavior that meets someone's definition of intellectual folly, but to the hostile interrogator they blur, making it especially necessary for such a witness to commandeer the privileges of the author. To judge from another comment in his Introduction, Mayne had been offended by religious discourse of the recent past which, deliberately or not, was only too Menippean, and he uses Menippean terms to satirize it. As Mayne defines the moral arena, it is laudable to be Lucian himself, generally speaking, but deplorable to be one of his characters: a similar judgement to Carpenter's, when he captures the moral high ground by casting himself as protagonist in his own Menippean satires. The anticipation of hostile response in Mayne's introduction is probably prompted by and awareness of conflicting opinions about Lucian's moral efficaciousness, but it is deflected by Mayne's placing himself at the right hand of Lucian, and giving an instant character-sketch of a lunatic sectarian, a target on which, in the early 1660s, most people would have agreed:

> [H]ad [Lucian] seen a self-conceited Preacher goe up buskind into the Pulpit,[54] and there in a Tragicall stile, and voyce as Cothurnall, entertain his Hearers with a Romantick showre of words, which promised Demonstration, the great Mountain of Discourse, but brought forth an abortive, poor, topicall Mouse; If he should hear a Text of Scripture transformed into a Chaos, pursued without just order, & stuffed with Bombast, & confusion; sometimes flying aloft into a thin cloud of Non-sence, as if the Preacher aymed at some high preferment in the Moon; or else had stolne his Sermon from Lucian's true History ... he would doubtless send such Garagantua, tumid Orators to the Doctor who cured his Lexiphanes of the Fustian disease, who upon the taking of a purge[55] was deliver'd of a Tympany, and made to vomit all his tuffe, affected words, his Anodynes, Efforts and Exertions up againe. (A3^v)

Writing after the Restoration, Mayne is making a particular effort to reclaim Lucian for the restored hierarchy, and hence to dissociate him from the previous regime.[56] Because of the Lucianic tropes in popular satire of the 1640s and 1650s, it was a necessary dissociation, but still more necessary is Mayne's assumption of control within the miniature narrative of his introduction. His is a normative mission, and he demonstrates that one can invoke polyphony and babel, yet not be drowned by it.[57] Despite Carpenter's obvious peculiarities, I would argue that his quest is similarly normative: both he and Mayne use Menippean satire to diminish opponents to the status of satiric types, and to aggrandize editors, writers, narrators, protagonists and all who can be seen to have some degree of control over what goes into a text.

This may seem surprising, not least because of the emphases of recent criticism. Bakhtin's notion of the carnival is interwoven with his definition of Menippean satire as a generic free-for-all; and of recent years it has figured often in historians' and literary critics' studies of the Civil War, to describe and explain the period's extraordinary linguistic variety. It has also lent itself to reflexive romanticizing (which says more about the twentieth century than the mid-seventeenth).[58] To indulge in *decorum personae* for a moment, the assumption (sometimes stated, sometimes not) runs like this: just as anything goes within Menippean satire or a carnival, the English Revolution permitted a heady relativism, and the free spirits who cared to respond must have experienced it as liberating. At its most simplistic, this elides the fact that all sides were making truth-claims, and that truth-claims make frightening demands on belief and personal behavior.

In Lucian's dialogue 'Philosophies for sale', Pythagoras, Democritus, Diogenes and others are put up for auction;[59] and those transferring between ideologies in the Civil Wars would, like a protagonist in a Menippean satire, certainly have known the claims of several different varieties of belief. But the parameters of debate at this period were governed by the claims of Christianity, and hence usually by real questions of salvation and damnation; in these circumstances, the proliferation of alternatives could be agonizing to the irresolute. Petrus Cunaeus's *Sardi venales* (1612) anticipates this by showing theological debate taking place in 'Epicuri inter mundia' (the space between the worlds), an indeterminate geographical locus which allows experimentation: very similar, one might say, to the gap in religious continuity which the

Civil Wars had brought about. But the character of Menippus appears accompanied by the ghost of a young man who committed suicide after having been posed insoluble theological questions: a reminder that dialogic freedom could often bring on despair.[60] Carpenter survived, but this is why he asserts the moral superiority of the narrator so anxiously, and why he wrote and lived as he did.

III

Nearly everything that Carpenter wrote is characterized by two things: first, a dogged protestation of certainty in his current calling (conformist or Independent, since he seems not to have written during his Catholic phases) and second, a rehearsal of his conversion. This is relativized by a number of generic factors, but takes its initial bearings from the expectations set up by conversion-narratives at this date, and so it will be helpful to discuss these first.

Apostasy was surrounded by a number of literary and theatrical conventions. A number of rituals were associated with it, ranging from recantation sermons at Paul's Cross to book-burnings. These had a prolonged and vigorous life well past Carpenter's time, into the late seventeenth century. In *The converted fryar*, a pamphlet dialogue of 1673, an ex-mendicant makes public declaration of the error of his ways by burning his books and rosary in a public bonfire, and in 1689 the comedian Joseph Haines delivered a humorous recantation prologue dressed in a white sheet with a burning taper in his hand, asking forgiveness for his temporary conversion to popery.[61] Somewhat earlier, William Gouge's *A recovery from apostasy* (1639) had, quite literally, dramatized the conversion of Vincent Jukes from the Islamic faith. Taking as his text the last sentence of the parable of the Prodigal Son, 'He was lost, and is found', Gouge describes it as 'the Catastrophe or sweet close of a Parabolicall History, or Historicall Parable, which is full of trouble and confusion throughout the greatest part of it, but endeth with a joyfull issue' (7). He gives a numbered list of the characters in the drama, ranging from 'God himselfe' and the 'Penitent Apostate' to 'Lewd tempters' and 'Sympathizing Friends', then divides the narrative into five acts. This demonstrates how naturally conversions came to be cast in generic moulds: in this case, first the biblical parable, and second the tragi-comedy.

This kind of publicity had many implications for the apostate's sense of identity. To be an apostate, and to testify to one's apostasy continually, gave a pamphleteer a number of rhetorical advantages: he could invite an audience to exercise magnanimity as well as to approve controversial points, and he could display specialist knowledge. Throughout the late sixteenth and seventeenth centuries there were issued many recantations, autobiographical accounts of conversion and pamphlet exposures of Catholicism from within often, as with Carpenter, mingling fact with fiction.[62] Robin Clifton has noted that 'these ideological refugees were writing to acquire new friends and patrons and therefore reflected most carefully Protestant conceptions of popery':[63] a comment which suggests the constraints which apostates faced in their new career, and the effect which apostasy had on conceptions of selfhood. In the language of new historicism, the apostate was or rather, had been the site of competing denominational discourses; inevitably, and very publicly, this destabilized the selfhood of the victim. Anthony Tyrrell, a Catholic priest spying for the Elizabethan government in the 1580s, frequently complained of the conflict and horror which his actions generated within his conscience.[64] His case, like Carpenter's, spectacularly illustrates the phenomenon of the serial apostate, something rather different from the convert whose conversion proved to be permanent. Another such, William Alabaster, was attacked in a pamphlet with the title *A booke of the seven planets, or, seven wandering motives of W. Alablasters wit* (1598).[65]

This title illustrates how converts to Catholicism had their sanity impugned; and because Catholicism stood in polemical terms for the very antithesis of what Protestant England desired, being drawn towards it did sometimes accompany irrationality. Dionys Fitzherbert, a seventeenth-century woman who wrote an account of her own mental instability, was tempted during her crisis by a wish to convert to Catholicism and join the strictest religious order she could find.[66] Heresy and madness could be thought of as synonymous by Catholics too, and a poem surviving in the library of Trinity College, Dublin, reproaches an apostate to Protestantism in terms which make this unusually clear:[67]

> Y[r] madd conceit, the madder is
> y[o][w] know w[t] net[68] y[o][w] doe in this.
> If y[o][w] had seen as others see
> the glistering light w[ch] fails in thee
> you might y[r] darkness soon perceive

And thus y^r self wo'd not deceive… .
When then I cannot neare yow draw
send me for gods sake, by ye law,
of friendship, wch our fathers had
w^t is the cause that makes y[o]^w madd.
Is it ye witt thats allways blind
or is't the will to flesh combin'd
wch doth y^r mind soe much besott
the light of faith that y[o]^w see not… .

Still, the comments of Carpenter's contemporaries prove the difficulty of distinguishing madness from deliberate indecorum. Gataker asked of Carpenter's rhetoric: 'is not this down-right ranting, and raving with a witness? or is not the man, think we, not staring, but stark mad?' (86); and in weighing this accusation, the reader is being asked to bear Carpenter's ideological wanderings in mind. But, in fact, the passages which Gataker offers the reader as proof are, almost without exception, ones where Carpenter is engaging in abuse of his enemies: in other words, where Carpenter is imputing madness to others, and so fitting his language to the decorum of insanity. One such passage is Gataker's catalogue of Carpenter's anti-Presbyterian epithets:

As for the Presbyterians, he can find no language foul, or broad enough to belch up against them, or spew out upon them, whom therefore … he bedawbs and bespatters with these, and other the like satyrical and scurrilous Titles[:] Scotch Pharisees, Scotch Manichees; Scotch Barnacles; Scotch Balaks and Balaams with their speaking Asses; Brethren of the Scotch Mist; Jockey Preachers; Tincking-toned Presbyters; new-found Pulpit men, black Knights of the blew Bonnet, that would tuck up all powers under a Geneva girdle; Pulpit Petifoggers, Saint-mouthd things, in a brown, or blew covering, low sqare [sic] Knights of the round Hoop; with a Montebank boldness, and tumbling devotion shewing tricks in a round Hoop; Pulpit Meteors; Jewish Cabalists; Kirk Sea-monsters; Hungrie Dogflies; Northern Locusts; home-spun Jesuits; the Devils Janisaries. Thus he, who reqires [sic] forsooth … of those that deal with him, to forbear, and banish all undecent, foul, and filthie language; and yet would not have anie to be scandalized with these overgone, or overgrown expressions (so himself terms them) …. (85)

Similarly, one should be cautious about citing the portrait-frontispieces to Carpenter's works as manifestations of eccentricity. Undoubtedly conceived by him, if not necessarily drawn by his hand, they demonstrate something of the same festive anger as the catalogue above, but also the same consciousness of the satirist's defamatory duties.[69] It is perhaps fairest to remark that, if not eccentric, they are unusual. Controversial engravings were, of course, a commonplace in the seventeenth century, but they tended to be sold as separate entities; given the fact that engravings were an expensive addition to a book, and that it was highly unusual to commission original engravings for works of religious controversy, one can speculate that Carpenter financed the actual engraving himself.[70] Their unusualness stems from an interpenetration of two conventions. Portrait-frontispieces aim to depict an individual,[71] usually in a stately and commanding manner; controversial engravings are concerned with types and caricatures. But Carpenter places himself next to the religious monsters whom he condemns, not merely as a type of sanity, but as author and individual; and on one occasion, he represents himself in a posture as ignoble as theirs. As portrait representations, they are like no other.

The first of Carpenter's portraits occurs in front of Carpenter's first book, *Experience, historie and divinitie.*[72] In many respects a straightforward portrait frontispiece, it follows the common early-modern convention of representing previous events by means of an inset scene; in the top left-hand corner Carpenter is shown being blessed by the Pope, who gives the injunction *Mitto te in Angliam ad pascendos Catholicos, et Hæreticos reducendos* (I am sending you into England to foster the Catholics and lead heretics home). The main picture of Carpenter himself shows him being struck by a beam of light (as opposed to the clouds which lower over the Pope) saying *Quod innuebat, facio; non quod volebat* (I do what he signified; not what he wished) (Fig. 7.2).[73] *Experience, historie and divinitie* is a conversion narrative punctuated by meditational rhapsodies, the most straightforwardly autobiographical of Carpenter's works, and this image gives added legitimacy to Carpenter's claim to speak with authority about popish manners.

Soon, however, the displaced papists reassert themselves in the company of other religious grotesques. One edition (probably the first) of *The anabaptist washt and washt* (1653) (Fig. 7.3) has a frontispiece divided into five compartments[74] and displaying a lion-mouthed Jesuit and dragon-tongued Presbyterian at the top. In

Figure 7.2   Frontispiece, Richard Carpenter, *Experience, historie and divinitie* (1641).

Figure 7.3   Illustration from *The Anabaptist washt and washt*.

'The Author's Admonition to the Reader, concerning the Picture', Carpenter explains:

> I know not, that all Jesuits are lion-mouth'd in the Picture-Sense: Nor that all Presbyterians are tongu'd like the Dragon .... I rather beleeve, that the Lion mouth'd Jesuit is the Pragmaticall Jesuit, descended from the roaring Lion in St Peter; who gives devouring and murderous Counsill ... And that many Presbyterians have peaceable Natures, & are not infernall-Dragon-tongu'd; but are inconsiderately engaged by the simple and unballanced Apprehension of Morall Circumspection in such Persons ....

As W. Scott Blanchard has commented, Menippean satire has strong affinities with the grotesque; like the satyrs with whom etymologists then associated the Menippean genre, grotesques conflated man and beast.[75] Carpenter's image is one of process, alluding to the grotesque tradition but specifically concerned with its moral etiology: how man will begin to demonstrate bestial characteristics himself if he keeps company with animals. At the base is a fire-breathing Anabaptist with a grotesque hell-mouth behind, intended to be reminiscent of the two monstrous animals above, and reminding the viewer of the inevitable fate of men who cultivate the beast. In the center is Carpenter himself.[76] Demonstrating no animal features, and poised against a bookshelf, he seems iconically and spatially representative of learning, good sense and moderation; like conformist depictions of sound churchmen pitted against Papist and Puritan, he personifies the golden mean.[77]

But the bottom right-hand compartment, the last at which the eye arrives, shows Carpenter again; and here he is engaged in a vomiting competition with a devil. The Latin caption reads *Per Vomitum Scurra fæculuntus*[78] *obstrepens* [The filthy jester making a protest by means of vomit]. Improbably, this is a genre signal: Lucian's dialogue *Lexiphanes* has a scene where a bad poet is purged and vomits, and Jonson, the most Menippean of seventeenth-century dramatists, borrows the idea for the climax of *Poetaster*.[79] This frontispiece makes a similar equation of disorderly text and physical indigestion – and the difference, very obviously, is that Carpenter is the protagonist, demanding respect for a supremely undignified action. But the seeming contradiction can be resolved if one remembers two things, both also part of satiric strategies other than Carpenter's. Bodily activity unrestrained by convention was part of the Cynic ideal of honesty: famously, Diogenes is said to have masturbated in market places.[80] Moreover, as with all confutations, the ideal of Carpenter's piece is to pay the adversaries back in their own coin, while the author reserves to himself the power to decide moral norms. The devil's vomit is black, Carpenter's white: the implication is that black vomit figures internal corruption, while Carpenter's is both moralistic and personally purgative. One could call this picture an extreme instance of *indecorum personae*.

Bodily emissions are a constant in Carpenter's satire, and an analogue to this frontispiece occurs in the prologue of Carpenter's quasi-drama, *The pragmatical Jesuit new leaven'd* (c.1660). A physician, Galen Junior, appears with a urinal and uses it to diagnose the ills from which his patient suffers; these prove to be those expected of a satirist, and finally, Galen explains that the urine is Carpenter's:

> It is high-colour'd, shews the blood's inflam'd,
> Yet pretty clear. Th'Evil may well be nam'd
> Without offence. Somthing I find of waight
> Sink to the Deep; which Mist-like, rises straight,
> And clears again. I cannot rightly call
> This a Distemper, when I judge of all.
> Gentlemen, help a little, look with me,
> Whose Water judge you this I cast to be?
> You know not. No? Nor shall I tell in hast,
> Lest then perhaps the man himself be cast,
> More than his Water. This I freely say,
> The Poets Water 'tis that made the Play.
> And yet no Water-Poet's.[81] The Play then,
> Is high, and clear, and deep, and clear again
> Just as the Poets Water. Who indeed. [sic]
> Had he not been a Patient forc'd to bleed,
> Had never Poetiz'd. By this I know
> He's render'd Poet from this Comick Shew.

(A3)

The satiric text, then, is equated with its author's bodily waste: low, but not bad in itself, and expressing a natural intolerance of accidentally ingested moral and religious evil. The nubecula observed by Galen, being cloudy, figures the opacities of sin and does indeed 'Sink to the Deep'; but then it rises and disperses. The play is an exposure, the exposure of evil Catholics, and therefore both a depiction of sin and an exercise in clarification: as Galen says, 'I cannot rightly call / This a Distempe ...' In Carpenter's satire as in early modern medicine, the subject's emissions are symptomatic of imbalance or evil, and can be used diagnostically.

This is something rather different from outwardly directed scatological abuse, which Carpenter condemns elsewhere: of some seminary scholars who believed that John Foxe 'was of so weake a braine, that hee thought his head was an Urinall' he comments, 'Is not this a pretty way to transforme people into a belief, that all the doctrine and history, which came out of that head, was no better than Urinall proofe?'[82] It is not that Carpenter never uses this himself as a satirical motif: within *The Pragmatical Jesuit*, Galen takes an emetic and Ignoro the lawyer a purge in order to be freed of all traces of religious devotion, and, pursuing the equation of language with vomit, Galen complains: 'Still my Stomack is upon a blabbing account, it utters all ...'(9).[83] One is meant to take this in conjunction with the prologue – but to observe the difference between artificially induced purgations undertaken for immoral reasons, and the emissions of a satirist, which are a reliable diagnosis of evil. Referring back to Carpenter's frontispiece, it becomes even clearer that the satirist himself vomits as an act of protest (not to expel devotion, but ultimately to promote it). The jester, an icon of indignity, was a common enough persona for satirists to adopt or to be given: Nicholas Perrot d'Ablancourt's French edition of Lucian, published in 1654, is prefaced by a portrait showing Lucian as jester in cap and bells with a mask.[84] Carpenter, though, is not merely a jester but a filthy jester: in the Cynic spirit he treats satire as performance art, and, like the Cynic, risks implicating himself in his own satire where the reader is not prepared to accept authorial claims to moral centrality.

Exorcism is a sacred emetic. A frontispiece to Carpenter's sermon *The Jesuit and the monk* (1656) shows Carpenter faced by a man in profile with a monstrous creature issuing from his mouth. (Fig. 7.4) The caption is in Latin verse, and can be translated as 'R. Carpenter declares silence to a kind of sacred piglet of the Gerasians, hasty in everything – of course – and cursed by the waves.[85] He is just as talkative as he is menacing and lying. "Be silent."'[86] Introducing his text, Carpenter uses the picture to proclaim the satirist's traditional mission:

R. Carpenterus Sac. Porcello cuidam Gerasenorum,
    Scilicet in omnia præcipiti, fluctibusq̃ deuoto,
Eidem porrò loquaci pariter et minaci mendaciq̃s,
    Silentium indicit atq̃s obmutesce.

Figure 7.4   Frontispiece, Richard Carpenter, *The Jesuit and the monk* (1656).

Now therefore, as the Monks and Jesuits are, in our Saviour's dialect, thistles and thorns, I shall be as Thorns in their sides; and endeavour by all means possible and imaginable, to fetch the Gerasen Hog, and the dirty Devil out of their mouths, that Wallows in all the mire, and impurities of Fraud, Fallacy, Falshood &c. ... And when they call me to it by their new Uncivilities, I will plainly shew you, as ye view in the Picture of the Jesuit or Monk here, the very Hog-Devil in their Teeth, and at the end of their Tongues; and lay down the reasons before your Eyes, why I charge the Monks so highly, and why they are so monstrous in my Glass. (A2^v)

The Gerasen hog is Carpenter's most elaborate grotesque, referring to and combining elements from the *Anabaptist* frontispiece: a pig with draconian horns and the forked tongue of a snake, breathing fire and functioning itself as tongue to the Jesuit/monk. Within the main body of the text, Carpenter accuses his targets of being serpents swelled into dragons: 'these denote their crooked and uneven motions, turnings, and winding ...' (24). This creature's protrusion from a mouth alludes to the usual pictorial conventions of exorcism, but also reflects how the mouth, particularly the tongue, is the source of language and therefore the locus of falsity.[87]

The serpentine twists of a tongue represent Carpenter's omnipresent satirical suspicion of linear mobility. In an anecdote in *The Jesuit and the monk*, a sermon preached to commemorate the Gunpowder Plot, he even uses Greek characters as hieroglyphs for straight and crooked personalities.[88] The abbot Pachonius was put in charge of over a thousand abbots, and as a means to help himself remember them all, he divided them into twenty-four classes according to the letters in the Greek alphabet:

> that in what Letter soever they were placed, their Natures and Manners should be deciphered and represented by the shape of the Letter. Those whom Nature had endowed with a direct and simple Disposition ... he put into the *Classis* of Iota ... it being but one right little line struck downwards. But his involv'd, cunning, and obscure-hearted Monks, if less cunning, he called ζ, if more ξ, because these are Serpentine, Dragonish, and winding Letters.

Carpenter goes on: 'I never saw ... an Iota Jesuit or Monk in all my life, but of ζ and ξ Jesuits and Monks I have seen whole swarms, being people of dark and crooked Hearts, and of tongues having all irregular motions, and moving through every dark place in the labyrinth of a Lye' (24). The story is doubly significant, with the pun on ι and 'I' representing Carpenter as a plain dealer, and his subjects as possessing a serpentine versatility; and in *The Pragmatical Jesuit*, Carpenter's *alter ego* Aristotle Junior introduces himself, 'I am a Graduate in the University, intending by a right Line forward' (2). The interplay between the physical appearance of words and their signification permeated Renaissance imaginative writing, and had a particular charge within the formal maledictions of satire.[89] There is a direct equation here between the windings of a snake, the motions of a tongue and the circuitous paths of the ungodly. In tracing the character, the pen's retractions figure retractation: not simply movement, but change and deceit.

Donne's satirical epic *Metempsychosis*, which he wrote at a time of religious uncertainty, and of which the Menippean inspiration has long been recognized, shows that Carpenter was not alone.[90] Though neither *Metempsychosis* nor Carpenter's works can be read as straightforwardly autobiographical, both are converts writing conversion-narratives, and exploiting the freedoms of Menippean satire to say the unsayable. Charting the progress of the soul of Eve's apple through its many subsequent homes, *Metempsychosis* uses the Pythagorean notion of the transmigration of souls to explore the moral implications of linearity, and the physical charting of progress and regression: a topic that is constant throughout Carpenter's writing. In *The Jesuit and the monk*, quoted earlier, Carpenter links his usual condemnation of evasiveness to Donne's topic and the topic of any moralist, the fall of man:

The Cain's Mark of a Jesuit or Monk ... is a Face figuring it self into all the Shapes of a nimble Fancy, and a Body that croutches, cringes, and winds any way, every way, all waies, especially, when a Plot's upon the anvile, or, when there is *Odor lucri*, any sent of gain; or, of a good Dinner. This Way, as it was not the Way of the Saints of God, but of the Serpent, and of Cain: so was it not the Way of the Prince of Saints, Christ Jesus. And first, because when he came into the World, as delegated by his Father to direct the World into the good Way, his Forerunner cried out, John 3.3. *Prepare ye the way of the Lord*, make his paths streight. The Latin inserts, *Rectas facite semitas ejus*: make his paths right. (7)

Carpenter is evoking, in words, a satirical representation that corresponds to the grimacing religious maniacs on his frontispieces; the physical distortions of their face or form convey a moral warning that their paths are crooked. His satirical mission could hardly be expressed more clearly.

IV

During the Civil Wars a number of interiorized epics were written, charting the progress of the soul onward and upward – for example, Henry More's *Psychozoia* (1642) and Edward Benlowes's *Theophila* (1652).[91] Donne's *Metempsychosis* is a satirical epic, chronicling a downward quest which, in unmistakable Menippean style, shatters ideals of heroic integrity by the bodily fragmentation of its protagonist. Carpenter combines the two traditions, and yet arrives at something distinctive. His self-presentation has elements of the Cynic protagonist, especially in his assumption that violations of decorum are an assurance of good faith; the audience is asked to side with him in his discontented search for truth, and see him as a type of the soul in a divided Christendom.

But this chapter has described how there is a paradox in this very search: search implies continuous alteration in state, and the Jesuits and other villains whom Carpenter condemns are villainous precisely for their hypocrisy, or capacity to mutate. This highlights a division integral to the Menippean genre, arguably its built-in flaw: psychological complexity is something which is allowed to the voyaging protagonist, and denied to the types he encounters. In Carpenter, this manifests itself in a distinction between development, which is admirable, and change, which is to be deplored; yet the distinction is an uneasy one, as unstable as its subject matter. Carpenter conceptualizes development as the growing ability to identify falsity; yet falsity itself is identified through its propensity to change. In *The perfect-law of God* Carpenter exemplifies his perennial connection between perpetual movement and untruth, or lying and heterogeneity, when he exclaims:

Go then, O ye Priestbyterian Ministers .... Go then, with your lyes of Defence, lyes of Offence, whole lyes, half lyes, quarter lyes, lyes with heads, but not with feet; lyes with feet, but not with heads; lyes with neither head nor foot; lyes that are all belly;

short lyes, long lyes, and lyes of a middle size; lyes whisper'd, and loud lyes; lyes of any bredth, of any length, of any bignes; a lye that playes or sings the tenor, a mean lye, and a base lye; lyes of all sorts, of all colours, of all fashions; (a lye will ye buy?) lyes that still, and ever lye, and yet, never lye still'. (226)

Change often equates with spiritual danger. To turn away from ungodliness was part of the Christian experience of grace, and did not necessarily mean a change in doctrinal allegiance;[92] but where conversion had the effect of making the convert switch denominations, it was, inevitably, declared a sign of grace among those whom the convert had joined, and a perilous fall by those whose cause had been deserted. A convert could not avoid being the site of interpretive clashes, and Carpenter's uniqueness was to imagine his conversion – indeed, his multiple conversions – into a genre which, since its genesis in the Socratic dialogue, had been better equipped than any other to reflect on the dialogic nature of human thought. Yet this provoked the last, most powerful and most painful clash: the terrible disjunction between the variability of religious truth according to individual doctrinal standpoint, and the eternal penalties of misaligning oneself.

Donne ends his *Metempsychosis*: 'There's nothing simply good, nor ill alone, / Of every quality comparison, / The only measure is, and judge, opinion' (ll. 518–20). Whether one reads this as flippant, or sceptical, or Erastian, or as a sober description of the condition of faith,[93] it is a pragmatic conclusion. Working in the same genre, Carpenter uses it to expound the very opposite trait: a constantly frustrated, consistently hopeful idealism. Where Donne delicately implies that his topic might have relevance to himself, Carpenter's writings are linked almost obsessively to autobiographical justification. Both show the suitability of Menippean satire as a means to describe ideological voyaging within a writer, and both demonstrate how the genre was thoroughly implicated in the conventions of seventeenth-century religious controversy. The point of this chapter has been to postulate, in the case of Richard Carpenter, a trinitarian procession between Menippean satire, religious exploration and the self-depiction of a serial convert. Within both Carpenter's life and his works, it has identified a shaping anxiety which gave rise both to a vividly imagic conception of good and evil plots, and a readiness to change, accompanied by a hatred of evasiveness.

This anxiety problematizes Bahktin's definition of the Menippea, the most perceptive and wide-ranging ever attempted, and perhaps the most influential. Like all the best generic criticism, it makes sense of texts which the critic probably never knew; as quoted in the preceding pages, his observations often illuminate the specificities of Carpenter's case. Yet Bakhtin's elaborate hostility to dogmatism, precisely that quality which made him an original thinker, is also a handicap here; it means that his version of the menippea develops gaps and contradictions when read against such Menippeans as Carpenter. Bakhtin speaks of the biblical and early Christian contexts in which the genre has been used, but fails to recognize how these heighten the genre's potential for purveying Christian dogma; he rightly identifies its huge importance in the Renaissance, yet does not extend his gaze to the Reformation.

Even while identifying the central importance to the genre of a search for truth, Bakhtin ignores the greedy effect that truth-claims have where the author is less than perfectly objective, where the claim is one with which the reader has been conditioned to sympathize, or where, as often, both these factors are present; other voices may be heard, but only one is allowed to dominate. This oversight may arise from his overt preference for 'debates which [do] not permit thought to stop and congeal in one-sided seriousness or in a stupid fetish for definition or singleness of meaning'.[94] While making his famous identification of the Menippea with the carnivalesque, he proclaims, most intolerantly of all, that carnivalistic 'joy at change and its joyful relativity is opposed to that one-sided and gloomy official seriousness which is dogmatic and hostile to evolution and change, which seeks to absolutize a given condition of existence or a given social order' (p. 160). Bakhtin-inspired criticism of the literature of the English Revolution has fastened on the period's polyphonic liberty, and often risks, or achieves, sentimentality; a proliferation of sects guarantees that more voices will be heard, but not that the individuals behind those voices accorded greater toleration to other voices with which they did not agree. But comments like Bakhtin's own go some way to explain where critics find the bias.

The privileged position of narrators, authors and other selectors within Menippean satire has already been stressed; and if an author chooses to be dogmatic, the genre can be made dogmatic too. There may be many voices, and the reader may potentially be able to identify with any or none; but the privileged one, like a soloist, will be louder than the rest, and to disagree with it involves the positive effort of reading against the text. Alternatively, as with Carpenter, the author is able to dictate both the allegiances of the protagonist and the religious proclivities of the surrounding satiric types; since satirical treatment implies dissociation, this inevitably creates an imbalance in the reader's sympathies. In the religious provisionalism of his life, Carpenter might seem to be a classic Bakhtinian hero: searching for truth, and never quite finding it. But, combined with his capacity for easy disillusionment, he also manifests a fierce *provisional* dogmatism – the two are necessarily connected, since present disillusion implies past belief. Taking his life and writings as a whole, Carpenter is less an apologist for any one version of Protestantism than a seeker after certainty (or dogmatism) in the abstract. Because he could not find it in mid-seventeenth-century Europe, his writings are angry. He used Menippeanism because it could combine a strong biographical thrust with an unparalleled ability to depict babel: yet to depict a social state is not to endorse it, and Carpenter believed that the times were out of joint.

Bakhtin's phrase 'joyful relativity' was coined to endorse, not simply to describe; but both description and praise need modification. The same Menippean muscles are needed for a smile or for a mad dog's snarl; and Carpenter's case shows how the genre can lend itself to *sorrowful* relativity, as well as joyful. Through Galen in *The pragmatical Jesuit*, he hints that personal unhappiness has forced him into writing, 'Had he not been a Patient forc'd to bleed ...', and this unhappiness was undoubtedly religiously inspired. It seems appropriate, therefore, to end with Carpenter's own summary of the state of religion during the English Revolution, which, like so many of his satirical descriptions, could just as well be applied to himself as to his targets: 'the Nation is like a Forrest on the Coasts of Barbary; where every Beast proudly forrageth for himself according to the latitude of his strength, and combates with every living thing he comes near .... So that forsooth, this may truly be called ... *Religio Deserti*, the Religion of the ... Wilderness, or the wild Boar's and Bear's Religion'.[95]

ACKNOWLEDGEMENTS

I would like to thank David Crandshaw, Cynthia Frame (Union Theological Seminary), Arnold Hunt, Jeremy Maule, Michael

Questier, Ingrid de Smet and Nigel Smith. I am also grateful to the English Department of University College London, where I wrote much of this, for helping to pay for the photographs, and to the library of Trinity College, Dublin for allowing me to quote from one of their manuscripts.

NOTES

1. For reasons of space it has not been possible to include a detailed study of this play in what follows, but I am writing an article on it.
2. For Wood's biographical notes on Carpenter, see *Athenae Oxonienses,* 2 vols (1691–2), 2: 438–40.
3. Raymond A. Anselment, *'Betwixt jest and earnest': Marprelate, Milton, Marvell, Swift and the Decorum of Religious Ridicule* (Toronto: University of Toronto Press, 1979) discusses the relationship – first asserted in England by Martin Marprelate – between the rhetoric of religious controversy and Horace's principle of *decorum personae,* where action and speech have to agree with character.
4. Nigel Smith, *Literature and Revolution in England, 1640–1660* (New Haven: Yale University Press, 1994), 4; K. Riikonen, *Menippean Satire as a Literary Genre, with Special Reference to Seneca's 'Apocolocyntosis'* (Helsinki: Societas Scientiarum Fennica [Commentationes Humanarum Litterarum 83], 1987), 12, 51.
5. See Benne Faber, 'The Poetics of Subversion and Conservatism: Popular Satire, c.1640–c.1649' (Oxford D.Phil. thesis, 1992). In *Menippean Satire: an Annotated Catalogue of Texts and Criticism* (New York: Garland, 1980), Eugene Kirk comments that 'Dialogues peopled by caricatures of Puritans, Catholics, and Anglicans, who dropped here and there into bits of verse as they wrangled with each other, became the everyday fare of the bookstall and handbill-hawker' (xxix). His bibliography is referred to as 'Kirk' hereafter.
6. Bakhtin's most extensive discussion of Menippean satire appears in *Problems of Dostoevsky's Poetics,* ed. and trans. Caryl Emerson (Minneapolis: University of Minnesota Press, 1984), ch. 4. A recent critique of Bahktin appears in Joel C. Relihan, *Ancient Menippean Satire* (Baltimore: Johns Hopkins University Press, 1993). See also Philip Holland, 'Robert Burton's *Anatomy of Melancholy* and Menippean Satire, Humanist and English', PhD diss., University of London, 1979, 36–7.
7. Eugene Kirk, 'Introduction'.
8. *Menippean Satire and the Republic of Letters, 1581–1655,* Travaux du Grand Siècle, II (Droz: Geneva, 1996), 70. Another recent discussion is W. Scott Blanchard, *Scholars' Bedlam: Menippean Satire in the Renaissance* (Lewisburg: Bucknell University Press, 1995).
9. Raymond Astbury, ed., *M. Terentii Varronis saturarum Menippearum fragmenta* (Leipzig: Teubner, 1985), 78–80.

10. De Smet, 70 (and see the reference to Thomas Coryate below).

11. Quoted in Christopher Robinson, *Lucian and his Influence in Europe* (London: Duckworth, 1979), 177.

12. Though given the links of Menippean satire with Cynic philosophy, his behavior could perhaps have been justified as adhering to Cynic ideals of honesty: Diogenes Laertius reported of Diogenes that, on being asked what he had done to be called a hound (the derivation of the term Cynic), he replied 'I fawn on those who give me anything, I yelp at those who refuse, and I set my teeth in rascals' (quoted from the 2–volume Loeb Classical Library translation by R. D. Hicks [London: Heinemann, 1965], 1: 63 [VI, 60]). See also John Leon Lievsay, 'Some Renaissance Views of Diogenes the Cynic', in James A. McManaway et al., eds., *Joseph Quincy Adams: Memorial Essays* (Washington, DC: Folger Shakespeare Library, 1948), 447–55.

13. For general biographical details about Carpenter, see DNB; Wood (see n. 3) says that Carpenter studied in Flanders, Artois, France, Spain and Italy; The Revd W. Cole, 'Cambridgeshire Collections, vol. XV', BL, Add. MS 5816, ff. 97ᵛ–100; Godfrey Anstruther, *The Seminary Priests*, 4 vols. (Great Wakering: Mayhew-McCrimmon, 1975), 2: 45–6; Charles Dodd (*vere* Hugh Tootell), *The Church History of England*, 3 vols, 1737–42, 3: 309–10. Other early sources (such as those cited by the DNB) tend to copy Wood. A piece of juvenilia survives in Cardiff Central Library (MS 2.1089), a prosopopoeia in which Satan laments his lot. See also *The English College at Valladolid. Registers 1589–1862*, Catholic Record Society 30 (London: CRS 1930), 146.

14. Carpenter also preached at St Bartholomew the Great on 19 August 1638: see the parish's 'Preachers' book', Guildhall Library, MS 4005/1, f. 6ᵛ. I am grateful to Arnold Hunt for this reference.

15. Cole, however, says that after returning to England in 1637 he was beneficed near Brandford, Middlesex (f. 98).

16. Given that Laud had first tried to present Carpenter to a living in Lancashire, a county notorious for Catholicism, he may have been deliberately trying to use Carpenter as a tool to win over Catholics.

17. Though he claimed that the parish was full of papists, the protestation returns for 1641 were signed by all male inhabitants over the age of 18: see R. Garraway Rice, ed., *West Sussex Protestation Returns, 1641–1642* (Lewes: West Sussex Record Society, 1906), 139–40.

18. *A discourse apologetical (1654)*, 65.

19. BL Stowe 743 (f. 163), endorsed 2 December 1640; eighteenth-century summary in BL Add. MS 4107, f. 69ᵛ.

20. No evidence from Carpenter occurs in Laud's trial; by the time this eventually took place, his continued vacillations would have made him an even less impressive witness than before.

21. Lambeth Palace MS 943 (papers of Archbishop Laud), 729–32, n.d. [1640–5].

22. *Proceedings, Principally in the County of Kent … Especially with the Committee of Religion*, ed. from the collections of Sir Edward Dering by Lambert B. Larking (London: Camden Society, 1862), 85. Though only the surname is given, Carpenter may also have been the individ-

ual interviewed on 8 December 1640 with a story that he was reproved by Windebank after complaining to Fr Price, a Benedictine, about some injury received; however, Carpenter says nothing of this in his letter to Dering. See also Anthony Milton, *Catholic and Reformed: The Roman and Protestant Churches in English Protestant Thought 1600–1640* (Cambridge: Cambridge University Press, 1995), 70. William Prynne, *Canterburies Doome* (1646), 184, 255ff., records other instances of Baker's forbidding or purging anti-Catholic material.

23. If Baker did indeed edit and rewrite Carpenter's recantation sermon, it is odd that he should then have forbidden it to be published; but if Carpenter did subsequently preach anti-Catholic sermons, Baker's position becomes more understandable as a fear that all Carpenter's productions would be read in a more pronouncedly anti-Catholic light. There may, too, have been unpredictable reactions to the sermon as Carpenter delivered it. However discreet an apostate from Catholicism was in his references to Rome, his significance was more locatable in his physical presence and the genre of the recantation sermon, than in the nuance of what he actually said; and a printed sermon was more accessible for consultation and potential agreement than one that was only delivered orally. The combination of these two factors could have resulted in an unexpectedly great utility to those who wished to denigrate Rome more than the Laudians did. However, parts of Carpenter's earlier anti-Catholic sermons may survive in *Experience, historie and divinitie* (first issued 1641), which combines elements of autobiography, sermon and meditation; by 1641 it would have been more possible to publish the material that Baker had vetoed earlier.

24. *The pragmatical Jesuit new-leaven'd* [1660], 65.

25. In *Winter Fruit: English Drama, 1642–1660* (Lexington: University of Kentucky Press, 1995), 56–7, Dale Randall suggests – interestingly but unprovably – that Carpenter may be the carpenter who holds Laud's nose to the grindstone in the quasi-drama *Canterburie his change of diot* (1641).

26. Dodd, *Church History of England*.

27. Cole, 'Cambridgeshire Collections', claims that while Carpenter was in Paris he wanted to reconvert to Catholicism, but was cast into prison for his anti-Catholic writings.

28. However, there may be a gap in Dodd's account. In 1647 a Richard Carpenter resigned the living of Woodnesborough, Kent, to the Committee for Plundered Ministers, and another was curate of St James's Duke Place in 1648, having been chosen by some parishioners. In that year the Corporation of the City of London ordered him to desist from preaching, there being 'some fowle things now informed against him'. See A. G. Matthews, *Walker Revised* (Oxford: Oxford University Press, 1988), 43–4 (the order is dated 28 November 1648); Corporation of London Record Office, Guildhall Repertories, vol. 59, ff. 317ᵛ–318. See also BL Add. MS 15,671 (Proceedings of the Committee for Plundered Ministers), f. 78. Though Richard Carpenter is not an uncommon name in the seventeenth century, the

juxtaposition of dates is suggestive, and the tone of the condemnation familiar from accounts which definitely relate to him.

29.   These were often reported in dialogue-form. See Ann Hughes, 'The
       Pulpit Guarded: Confrontations between Orthodox and Radicals in
       Revolutionary England', in Anne Laurence et al., eds., *John Bunyan
       and his England, 1628–1688* (London: Hambledon, 1990), 31–50.

30.   The reference (clearly sarcastic) is to Thomas Coryat (1577?–1617),
       author of the travel-book *Coryats Crudities* (1611), who had a contem-
       porary reputation as a buffoon (DNB). Kirk classes him as a
       Menippean satirist on the grounds that he affected prosimetrum,
       ironic eulogy and fantastic travelogue (nos. 514–17).

31.   The pamphlet is reprinted, with the scatological rhetoric deleted, in
       William McMurray, ed., *The Records of Two City Parishes: A Collection of
       Documents Illustrative of the History of SS. Anne and Agnes, Aldersgate,
       and St. John Zachary, London* (London: Hunter & Longhurst, 1925),
       95–8. He transcribes (282) a passage referring to the event from the
       Commons' Journals dated 26 July 1641 (the date on the pamphlet is
       probably the publication date, and not the date of the event). In
       December 1642 the churchwardens and inhabitants of the parish,
       'haveing bin longe destitute of a painefull and godlie Minister
       amongst them almost the space of these Twentie five yeares last past'
       petitioned Parliament to appoint a Sunday afternoon lecturer
       (McMurray, 99 & 282). I am grateful to Arnold Hunt for all these
       references.

32.   Reissued in 1642, 1644 and 1647 (on the last two occasions with the
       title *The down-fal of Anti-Christ*). The Wing descriptions incorrectly
       imply that these were separate editions. The response to the episode
       at St Anne's Aldersgate dates the text to the second half of 1641.

33.   Cf. *Experience, historie, and divinitie*, 327–8 (quotation p. 328), where
       Carpenter makes the distinction between the Spouse of Christ speak-
       ing all languages when she prays, and the Church of Rome, whose
       'tongue speakes strange languages, she knowes not what ...'.

34.   *The Anabaptist washt and washt* (1653), B2ᵛ.

35.   Marilyn Lewis, 'John Gibbs, a Newport Pagnell puritan, 1627–1699',
       typescript, Newport Pagnell, 1995 (copy held at Dr Williams's
       Library), 37. Lewis maintains (42–4) that he was not, in fact, an
       Anabaptist; like Bunyan, he appears to have argued that the elect
       were saved by a baptism of the Holy Spirit.

36.   This is found on the undated [*c.* 1653] edition of *The anabaptist washt
       and washt*: for the other frontispiece on the dated (and probably
       earlier) edition, see below. The inspiration is probably the engraved
       frontispiece to Daniel Featley's *The Dippers dipt* (1646), described in
       A. F. Johnson, *A Catalogue of Engraved and Etched English Title-pages
       Down to ... 1691* (Oxford: Bibliographical Society, 1934), Marshall 97.
       William Marshall also engraved the frontispiece to *Experience, historie
       and divinitie*.

37.   Gataker is responding to a postscript in Lilly's *Almanack* for 1654.

38.   This appears to be a coinage of Carpenter's. The OED cites only one
       other instance, again from the *Discourse apologeticall* where Gataker is

quoting Carpenter: 'Also his pleading for the setled and immoveable Font for the baptizing of Infants, which the Presbyterians, he saith, have brought to a moveable and unsettled Pue-dish' (67).

39. Carpenter wrote this sermon during his period as an Independent, and on one level, this title probably refers to the constitutional peculiarities of the Independents.

40. *Experience, historie and divinitie*, the first of Carpenter's published writings, is also the most stylistically conventional.

41. Independently of Bakhtin, Northrop Frye also revived the term within literary criticism with the suggested alternative 'anatomy': see *Anatomy of Criticism* (1957; Harmondsworth: Penguin, 1990), 308–14.

42. Blanchard, *Scholar's Bedlam*, 47, claims that from the mid-fifteenth century 'scholarly invective began to display many characteristics that are found in Menippean satire'. The genre also lent itself to religio-political tracts, e.g. *Satire Menippée* (1594), which Charles M. Coffin has argued was one of the sources for Donne's Lucianic *Ignatius his Conclave* (*John Donne and the New Philosophy* [New York: Columbia University Press, 1937], 197–8); see also his introduction to the facsimile edition of *Ignatius his Conclave* (New York: Columbia University Press, 1941). The introduction to T. S. Healy's edition of *Ignatius his Conclave* (Oxford: Clarendon, 1969), xvi–xvii, discusses Donne in the context of Justus Lipsius's *Satyra Menippaea* (1605).

43. Frye, 309.

44. A number of controversial dialogues are included in Kirk, for example, Oliver Ormerod, *Picture of a papist* (1606) (Kirk , 511).

45. See Smith, 305, 315–16; Faber, 'Poetics of subversion', *passim*; Benjamin Boyce, 'News from Hell: Satiric Communications with the Nether World in English Writing of the 17th and 18th Centuries', *PMLA* 58: 1 (1943): 402–37, though badly dated, has a useful bibliography of Lucianic heaven- and hell-pamphlets in England.

46. Faber, 'Poetics of Subversion', 84, discusses learned allusion in popular pamphlets. For recent discussions of the Menippean tradition in the Renaissance, see the introduction to Seneca's *Apocolocyntosis* (ed. P.T. Eden [Cambridge: Cambridge University Press, 1984], 19–22); Robinson, 95–163; Douglas Duncan, *Ben Jonson and the Lucianic Tradition* (Cambridge: Cambridge University Press, 1979), *passim*. All references to Lucian are taken from the Loeb Classical Library edition, trans. and ed. A.M. Harman et al. (London: Heinemann, 1959–67). Menippus's own writings are lost, and it is still debatable how many of Lucian's dialogues are 'Menippean' (see de Smet, 24–5), but I believe early modern writers would normally have regarded Lucian's works as a whole when it came to Menippean imitation.

47. See J. Wight Duff, *Roman Satire* (Cambridge: Cambridge University Press, 1937), 104–5.

48. Lucian, 2: 60–87.

49. Robinson, 95–8, 168–97. See also R. Bracht Bramham, 'Utopian Laughter: Lucian and Thomas More', *Moreana* 86 (1985): 23–43.

50. *A wise and moderate discourse, concerning church-affaires* (first printed 1641), 7.

51. See also A6, concerning Lucian's supposed atheism: 'They might as
     well affirme that Clemens of Alexandria, Arnobius, Justin Martyr,
     St Austin, and as many Fathers of the Church, as armed their Pens
     against the Superstitions of those Times ... were Atheists too.'
     Arguing that the debate about the propriety of religious laughter was
     particularly to the fore during the 1660s and 1670s, Anselment dis-
     cusses Isaac Barrow's sermon on Ephesians 5: 3–4 (printed in *Several
     sermons against evil-speaking*, 1678): 'But fornication, and all unclean-
     ness, or covetousness, let it not be once named amongst you, as
     becometh saints; neither filthiness, nor foolish talking, nor jesting,
     which are not convenient ...' Barrow reasserts what had become a
     traditional opposition, between innocent and harmful jesting. John
     Fell's sermon, *The character of the last daies* (1675), also contributes to
     the debate, warning that 'The brightest evidence and vertue disguis'd
     and render'd monstrous by burlesque, like the Primitive Christians
     in the skins of wild beasts, will easily be worried and destroied. Nay
     so it fares, that the most venerable persons, things, and actions, are
     most liable to be thus expos'd and made ridiculous ...' (20).
52. The introductory material is by Francis Hickes's son Thomas.
53. They were, however, translated about 25 years earlier (see
     Dedication, A2) when Mayne's comments seem to imply that they
     were forbidden the press at the time. This edition also reprints the
     Hickes translations, and Mayne's introduction borrows considerably
     from Hickes's. The verse on the frontispiece reads: 'Such was sharpe
     Lucian, who reform'd ye Times, / Whose Gods, & Temples were their
     Sacred Crimes. / Who gave ye blinde Worlde Eyes, & new Heavens
     taught. / By which he Idols from their Altars laught ...'
54. Smith comments on the 'fusing of theatrical vocabulary with that of
     other institutions and sites of authority' including the pulpit, at this
     date (74–5). See also Lois Potter, 'The Plays and Playwrights,
     1642–1660', in Philip Edwards et al., eds., *The Revels History of English
     Drama*, vol. 4 (London: Methuen, 1981), which discusses how theatri-
     cal forms pervaded a number of genres at a time when theatres were
     ostensibly closed; and the discussion of *A true relation of a combustion*
     above.
55. See below, n. 80.
56. Again on Lucian's detractors, Mayne declares: 'I do not wonder that
     such Opinionators should be sick of this Disease: who having suc-
     ceeded a canting Generation of men, whose Rhetorick was as rude, &
     mechanick as their persons, do defile the English tongue with their
     Republick words, which are most immusicall to the Eare, and scarce
     significant to a Monarchicall understanding' (A4).
57. More broadly, pamphlets in the Civil Wars are well known for their
     generic inclusiveness. 'When the purpose of the pamphlet was to
     persuade or convince, every significant cultural resource which could
     signify in a pamphlet was used' (Smith, 96).
58. As the conclusion to this essay will contend, it is not a problem which
     Bakhtin himself sufficiently anticipates.
59. Lucian, 2: 450–511.

60. For the relationship between religious controversy and suicidal despair, cf. John Stachniewski, *The Persecutory Imagination* (Oxford: Clarendon, 1991), though his study concentrates on the despair engendered by belief in predestination.

61. Given that Haines was playing Bayes in a revival of Buckingham's *The Rehearsal* (1671), an added satirical reflection on Dryden's conversion seems intended. The prologue, written by Thomas Brown, was published separately as *Mr. Haynes his recantation-prologue* (1689), and a second one was offered in 1690; Brown also wrote three Lucianic *Letters from the dead* purporting to come from Haines (discussed by Boyce, 420–2). See Philip J. Highfill, Jr. et al., *A Biographical Dictionary of Actors, Actresses, Musicians, Dancers, Managers and Other Stage Personnel*, 14 vols. (Carbondale: Southern Illinois University Press, 1982), 7: 7–8, 12–14. This account quotes (12) the anecdote in Anthony Aston, 'Supplement to Cibber's Apology', in Robert W. Lowe, ed., *An Apology for the Life of Mr. Colley Cibber*, 2 vols. (London: John C. Nimmo, 1889), 2: 314–15: Haines, admonished by Judge Pollexfen for presenting the puppet-show *The whore of Babylon, the devil and the Pope* in July 1685, replied that 'he did it in respect to his Holiness; for, whereas many ignorant People believed the Pope to be a Beast, he shew'd him to be a fine, comely old Gentleman, as he was; not with Seven Heads, and Ten Horns, as the Scotch Parsons describe him'.

62. The only full-length study of conversions to and from Catholicism in the early modern period is Michael C. Questier, *Conversion, Politics and Religion in England, 1580–1625* (Cambridge: Cambridge University Press, 1996); see also his article 'English clerical converts to Protestantism, 1580–1596', *Recusant History* 20 (1991): 455–77. Among the conversion-narratives which Carpenter might have known, before his first conversion to the Church of England and directly after, are *A declaration of the recantation of John Nichols* (1581), and *John Nichols pilgrimage* (1581); *The recantation made at Pauls Crosse, by William Tedder, seminarie priest . . . whereunto is adioyned: The recantation or abiuration of Anthonie Tyrrell* (1588); Richard Sheldon, *The motives of Richard Sheldon priest for his. . . renouncing of communion with the Church of Rome* (1612); Fernando de Texeda, *Texeda retextus* (1623); John Gee, *The foot out of the snare* (1624), and *New shreds of the old snare* (1624); James Wadsworth, *The English Spanish pilgrime* (1629); Henry Yaxlee, *Morbus et antidotus* (1630); Thomas Abernethie, *Abjuration of poperie* (1638), and *A worthy speech by Mr. Thomas Abernethie, wherein is discovered the hellish plots . . . wrought in the Pope's court* (1641); *The Capuchin, or the recantation of Father Basil Clouet, Francois* (1641); *The convertion of Francis de Neville* (1644). Examples of the related controversial genre witnessing to the results of popery are Lewis Owen, *The Running register* (1626); and *Speculum Jesuiticum* (1629).

63. 'The popular fear of Catholics during the English Revolution,' *Past and Present* 52 (1971): 23–55 (quotation p. 37).

64. See 'Reading and Misreading the Body Politic: the Conscience of Anthony Tyrrell, Spy and Apostate', ch. 3, in Lowell Gallagher, *Medusa's Gaze: Casuistry and Conscience in the Renaissance* (Palo Alto,

CA: Stanford University Press, 1991). John Morris, *The Troubles of our Catholic Forefathers*, 3 vols. (London: Burns & Oates, 1872–7), vol. 2 (1875), reprints Persons's narrative under the title, 'The Fall of Anthony Tyrrell'.

65. This is responding to 'Seven motives' which Alabaster issued, giving reasons for his conversion; though these do not survive, their content can be gleaned from this pamphlet and STC 10799. Alabaster reconverted to Protestantism subsequently.

66. See Katharine Hodgkin, 'Dionys Fitzherbert and the Anatomy of Madness', in Kate Chedgzoy, Melanie Hansen and Suzanne Trill, eds., *Voicing Women: Gender and Sexuality in Early Modern Writing* (Keele: Keele University Press, 1996), 69–92 (esp. n. 15).

67. TCD MS 1373, 22–36. This is the English translation (by 'Dr. M') of a Latin poem attributed to Bonaventure O'Hussey, and said to be addressed to Miler Macgrath, Archbishop of Cashel. See T. K. Abbott and E. J. Gwynn, *Catalogue of the Irish Manuscripts in the Library of Trinity College, Dublin* (Dublin: Dublin University Press, 1921), 224.

68. Probably 'you know not what … '.

69. Listed in Johnson (Marshall, 85).

70. One of Carpenter's last books, *The last, and highest appeal* (1656) was printed for the author.

71. Though one must distinguish between woodcut portraits, which aimed only to depict a type and were designed to be used several times, and the more individuated nature of engraved portraits.

72. Dated 1641, it probably accompanied the first issue of the book (though no example of this has been seen with a frontispiece).

73. Alternative translations of *innuebat* are 'meant' and 'intimated'; Carpenter's comment probably refers to the conventions of equivocation, whereby one could interpret and act upon an opponent's remark with reference to other meanings than those intended. Converts were often represented in a heavenly shaft of light: cf. frontispiece from John Gennings, *The life and death of Mr Edmund Geninges* (1614), reproduced on the jacket of Questier, *Conversion*.

74. Cf. Ephraim Pagitt, *Heresiography* (first edn 1645: 1646 edn the first seen with an engraved title-page).

75. Blanchard, *Scholars' Bedlam*, 32; cf. de Smet's discussion of satyrs (60).

76. The other edition, discussed above (Wing C618), has a frontispiece depicting the activities of the Anabaptists themselves (Fig. 7.1).

77. For example, 'Sound-Head', 'Rattle-Head', 'Round-Head' (BL 669, f. 6, Tract 94) reproduced on the jacket of Milton's *Catholic and Reformed.*

78. There may be a pun on *facundus* (eloquent).

79. Act V: i. See Robinson, 105–6; Duncan, 130.

80. Diogenes Laertius, trans. Hicks, 2: 46.

81. The nickname of John Taylor (1580–1653).

82. *Experience, historie and divinitie*, 201–2 (2nd sequence); the anecdote recurs in *The Pragmatical Jesuit*, 33.

83. At the end of the play, Lucifer vomits a baby Jesuit, and defecates, producing a baby monk.

84. Cited in Duncan, 12.

85. The reference is to Mark 5: 2–16, where Jesus casts a horde of devils out of a man, who then enter a herd of swine and cause them to drown.

86. This appeared first in *The Jesuit and the monk* (1656), then in *Astrology proved harmless* (1657) , then in *The pragmatical Jesuit* (c.1660). Cole has a description of Carpenter's frontispieces.

87. There is an account of an exorcism in *Experience, historie and divinitie*, 177–9 (2nd sequence).

88. This probably borrows from Lucian's dialogue 'The consonants at law' (1: 396–409).

89. Faber, 28, 34.

90. John Klause, 'The Montaigneity of Donne's *Metempsychosis*', in Barbara Kiefer Lewalski, ed., *Renaissance Genres,* Harvard Studies in English, 14, (Cambridge, MA: Harvard University Press 1986), 418–43. For Donne's conversion, see M. Thomas Hester, *'Kinde pitty and brave scorn': John Donne's Satyres* (Durham, NC: Duke University Press, 1982), chs. 3–4, Appendix A; for the 'lingering Catholic sympathies' demonstrated in *Metempsychosis*, see John Carey, *John Donne: Life, Mind and Art,* 2nd edn, (London: Faber & Faber, 1990), 134. The word 'progress' had begun to have two distinct moral implications around this date: the journey, with no especial moral implication, and the quest for something better (OED).

91. Smith, *Literature*, discusses the former (218–21). See also Harold Jenkins, *Edward Benlowes* (London: Athlone, 1952), ch. 17.

92. This is one of the central arguments in Questier's *Conversion*.

93. In his sermons Donne calls opinion the 'middle station, betweene ignorance, and knowledge'. See *The Sermons of John Donne*, ed. Evelyn M. Simpson & George R. Potter, 10 vols (Berkeley: University of California Press, 1953–62), 6: 317.

94. *Problems of Dostoevsky's Poetics*, 132. Cf. the critique of Bakhtin in Peter Stallybrass and Allan White (eds.), *The Politics and Poetics of Transgression* (Ithaca and London: Cornell University Press, 1986).

95. *The pragmatical Jesuit new-leaven'd*, 14.

8

Milton's Paradise of Fools: Ecclesiastical Satire in *Paradise Lost*

John N. King

Anti-Catholic satire dominates the futuristic account of the Paradise of Fools in Book Three of John Milton's *Paradise Lost* (1667).[1] Located within the sphere of the fixed stars, it is the next stop on Satan's itinerary after he leaves Hell and passes through Hell Gate (3.430–97). Although many critics have expressed profound regret for the episode ever since the time of Joseph Addison, John Dryden and Alexander Pope pay homage to Milton's burlesque in their own mock-heroic satires: *Mac Flecknoe* and *The Rape of the Lock*.[2] Milton adds a polemical twist to the lighter comedy of the flight to the moon undertaken by Astolfo to collect Orlando's lost wits under the tutelage of St John the Evangelist at Ariosto's Limbo of Vanity (*Orlando furioso*, 34. 70–91). Confined to a passing reference to the Donation of Constantine in the Ariostan original, religious satire is such a slight presence that it receives no comment in the annotations on *Orlando Furioso in English Heroical Verse* (1591) by Sir John Harington. Milton frames the Paradise of Fools very differently.

In contrast to Harington, Milton's translation of Ariosto's verses in *Of Reformation Touching Church Discipline in England, and the Causes that Hitherto Have Hindered It* (1641) sets the Limbo of Vanities in the context of an attack on Archbishop Laud's policies as the most recent manifestation of Antichrist's takeover of the Church, which began during the reign of Emperor Constantine I:

> Then past he to a flowery mountain green,
> Which once smelled sweet, now stinks as odiously,

198

This was that gift (if you the truth will have)
That Constantine to good Silvestro [Pope Sylvester] gave.

(st. 79)

Milton's anti-prelatical tract styles Ariosto as an anti-clerical compeer of Dante, Petrarch and Chaucer. The archaism of the satire on Purgatory, medieval monastic abuses and justification by good works in the Paradise of Fools episode helps to style that attack against Roman religious practices partly as a screen to conceal mockery of the Caroline and Restoration Church of England.[3]

Even though Satan experiences absolute solitude at a location where 'other creature in this place / Living or lifeless to be found was none', the narrator's proleptic (i.e., anticipative) account fills the void with 'all things transitory and vain' (3.442–6). Roman Catholic belief in Limbo as the residence of souls temporarily or permanently denied entry into Heaven (e.g., the patriarchs under the Old Law, unbaptized infants, suicides and virtuous pagans) constitutes an immediate object of satirical attack. The attack ramifies into an affirmation of justification by faith alone versus justification by good works, the alleged Catholic belief that human beings take an active part in the reception of divine grace. Indeed, that 'superstition' takes on a demonic aspect because trust in 'works', which find their source in Sin, the parthenogenetic offspring of Satan, verges upon Pelagianism:

> … when Sin
> With vanity had filled the *works* of men:
> Both all things vain, and all who in vain things
> Built their fond hopes of glory or lasting fame,
> Or happiness in this or the other life;
> All who have their reward on earth, the fruits
> Of painful superstition and blind zeal,
> Nought seeking but the praise of men, here find
> Fit retribution, empty as their deeds… .

(3.446–54; emphasis mine)[4]

Of course, the Lutheran principles of faith alone and grace alone (*sola fide* and *sola gratia*) represent a readjustment of fundamental Christian belief, shared by Catholics and Protestants alike, in both good works and faith.[5]

The narrator's use of 'vanity', a highly suggestive term identified with religious error in the Protestant tradition,[6] parodies Catholic salvation theology, on the one hand, by defining 'the works of men' and 'fruits/Of painful superstition and blind zeal' as weightless errors that would fly 'Up hither like aerial vapours' (3.445–52). In *De Doctrina Christiana*, on the other hand, Milton advances the standard Protestant view that good works play an essential role as *posterior* signs of a living faith: 'So we are justified by faith without the works of the law, but not without the works of faith; for a true and living faith cannot exist without works, though these may be different from the works of the written law' (*CPW* 6: 490).

At issue is the Reformation controversy concerning the doctrine of justification, which hinged on Luther's insistence upon the priority of faith over works. We can locate an antecedent of the Miltonic position in Cranmer's sermon 'Of Good Works' in the first *Book of Homilies* (1547), which concludes with a satirical catalogue of alleged Roman Catholic abuses akin to the one in the Paradise of Fools episode. In employing the 'imagery of weight and lightness to stress the distinction between true merit and vanity',[7] Milton modifies a medieval iconographical figure for the Last Judgment in which an attendant demon cannot tip the Scales of Justice in favor of souls of the damned. The demon's upward movement resembles the trajectory of Satan's flight to Limbo, a false paradise whose close proximity to Heaven belies its ontological status as a different kind of Hell, where all is 'Abortive, monstrous, or unkindly mixed' (3.456).[8] The iconography of the Weighing of Souls becomes explicit when the Father employs 'his golden scales' (4.997) to weigh Satan:

> The fiend looked up and knew
> His mounted scale aloft: nor more; but fled
> Murmuring, and with him fled the shades of night.

> (4.1013–15)

The catalogue of members of religious orders and 'false' religious practices in the Paradise of Fools episode constitutes the most extensive and topically explicit satirical outburst in the whole of *Paradise Lost*:

> … eremites and friars
> White, black and gray, with all their trumpery.

Here pilgrims roam, that strayed so far to seek
In Golgotha him dead, who lives in heaven;
And they who to be sure of Paradise
Dying put on the weeds of Dominic,
Or in Franciscan think to pass disguised;
They pass the planets seven, and pass the fixed,
And that crystalline sphere whose balance weighs
The trepidation talked, and that first moved;
And now Saint Peter at heaven's wicket seems
To wait them with his keys, and now at foot
Of heaven's ascent they lift their feet, when lo
A violent cross wind from either coast
Blows them transverse ten thousand leagues awry
Into the devious air; then might ye see
Cowls, hoods and habits with their wearers tossed
And fluttered into rags, then relics, beads,
Indulgences, dispenses, pardons, bulls,
The sport of winds: all these upwhirled aloft
Fly o'er the backside of the world far off
Into a limbo large and broad, since called
The Paradise of Fools, to few unknown
Long after, now unpeopled and untrod.

(3.474–97)

In targeting pilgrims and the four orders of mendicant friars – the Carmelites, Dominicans, Franciscans and Augustinians – the narrator echoes a tradition of anti-fraternal satire that stretches back into the Middle Ages. Milton thus returns to territory traversed by *Of Reformation* and *An Apology against Smectymnuus*, which cite objects of anti-clerical satire in Chaucer's *Friar's Tale*, the pseudo-Chaucerian *Plowman's Tale*, and Spenser's *Shepheardes Calender* as prototypes for prelatical 'abuses'.[9] Absent from England for more than one hundred years, friars lived on in polemical cartoons in Foxe's *Book of Martyrs* and contemporary broadsheets. As such, the friars supplied a screen for attacking the triumph of Laudianism in the newly restored episcopalian Church of England. Even though it is easy to identify 'false' clerics in *Paradise Lost*, we should remember that Milton's view of the priesthood of all believers attaches 'little significance to the distinction between clergy and laity'.[10]

The narrator's contempt for Catholic 'trumpery' invokes the rhetoric of Reformation polemics against Catholic devotional modes, rites and images. Milton's usage is the third recorded instance of a contemptuous Protestant expression for superstitious religious practices that had emerged by 1540 (*OED* 'trumpery' 2.c). It accords with E.K.'s polemical gloss on Spenser's May Eclogue, which defines the 'trusse of tryfles' carried by the Fox 'as a poore pedler' (ll. 237–40) by reference to 'the reliques and ragges of popish superstition, which put no smal religion in Belles: and Babes .s. Idoles: and glasses .s. Paxes, and such lyke trumperies'. *Loci classici* for Protestant attacks against Roman 'trumpery' may be located in the catalogue of Catholic 'abuses' in third part of the sermon 'Of Good Works' in the *Book of Homilies* and the preface to Thomas Becon's *Works* (1560–4; 1: C6ᵛ–7).

Although satires had mocked Puritan linguistic habits throughout the previous century (e.g., Samuel Butler's *Hudibras*), Milton unembarrassedly breaks epic decorum by attacking 'trumpery', a familiar cant term from anti-Catholic propaganda. Objecting specifically to the scurrilousness of that word, Richard Bentley proposes that the Paradise of Fools is a spurious addition in his 1732 edition *Paradise Lost*: 'all this long description of the outside of the world, the Limbo of Vanity, was not Milton's own, but an insertion by his editor .... in its several parts it abounds in impertinencies ... 'tis a silly interruption of the story in the very middle' (n. on 3.444–98). Like Bentley's other efforts to 'purify' *Paradise Lost* of textual 'errors', his emendation exemplifies newly fashionable neo-classical decorum. Concerning the particular term, he states: 'Tis a doubt, whether the word "trumpery" here in epic style is not as great a fault in a poet, as the thing itself in the friars' (n. on 3.475). Nonetheless, Bentley's objection affords a counterintuitive proof that Milton exploits a demotic lexical register to undercut Satan's false claim to heroic status. Thomas Newton's rejoinder defends the authenticity of both 'trumpery' and the episode as a whole: 'Bentley is for rejecting this verse and fifty more which follow as an insertion of the editor; but I think there can be no doubt of their genuineness.' Bishop Newton continues: 'Our author here, as elsewhere, shows his dislike and abhorrence of the Church of Rome, by placing the religious orders with all their *trumpery*, cowls, hoods, relics, beads, etc., in the Paradise of Fools, and not only placing them there, but making them the principal figures' (emphasis mine).[11]

Milton's use of 'trumpery', a contemptuous term for the superstitious religious practices as worthless rubbish, invokes the vernacular rhetoric of revolutionary broadsides that celebrated the downfall of Archbishop Laud, whose introduction of liturgical changes evoked the specter of Catholic 'peril' in the minds of militant Protestants. For example, the polemical woodcut of a 'Pack of Popish trinkets' in *A Discovery of the Jesuits' Trumpery, Newly Packed Out of England* (1641) features bell, book and candle in addition to other Roman Catholic devotional objects: rosary, Mass chalice, asperges and cross (Fig. 8.1). The peddlar's pack is conventional in ecclesiastical satires such as Spenser's May Eclogue, just as the attack on the friars for attempting to equivocate their way into heaven ('For we have Friars have been at Heaven and tried it') anticipates language used to describe the Paradise of Fools. Another inflammatory broadsheet, *Time Carrying the Pope from England to Rome* (1641), celebrates the downfall of Laudianism with a lurid burlesque of the Pope as another 'peddlar's pack'. The engraving by Wenceslaus Hollar allegorizes *Veritas Filia Temporis* ('Truth, the Daughter of Time'), a classical emblem adopted by both Protestants and Catholics during different phases of the English Reformation (Fig. 8.2). The winged figure of Father Time carries the Pope – 'This load of vanity, this peddler's pack / This trunk of trash & Romish *trumperies*' (emphasis mine) – on a return trip to Rome. Engraved verses define Truth as the daughter not of Time, but rather 'Time's great maker (the most high Eternal)'.[12] As in Milton's Paradise of Fools, Roman Catholic *vanity* is a key concern.

Yet again, Richard Bentley's rejection of the joking allusion to St Peter and his keys 'at heaven's wicket' as a 'low and doggerel' usage (n. on 3.484) constitutes an unwitting proof of the authenticity of the wording. Although the phrasing derives from Matthew 7: 13–14 – 'Enter in at the strait [i.e., narrow] gate: for it is the wide gate, and broad way that leadeth to destruction … and the way narrow that leadeth unto life, and few there be that find it' – the language constitutes yet another indecorous intrusion from Protestant tractarian discourse. Nonconformists used the 'wicket' or 'gate' as a figure for the progress of the elect soul through the vanity of the world and towards heavenly salvation. The best-known example, the Wicket Gate through which Christian passes *en route* to the Celestial City in *Pilgrim's Progress* (1678), is roughly contemporary to *Paradise Lost*, but the usage recurs in works ranging from a

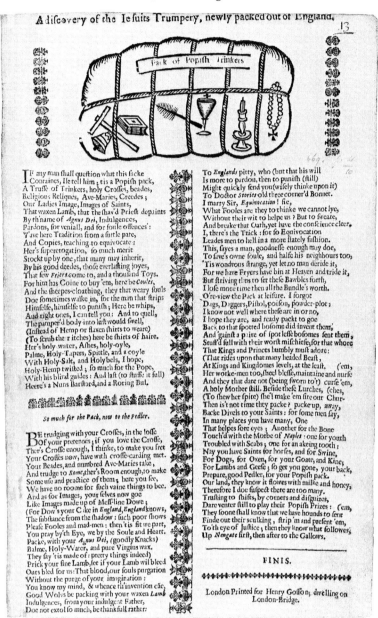

Figure 8.1   *A Discovery of the Jesuits' Trumpery, Newly Packed Out of England* (1641).

This Burden backe to *Rome*, I'le beare againe;
From thence it came, there let it ftill remaine.

When Times Great Maker (the most high Eternall) He to his daughter Truth gaue ftreight command   This trunke of trafh 'tRomifh Trumperies
In mercy loked from his Throne iupernall :   That fhee thofe dang'rous Errors fhould withftand Deluding fhower infernall forgeries
And faw the Euils which began to grow   Then vp I tooke vpon my aged backe   And therefore am I hence inpoft this riding
In his deare Vine here Militant below ,   This load of vanits, this Pedlers packe   To Rome againe, for here is no abiding

Figure 8.2   Wenceslaus Hollar, *Time Carrying the Pope from England to Rome* (c.1641).

sixteenth-century attack on transubstantiation and the Mass to pietistic writings of Restoration nonconformists.[13]

   The anticlerical topos of 'false feeding', found in *Lycidas*, Milton's anti-prelatical pamphlets and throughout *Paradise Lost*, governs the metaphorical flatulence ('A violent cross wind') that blows the mendicant friars with their 'Cowls, hoods and habits' over 'the backside of the world' and into the Paradise of Fools. In employing a scatological conceit to represent the corrupt offensiveness of an ontological disease that begins to infect the universe following the Fall of the rebel angels, the passage exemplifies the late seventeenth-century shift away from the belief that breaking wind constitutes a socially acceptable and healthy biological function.[14]

In treating the friars as objects of scatological satire, Milton employs abusive language of anti-fraternal attack typified by Chaucer's *Summoner's Tale* and Wycliffite tradition, which associates the friars with the arse of the Devil or Antichrist.[15] In John Bale's *Acts of English Votaries*, furthermore, friars are the 'tail which covereth his [i.e., Antichrist's] most filthy part' (D8ᵛ). Militant Protestants habitually directed scatological invective against the doctrine of transubstantiation and the Roman-rite Mass. Like his co-religionists, Milton is unconcerned with the violence of such abusiveness.

In an addition to the windiness of classical Limbo, a broad parody of the Epistle for Whitsunday (Pentecost) in the *Book of Common Prayer* (or the Roman-rite liturgy that underlies it) furthers Milton's scatological satire against the friars as 'false' apostles in an inversion of the birth of the Church at the descent of the Holy Spirit upon the apostles: 'And suddenly there came a sound from heaven, as it had been the coming of a mighty wind, and it filled all the house where they sat .... And they were all filled with the Holy Ghost, and began to speak with other tongues, even as the Spirit gave them utterance' (Acts 2: 2–4).[16] The Paradise of Fools mocks the birth of the 'false' Church. A learned pun upon prophetic 'inspiration' (from Lat. *inspirare*, 'to blow upon, inspire') confers a mordant twist upon this dramatization of the old expression, 'to break wind'. By contrast, 'false' inspiration parodies the creation of Adam by the 'breath of life', the life-giving spirit of the Father (7.525–6; from Gen. 2: 7). Allusion to apostolic speaking 'with other tongues' affords a witty contrast to the linguistic confusion of the 'builders next of Babel' (3.466), who precede the friars in the narrator's catalogue of future inhabitants of the Paradise of Fools.[17]

Symbolic flatulence affords a symbolic counterpoint to the absence of flatulence in prelapsarian Eden, where the 'pure digestion' of Adam soundlessly generates

… temperate vapours bland, which the only sound
Of leaves and fuming rills, Aurora's fan,
Lightly dispersed ….

$$(5.4–7)^{18}$$

According to Archangel Raphael, flatulence is analogous to the ontological disturbance soon to be effected by the disobedience of
Adam and Eve:

> But knowledge is as food, and needs no less
> Her temperance over appetite, to know
> In measure what the mind may well contain,
> Oppresses else with surfeit, and soon turns
> Wisdom to folly, as nourishment to wind.

$$(7.126–30)$$

The reader later learns that after the Fall, 'envious winds/Blown
vagabond or frustrate' (11.15–16), which emanate from the Paradise
of Fools, fail to deter the heavenward course of Adam and Eve's
prayers. Michael's concluding prophecy concerning ecclesiastical
history reverses the model of Limbo in its précis of the scriptural
account of the Apostolic Church that endured for a brief moment
following Pentecost and before its subversion by succeeding 'teach-
ers, grievous wolves', who necessarily include the proleptic friars of
the Paradise of Fools:

> … for the Spirit
> Poured first on his apostles, whom he sends
> To evangelize the nations, then on all
> Baptized, shall them with wondrous gifts endue
> To speak all tongues, and do all miracles,
> As did their Lord before them.

$$(12.497–502)$$

As in St Peter's attack against false shepherds, whose 'hungry
sheep look up, and are not fed, / But swoll'n with wind' (*Lycidas*,
ll. 125–6),[19] the satirical point is quite serious. The epic narrator

attacks the doctrine of transubstantiation, Roman-rite Mass and clerical aggrandizement in general for substituting coarsely material feeding and digestion for pastoral 'feeding' of the Christian flock with scriptural truth. An interconnection between the trope of false feeding and the diminishment of Satan's 'heroic' stature is apparent in the simile of 'a vulture on Imaus bred', which gorges on the 'flesh of lambs or yearling kids / On hills where flocks are fed' (3.431–5), in accordance with his status as progenitor of orgiastic feeders and prototype of the Pope as a 'false' St Peter and of other 'false' shepherds who fail to feed their congregations.

'False wit', Joseph Addison would say,[20] but Dryden, regardless of his disagreement with Miltonic politics and religion, imitates the burlesque satire of the wind-whipped friars, who undergo a precipitous drop following a fraudulent 'flight', when his 'yet declaiming bard' descends through the trapdoor of the Barbican stage at the conclusion of *Mac Flecknoe* (1682):

> Sinking he left his drugget robe behind,
> Born upwards by a subterranean wind.
> The mantle fell to the young prophet's part,
> With double portion of his father's art.

> (ll. 214–17)

Alliterative plosives contribute to the imaginary 'fart' that concludes the implied triplet that ends that poem by transferring the burden of Miltonic satire against the friars, and the English bishops who perpetuate their ways, to mock-heroic burlesque of bad poets as 'false prophets' who emulate the proleptic disguise worn by Satan.[21]

Reformation polemical discourse remains in play when Satan, like a prototypical friar, assumes the 'habit' of a 'stripling cherub' (3.636, 643) in preparation for his encounter with Uriel upon departure from the Paradise of Fools. Satan's disguise supplies a proleptic link to the vestments of its future residents: 'Cowls, hoods and habits'. That wry reference to clerical attire recalls polemical attacks on the Pope or English bishops as manifestations of demonic hypocrisy (from ὑπόκρισις, 'stage acting'). The trope of clerical disguising is a prominent device in Milton's anti-prelatical pamphlets, for example, *Of Reformation*, which yokes 'the unmasking of hypocrites' with attack upon 'the Pope and papists', and *Eikonoklastes*, which undermines *Eikon Basilike* for incorporating 'the common grounds of tyranny and popery, dressed up, the better to deceive, in a new Protestant guise, and trimly garnished over'.[22]

Of course, Roman Catholics lacked a monopoly on 'hypocrisy' in the minds of Milton and other nonconformists, whose 'stress on inwardness meant that for them, as for Puritans, hypocrisy and formalism were above all the vices to guard against'.[23] The first commentary on *Paradise Lost*, published in 1695,[24] parts company with Milton's republican politics in glossing 'zeal' with reference to 'those zealous hypocrites our author's contemporaries, an age so impiously godly, and so zealously wicked, that prayer was the prologue to the murder of a monarch' (n. on 2.486), but the annotation on Satan's status as a personification of Hypocrisy – 'a counterfeiting virtue, religion and piety, the better to gain an opinion of sanctity' (n. on 3.683) – accords with the epic narrator's view that Satan 'was the first / That practiced falsehood under saintly show' (4.121–2). Hypocritical costuming marks the degradation of Satan throughout *Paradise Lost*, as he conceals his nature, at the level of simile or outright metamorphosis, in the form of a toad, cormorant and serpent. Nevertheless, Satan's 'likeness of an angel bright' fails to conceal his family resemblance from Sin and Death, in a reversal of his outright deception of Archangel Uriel: Disguised he came, but those his children dear / Their parent soon discerned, though in disguise' (10.330–2). Satanic disguise affords a further contrast to the prelapsarian nakedness of Adam and Eve, who lack 'these troublesome disguises which we wear' (4.740).

Although Satan's assumption of the 'habit' of a 'stripling cherub' alludes primarily to the Devil's pose as an 'angel of light' (2 Cor. 11: 14), demonic disguising invokes a long satirical tradition in which personifications of Hypocrisy actually don clerical attire. Jesus' frequent applications of ὑπόκριτης ('a stage actor') in its figurative sense of 'hypocrite' to the Jewish priests, Pharisees, and Sadducees provide the scriptural source (e.g., Matt. 23: 27–8). Satanic soliloquies therefore bear a generic resemblance to ironic self-confessions by personifications of hypocrisy in religious attire, notably False Semblaunt in Jean de Meun's *Roman de la Rose*, and the narrator of *The Pardoner's Tale* whom Chaucer models on False Semblaunt. John Bale's imprinted satire of that kind with an anti-Catholic stamp in polemical interludes like *The Three Laws*, in which Hypocrisy wears the costume of a Franciscan friar and Sodomy appears as a monk. A host of analogues infiltrate interludes, poems and woodcuts produced by sixteenth- and seventeenth-century century Protestant satirists.[25]

We may locate highly compelling instances of Satan in the guise of a Roman Catholic cleric both in John Bale's *John Baptist's Preaching* (c. 1547) and in *Paradise Regained*, where Satan appears as

> ... an aged man in rural weeds,
> Following, as seemed, the quest of some stray ewe,
> Or withered sticks to gather.

> (1.314–16, 467)

Gunpowder Plot associations invade kindred seventeenth-century texts, moreover, when the reader recalls Satan's worldly disguise as a Franciscan friar in *In Quintum Novembris* (ll. 74–89) or Equivocus, the arch-Jesuit, in Fletcher's *Apollyonists* (2.8–9).[26]

Despite Uriel's status as the 'sharpest sighted spirit of all in heaven', his inability to see through Satanic disguise penetrable only by divine providence leads the narrator to comment on an epistemological problem fundamental the Reformation world view:

> So spake the false dissembler unperceived;
> For neither man nor angel can discern
> *Hypocrisy*, the only evil that walks
> Invisible, except to God alone,
> By his permissive will, through heaven and earth:
> And oft though wisdom wake, suspicion sleeps
> At wisdom's gate, and to simplicity
> Resigns her charge, while goodness thinks no ill
> Where no ill seems ....

> (3.681–9, 691; emphasis mine)

The Miltonic narrator's scorn for the latter-day 'trumpery' of the hermits and friars echoes William Tyndale's attack against the 'hypocrisy of outward works'.[27] Even an archangel must wrestle with the task of discriminating between 'true' and 'false' images, an important paradigm in Protestant literary tradition.[28] Stephen Fallon defines this moment in terms of 'the Uriel defense': the 'un-avoidability and moral neutrality of intellectual / perceptual error'.[29] The Protestant eradication of external, worldly authorities turned the search for 'truth' into an inward process capable of resolution only by individual believers.

The projection of this conflict onto the struggle of Adam and Eve to fulfill the divine commandment of obedience indicates how near Milton stands to John Bale, whose *Image of Both Churches* (1545) outlines the central problem of discriminating between the 'true' and 'false' churches, despite the gulf between Bale's blunt vernacular style and Milton's elegantly Latinate diction. Milton's *Of True Religion* similarly draws an absolute distinction between 'true worship and service of God, learnt and believed from the Word of God only' and 'false religion or … the Romish Church, Mother of Error, School of Heresy' (*CPW* 8: 419–21). Militant Protestants attacked Catholic devotion at the popular level and the Laudian 'beauty of holiness' for blurring the distinction between image and archetype, by contrast to the Pauline distinction between New Testament antitypes and later historical types that reflect them. Milton's defense of proliferating heretical sects in *Of True Religion* indicates how the passage of time had complicated Bale's neat binary oppositions between 'truth' and 'falsity', which leave no room for dissension among adherents of 'true' religion.

The epistemological problem of discriminating 'truth' from 'falsehood' is central to Satan's initiation of temptation by invading the dream world of sleeping Eve, whose 'fancy' (i.e., the image-making faculty of the fantasy) is most vulnerable when the reason is at rest. Satan accordingly assumes toad-like disguise in order to seek revenge against the Father:

> Squat like a toad, close at the ear of Eve;
> Assaying by his devilish art to reach
> The organs of her fancy, and with them forge
> Illusions as he list, phantasms and dreams ....
>
> (4.800–3)

The demonic projection of 'discontented thoughts, / Vain hopes, vain aims, inordinate desires / Blown up with high conceits' into Eve's mind supplies a mock-heroic link to the windiness and vanity of the Paradise of Fools (4.807–9), with all of its anti-fraternal associations. Indeed, Satan's whispering into her ear may even hint at a slur on Catholic images of the Annunciation, when the Holy Spirit delivered news of the Incarnation into the ear of Mary, the anti-type of Eve.[30] Protestant suspicion of the mimetic function of the 'fancy', a deceptive faculty capable of undermining human understanding by transmitting false and misleading ideas, permeates the scene.[31]

During the morning after Eve's disturbed sleep, in response to her anxiety over Satan's aural penetration of her dream in the form of a false angel who made the Tree of Knowledge appear 'Much fairer to my fancy than by day' (5.53), Adam instructs her on the proper function of the wakeful 'fancy' as a faculty subordinate to the reason, despite the subversion of rationality when 'mimic fancy' governs during sleep, 'most in dreams' (5.110–13). In doing so, Adam addresses the epistemological problem posed by Satan's employment of angelic disguise to deceive Uriel, and his reprise of that performance by invading Eve's mind with a bad dream:

> Evil into the mind of god or man
> May come and go, so unapproved, and leave
> No spot or blame behind.

> (5.117–19)[32]

Shortly before Satan's temptation of Eve by means of a dream, he takes part in an allegorical performance akin to a polemical mystery or morality play by John Bale. It begins when cherubim delegated to patrol Eden by night apprehend toad-like Satan in a farcical episode. The simile attached to the interruption of Satan's stratagem, when Ithuriel and Zephon arrest him at his victim's ear, fuses a ludicrous echo of flatulence at the Paradise of Fools with cartoon-like anticipation of the contemporary belief that the Gunpowder Plot was the invention of the Jesuitical Devil:

>   As when a spark
> Lights on a heap of nitrous powder, laid
> Fit for the tun some magazine to store
> Against a rumoured war, the smutty grain
> With sudden blaze diffused, inflames the air:
> So started up in his own shape the fiend.

> (4.814–19)

During the ensuing scene, Satan undergoes an involuntary costume change to play the role of a melodramatic Vice, familiar from John Bale's anti-Catholic interludes, engaged in psychomachic conflict with sober angelic Virtues. Aided by stage directions, Satan's interrogation proceeds by means of highly ironic, satirical dialogue which undercuts his continuing self-deception and leads him to assume a variety of indefensible positions in the unfolding debate. That the angels are only 'half amazed' suggests that they feign surprise at their apprehension of 'the grisly king' (ll. 820–1). Despite Satan's bombastic delivery of lines 'filled with scorn' to a lowly cherub whom he had once lorded over in heaven, Zephon counters 'scorn with scorn' in mockery of the loss of his resplendent 'glory' (ll. 827–40). That cherub's sharp retort renders the prisoner speechless as the butt of a cosmic joke: 'The fiend replied not, over-come with rage' (l. 857). When brought before Gabriel, commander of the angelic guards, Satan continues his histrionic delivery, 'with contemptuous brow' and 'frowning stern'. By contrast, the archangel cooly delivers a sardonic rebuke, 'disdainfully half smiling', that derides Satan's cowardice in fleeing from Hell as a 'courageous chief, / The first in flight from pain' (ll. 885–924). Angelic mockery reduces Satan's arguments to absurdity, forever destroying his pretence to heroism.[33]

The sardonic comedy that introduces Satan's initial temptation of Eve is in keeping with the ongoing importance of anti-Catholic satire in *Paradise Lost*. Satan's ludicrous interrogation functions as a sequel to the Paradise of Fools episode, which introduces clerical disguising as an important motif associated with polemics against the *hypocrisy* of Roman-Catholic (and English) prelates. Ramifying intertextual associations infiltrate those episodes in proleptic antici-pation of a tradition of Reformation allegory that extends from morality plays by John Bale to Book One of Spenser's *Faerie Queene* to scabrous anti-Catholic cartoons of Milton's own age (see Figs. 8.1–2). The guardian angels' hilarious debasement of Satanic claims to heroic stature complements divine laughter at demonic intrigue, which reverberates in Heaven to the chagrin of William Empson.[34] Caustic humor distances the reader from the imminent Fall of Adam and Eve, thus highlighting the centrality of divine comedy in *Paradise Lost*, despite the tragic cast of the enactment of the Fall of Adam and Eve and its aftermath in Books Nine and Ten. Anti-Catholic polemics play an important role in a previously unno-ticed satirical dynamic that radiates outward from Milton's Paradise of Fools.

214   *John N. King*

ACKNOWLEDGEMENTS

I would like to thank Stephen R. Honeygosky, John G. Norman, John T. Shawcross and members of the Newberry Institute of Renaissance Studies Milton Seminar for comments on earlier versions of this chapter. I also acknowledge the very helpful assistance in research of Kevin Lindberg, Nancy W. Miller and Thomas G. Olsen. An Andrew Mellon Foundation Fellowship at the Huntington Library, an NEH Fellowship for University Professors, and assistance from the College of Humanities, Center for Medieval and Renaissance Studies, and Department of English at The Ohio State University have supported completion of this chapter.

NOTES

1.   Unless otherwise noted, London is the place of publication and reference is to first editions. The abbreviation sig. is omitted from signature references. Scriptural texts are from *The Geneva Bible*, facsimile of the 1560 edition with introduction by Lloyd E. Berry (Madison, University of Wisconsin Press, 1969). Miltonic texts are from *Complete Prose Works of John Milton*, 8 vols., ed. Don M. Wolfe et al. (New Haven: Yale University Press, 1953–82), hereafter cited as CPW; and *The Poems of John Milton*, ed. John Carey and Alastair Fowler (London and New York: Longman, 1968). Notes to PL are cited by reference to Fowler. All texts are modernized. Italic type supplies added emphasis.
2.   Joseph Addison and Richard Steel, *The Spectator*, ed. Donald F. Bond, 5 vols. (Oxford: Clarendon Press, 1965), no. 297. Pope models the apotheosis of Belinda's lock in *The Rape of the Lock*, 5. 123–8, on *PL* 3.459, 481–3. See below concerning *MacFlecknoe*. See also Robert A. Kantra, *All Things Vain: Religious Satirists and Their Art* (University Park: Pennsylvania State University Press, 1984), ch. 4.
3.   CPW 1: 553–60; quoting p. 560. Pope Sylvester I received the alleged gift of temporal authority from Emperor Constantine I.
4.   Capitalization of Sin as a personification follows *Paradise Lost*, ed. Roy Flannagan (New York: Macmillan, 1993), 3.446.
5.   Jaroslav Pelikan, *The Melody of Theology: a Philosophical Dictionary* (Cambridge, MA: Harvard University Press, 1988), 86–9. On the proleptic aspect of Limbo, see John Wooten, 'The Metaphysics of Milton's Epic Burlesque', *Milton Studies* 13 (1979): 256; Marshall Grossman, *'Authors to Themselves': Milton and the Revelation of History* (Cambridge: Cambridge University Press, 1987), 66.
6.   E.g., Vanity Fair in John Bunyan's *Pilgrim's Progress*, ed. Roger Sharrock (Harmondsworth: Penguin Books, 1965), where 'as in other fairs, some one commodity is as the chief of all the fair, so the ware of

Rome and her merchandise is greatly promoted in this Fair: only our English nation, with some others, have taken a dislike thereat' (125).
7. John M. Steadman, *Milton and the Renaissance Hero* (Oxford: Clarendon Press, 1967), 150.
8. See John N. King, *Tudor Royal Iconography: Literature and Art in an Age of Religious Crisis*, Princeton Essays on the Arts (Princeton: Princeton University Press, 1989), fig. 56, 171–2; and Eugene R. Cunnar, 'Milton's "Two-Handed Engine": The Visionary Iconography of *Christus in Statera*', *Milton Quarterly* 17 (*1983*): 29–38.
9. See Michael Lieb, 'Milton among the Monks', in *Milton and the Middle Ages*, ed. John Mulryan (Lewisburg, PA: Bucknell University Press, 1982), 103–14.
10. Christopher Hill, *Milton and the English Revolution*, 2nd edn (1977; Harmondsworth: Penguin Books, 1979), 421.
11. *PL*, ed. Newton, 2nd edn (1750), nn. on 3.444, 475.
12. See King, *Iconography*, 103, 151n, 175, 189, 191–95, 228–31.
13. Anonymous, *Wyclif's Wicket* (Nuremberg, i.e., London, 1546); N. H. Keeble, *The Literary Culture of Nonconformity in Later Seventeenth-Century England* (Athens: University of Georgia Press, 1987), 268–72.
14. Norbert Elias, *The Civilizing Process: The History of Manners*, trans. Edmund Jephcott (New York: Urizen, 1978), 82–3, 130–5. On the 'oral–anal–sexual imagery' of Chaos and Limbo, see Michael Lieb, *The Dialectics of Creation: Patterns of Birth & Regeneration in Paradise Lost* (Amherst: University of Massachusetts Press, 1970), 28–33.
15. The angelic command in Chaucer's *Summoner's Tale* may have a Lollard tinge: '"Hold up thy tayl, thou Sathanas!" quod he; / "Shew forth thyn ers, and lat the frere se / Where is the nest of freres in this place"' (ll. 1689–91). The ensuing burlesque of the division of the argument in scholastic disputation, which results in the ludicrous decision that each of twelve friars in a mendicant house 'sholde have yliche his part / As of the soun or savour of a fart' (ll. 2225–6), indicates that crude anti-fraternal humor remains a living feature of ecclesiastical satire until Milton's lifetime. See Alan Levitan, 'The Parody of Pentecost in Chaucer's *Summoner's Tale*', *University of Toronto Quarterly* 40 (1970–1): 236–46; Penn Szittya, *The Antifraternal Tradition in Medieval Literature* (Princeton: Princeton University Press, 1986), 233.
16. John E. Booty, ed., *The Book of Common Prayer 1559: The Elizabethan Prayer Book* (Charlottesville: University Press of Virginia for The Folger Shakespeare Library, 1976), 169.
17. See OED 'wind' sb.1 10; and PL 11.14–16 and Fowler n.
18. For a catalogue of winds as false inspiration, see Janet Adelman, 'Creation and the Place of the Poet in Paradise Lost', in *The Author in His Work: Essays on a Problem in Criticism*, ed. Louis L. Martz, Patricia Meyer Spacks and Aubrey Williams (New Haven: Yale University Press, 1978), 66–7 and n. 9.
19. The wording may allude further to 2 Peter 2: 1, 18, which attacks 'false prophets' who 'speak swelling words of vanity'. See John C. Ulreich, Jr., '"And by Occasion Foretells": The Prophetic Voice in *Lycidas*,' *MS* 18 (1983): 3–21, p. 7.

20. That is, a punning association whereby a pair of words 'agree in the sound, but differ in the sense' (*The Spectator*, No. 61).

21. Dryden's travesty also alludes to Elisha's assumption of Elijah's mantle (2 Kings 2: 9–13). See J. B. Broadbent, *Some Graver Subject: an Essay on 'Paradise Lost'* (: Chatto & Windus, 1960), 263n.

22. *CPW* 1: 527; 3: 339. See also Milton's attack in *An Apology against Smectymnuus* against 'mitered hypocrisy' (1: 924) and instances in other tracts at 1: 590, 679, 894; 3: 195, 545. On acting as a trope for prelatical 'disguising,' see Jonas A. Barish, *The Antitheatrical Prejudice* (Berkeley and Los Angeles: University of California Press, 1981), 162.

23. Keeble, 219. On Milton's general disdain for hypocrisy, see Honeygosky, 8, 45, 49, 52, 63. Milton's *Civil Power* attacks re-establishment of a State Church because it would breed hypocrisy (*CPW* 7: 269). An account of the invisible church in *The Racovian Catechism* (Amsterdam [London?], 1652), publication of which Milton approved as a Commonwealth censor, affords a gloss on Satan's disguise: 'But it can hardly be known by the outward actions where true faith is; for outward actions, proceeding from a corrupt heart, may carry the same appearance with those that flow from a heart which is sincere. In short, he that is evil-minded, may put on the outward garb of a good man: but it is otherwise in a good man, who never laboureth to put on the garb of an evil man' (*STC* 20083.8; M6^{r-v}).

24. P. H., *Annotations on Milton's 'Paradise Lost'*; attributed to Patrick Hume.

25. See Barish, 91, 117, 125, 155; Paul Whitfield White, *Theatre and Reformation: Protestantism, Patronage, and Playing in Tudor England* (Cambridge: Cambridge University Press, 1993). On monastic disguise, see Michael Lieb, 'Milton among the Monks', in *Milton and the Middle Ages*, ed. John Mulryan (Lewisburg: Bucknell University Press, 1982), 103–14, p. 110; and John N. King, *Spenser's Poetry and the Reformation Tradition* (Princeton: Princeton University Press, 1990), 50–4, 57.

26. Giles and Phineas Fletcher, *Poetical Works*, 2 vols. (Cambridge: Cambridge University Press, 1908–9).

27. *Whole Works of William Tyndale, John Frith, and Doctor Barnes*, ed. John Foxe (1573), G4v.

28. See King, *English Reformation Literature*, 63, 153–60. Satan's 'posing as a cherub' suggests 'epistemological perversity' according to Kenneth Borris, 'Allegory in *Paradise Lost*: Satan's Cosmic Journey', *Milton Studies* 26 (1990): 117–18.

29. Fallon, 'Milton's "Peculiar Grace"': Self-representation, Intention, and Authority', forthcoming.

30. Roland Mushat Frye, *Milton's Imagery and the Visual Arts: Iconographic Tradition in the Epic Poems* (Princeton: Princeton University Press, 1978), 100. Satan's whispering into the Pope's ear is a conventional satirical device found in Milton's *In Quintum Novembris* (ll. 92–132).

31. See John Guillory, *Poetic Authority: Spenser, Milton, and Literary History* (New York: Columbia University Press, 1983), 108–13; and King, *Spenser's Poetry*, 65–79.

32. The icastic imagination is a 'peculiar instrument of grace' according to Paul Stevens, 'Milton and the Icastic Imagination', *Milton Studies* 20 (1984): 44. The aurality of Satanic temptation parodies the priority of hearing the Word versus seeing images in Puritan thought. See Stephen M Fallon, 'Milton's Sin and Death: The Ontology of Allegory in *Paradise Lost*', *ELR* 17 (1987): 329–50, p. 341, on Miltonic allegory as an expression of 'fallen epistemology, the perverse refusal of Satan and his devils to acknowledge the unity of a monist universe'. See also Guillory, *Authority*, 148–9.
33. This paragraph builds upon conversation with Stephen R. Honeygosky.
34. William Empson, *Milton's God* (London: Chatto & Windus, 1961), *passim*.

9

'The Wretched Subject the Whole Town Talks of': Representing Elizabeth Cellier (London, 1680)

Frances E. Dolan

The crisis known as the 'Popish Plot' was about the power of stories – testimony in court, rumors in the street and narratives in print – to persuade the English populace, and especially judges and juries, that Catholics were conspiring to reclaim the kingdom by force and by stealth. The power of stories to confirm, inflame or create anti-Catholicism was certainly not without precedent. Yet, the Popish Plot depended almost exclusively on one witness, Titus Oates, and his claim that Catholics, particularly Jesuits, were conspiring to kill Charles II and his councillors, massacre Protestants and set up a Catholic government under the Duke of York (the future James II). The rumor of yet another popish plot had legs because it served political needs. By discrediting Catholics, it fuelled the Exclusion Crisis, a Whig attempt to bar James's succession.[1]

Regarding the Popish Plot, then, it is impossible to distinguish between events and their narrative representations because those narratives – circulated as rumors, offered in court as testimony, published – were the event. Despite the Lord Chief Justice's claim, in one trial, that 'Narratives are no Evidence at all', another commentator explains that 'the whole Machine of this vast, and hideous Plott is built upon the bare testimony of the swearers'.[2] Narratives were indeed evidence, if not of what real people actually did, then of what writers and readers feared and believed. As Rachel Weil has argued, witnesses' credibility was determined not so much by what they said, or even who they were, since many of the key witnesses in these trials were 'infamous persons', but by how well their

218

testimony served dominant political interests, confirmed long-standing prejudices and conformed to familiar conventions.[3] On the 'evidence' of those narratives found most convincing, that is, those describing a Catholic conspiracy, at least twenty-two were executed, none of whom ever confessed. In these deaths, the traditions for representing Catholicism issue in material consequences, the discursive reveals itself as the real.

Although the trials of the alleged conspirators were, according to Jonathan Scott, 'not judicial events at all', but rather 'acts of political theatre, to express, and to that extent assuage, a general public concern', they could not have functioned as such if they had not been widely represented in print.[4] Without the press, these trials would have had limited audiences and limited impact; the press brought the 'Popish Plot' into the public sphere more than the courts or the scaffolds did. What gave the Popish Plot trials their cultural significance was the way that they were both spectacles and publication opportunities; coming at a crucial moment in the transition from a culture of spectacle to one of print, these trials formed a bridge between the two. Presses printed expanded versions of witnesses' testimony, rival accounts of the trials and executions, gossip about those suspected or accused, satires, 'news'. News also, obviously, circulated orally, at least in London. But this oral transmission, like the events in the courts, is accessible to us now only through the written record.

In the flurry of publication which not only represented but constituted the Popish Plot, and justified fierce retaliations against Catholics, queens and clerics assume prominence, as they so often did. In this chapter, however, I would like to look at a woman who was an *un*usual suspect. This less privileged woman who yet became a highly public embodiment of Catholicism was Elizabeth Cellier, the so-called 'Popish Midwife' implicated in the Meal Tub Plot, a belated offshoot of the Popish Plot. For Cellier, as for the other female figures for Catholicism, representations owe as much to rhetorical and iconographic traditions as they do to any observation of actual persons or events. Yet I also want to argue that the particulars of Cellier's persona and history exert more pressure on the representations of her than was possible in representations of more socially and conceptually remote figures (even living queens consort). However much she, too, was a figment of the culture's imagination, she also had a specificity, and consequently a vulnerability, stemming from a particular cultural moment. Representations of Cellier reveal the tension between, as well as the overlapping or collapse of, the realms of the real and the representational, the historical and the discursive.

Charges of a Meal Tub Plot arose after the Popish Plot executions, when the frenzy of prosecution and retribution had subsided, but the Exclusion Crisis was still on the boil. Purportedly a Catholic scheme to divert blame for the Popish Plot onto Presbyterians, the Meal Tub Plot might also have been a scheme by those who opposed James's succession to reanimate hostility toward Catholics. Regardless, it was understood from the start as an attempt to manipulate public opinion. Testing the power of a new charge to reanimate a tired controversy, the Meal Tub Plot focused on the provenance and proof-value of documents found hidden in Elizabeth Cellier's 'Meal Tub', or flour barrel. When one Thomas Dangerfield was arrested for trying to frame the Whig politician Roger Mansel for treason, he cast doubt away from himself by accusing Cellier (among others). As far as the written record is concerned, Dangerfield's accusation calls Cellier into being, as if she had not existed until he interpellated her. Cellier was available, so to speak, because she was using her mobility and her contacts as a midwife, with an aristocratic, even royal clientele, to monitor and relieve Catholic prisoners in Newgate, to smuggle correspondence into and out of the prison, and to support the defenses of Catholics on trial.[5] Funded by contributions from powerful Catholic patrons such as Lady Powis and Roger Palmer, Earl of Castlemaine, Cellier worked to relieve or provide bail for the more than two thousand Catholics imprisoned in the London area.[6] Cellier claimed that she had hired Dangerfield to provide information on how Catholic prisoners were being treated in Newgate and to work as a servant, courier and informant; he claimed that she had hired him to fabricate evidence of a Presbyterian plot to replace Charles II with his illegitimate son, Monmouth, and to plant material incriminating the Earl of Shaftesbury in a plot against the King.[7] Dangerfield testified that his written reports on his 'fact-finding' missions could be found concealed in a meal tub in Mrs Cellier's house, as, indeed, they were. Whichever side concocted the Meal Tub Plot, it brought to the fore the central question at which the Popish Plot prosecutions had hinted: might one faction invent a plot to incriminate and discredit another? If evidence could be fabricated, how could it be trusted as 'proof'?

Dangerfield's charges instigated a process which made Elizabeth Cellier notorious. She was indicted and tried for treason. Like everyone tried for treason before 1696, she had to act as her own defense attorney; unlike most, she did so successfully. Cellier was acquitted, in part because the fervor had passed and questions were already being asked about the legal procedures and witnesses used to convict the 'traitors'. However, anger at the verdict made it unlikely that she could proceed quietly with her life and work. Cellier compounded her notoriety when, in the three weeks following her acquittal, she wrote a self-justifying account of the trial, *Malice Defeated: Or a Brief Relation of the Accusation and Deliverance of Elizabeth Cellier* (London, 1680), which she had printed for her, despite the Privy Council's attempts to seize sheets while they were in press, and which she sold from her house.[8] For this text, Cellier was subsequently tried for and convicted of libel. Apparently, while the King's Bench was not willing to convict her of treason, the Whig-controlled Old Bailey could not allow so forthright an espousal of the Catholic cause in print to go unpunished, especially given Cellier's claim that Catholic prisoners were being tortured in Newgate. Although her treason trial was belated in regard to the Popish Plot, her libel trial reveals that much was still at stake.

The one thing about which Elizabeth Cellier and her detractors can agree is that paper and pens have become crucial weapons, and the page a terrain of struggle, one increasingly as or more important than the courtroom or the scaffold. Both court cases against Cellier revolve around texts: correspondence smuggled into and out of Newgate, lists and schemes hidden in meal tubs, libelous publications, witnesses' examinations. In accounts of her two trials, Cellier and her accusers fight over possession of papers, over authorship and accountability, over what papers can prove and how they can be manipulated, forged, altered, planted.[9] If we now understand these battles over texts only through texts, so, too, did the combatants. Asked how she knows something happened, Cellier replies: 'I read it in a Pamphlet' (*MD* H2ᵛ). Multiple accounts of both Cellier's trials survive, including *Malice Defeated*; she is referred to in the only regular account of news in print during the months of her notoriety, Henry Care's *The Weekly Pacquet of Advice from Rome*, and in multiple broadsides and ballads.[10]

It was Cellier's punishment for libel that really made her a public figure, not just because she was literally exposed to public view (and assault), but because this public spectacle became such a popular topic for visual and verbal representation. The sentence was strict: she was fined the huge sum of £1,000, and placed on the pillory on three separate occasions, where the crowd brutally ill-treated her. On each occasion, the hangman burned copies of her book. On her last two visits to the pillory, perhaps because she had complained in a petition to the King that 'she might as well have been sentenced to be stoned to death',[11] she was allowed to keep her head and hands out of the pillory and to wield a wooden shield 'as a kind of battledore' to defend herself.[12] While this protection may have saved her life, it made her even more vulnerable to ridicule, as I shall show. Enthroned on the pillory, depicted in woodcuts, represented in effigy in a pope-burning procession,[13] the target of at least twenty-five published attacks and a polemicist in her own right, Cellier was a highly public, visible and audible figure in the London street cultures of both spectacle and print. She was, as Henry Care remarked, 'a *wretched Subject*, that all the Town talks of'.[14] It is only as she becomes a 'wretched subject' of town talk that she becomes a subject to whom agency and speech are attributed; only as she is acknowledged as a topic of conversation is she also represented as a speaker and a schemer. Furthermore, it is only through this process that, given the absence of birth or death records for her, she comes into being at all as an object of study. It is almost as if, when Dangerfield accuses her, she comes into being; later, when polemic no longer refers to her, and when she has written and published her last text, she disappears. Yet if being the wretched subject of London discourse is what inscribed Cellier into the historical record, it was, like many processes of subject forma-tion, extremely risky; here, the risks of entering into representation were as concrete as being brained with rocks.

The image of Cellier on the pillory parrying rocks, an image created through woodcuts, pamphlets and broadsides, vividly depicts the dangers and humiliations of being the target or object of representation. Yet Cellier was sentenced to the pillory for being a subject in the opposite sense – an author and a legally accountable agent. Thus, at least in her case, exercising some control over repre-sentation – acting as a producer as well as a topic – did not necessar-ily either set the record straight, or protect her. Both Cellier's attackers and her defenders agree in censuring her movement into print as an act of aggression. A detractor describes her as 'a stout *Virago*, who having been Imprisoned for the *Cause*, and escaped the Law, now with bold and audacious Effronteries publishes her Adventures.'[15] Even Cellier's one Catholic defender, James II's Jesuit confessor John Warner, simultaneously praises Cellier for her skill and argues that she endangered herself (and her cause) by displaying it indiscreetly:

> Mrs. Cellier had won her laurels in this rather small affair of her trial; with her remarkable powers of endurance and of skill, she had fought alone against many and had vanquished all opposition. In her eagerness to add to these laurels by publishing the history of her trials, she came near to ruining everything. For in her book she gave free rein to her skill, ... thus she offered a handle to those who were looking for one, to charge her with libel.[16]

For Warner, it is publication, not 'remarkable powers of endurance and [legal] skill', that makes Cellier an insufficiently covert *femme*. Warner's location of danger in Cellier's 'publishing the history of her trials' and giving 'free rein to her skill' deserves closer scrutiny. Why was it in this, rather than in any of her risky, but more covert, political activities, that Cellier 'came near to ruining everything'?

Other early modern women made contested public appearances in the courts and in the press. For all who did so, there were real consequences not only of their skill – how well they could represent themselves, how successfully they could manipulate the available terms – but, more importantly, of how gender set those terms, determining the conditions under which authorship and agency might be attributed to women. Nor did gender act independently as a determinant; religious affiliation, for instance, combined with gender with uneven and unpredictable effects. For instance, Catholics, like other minority dissenters, such as Quakers, operated under legal restrictions and social prescriptions even more rigorous than those constraining all early modern women. If the limits were more clearly marked and stringently enforced for such women, and their transgressions of those limits more urgent and more harshly punished, then attention to such groups can reveal where those limits were set and what the possibilities for maneuvering within or pressing against them might have been. Since Elizabeth Cellier was often at risk, but never decisively defeated – that is tried, but not convicted, then convicted and pilloried, but not executed, denounced in court and in the press, but willing to venture into both arenas to defend herself, her books burned but not all of them – she offers an especially revealing limit case, I shall argue, for how gender and religious affiliation conjoin and conflict in limiting the options for representing women as agents and authors. Catholicism and femininity sometimes conjoin to create a double bind; at other times they cancel each other out. Neither category is adequate to explain the phenomenon of the 'Popish Midwife'. Furthermore, both 'Catholic' and 'woman' have provisional and contingent meanings, which become even more volatile when they are combined. Shifting the focus away from the 'wretched subject' of London talk in 1680 (that is, from what Cellier did or did not do, from her agency and responsibility, good or bad), I shall focus here on the various ways she is represented and what contingencies (which court, what genre, what year or even month) shaped these.

Since, for many early modern women, writing for public circulation and consumption could be incriminating in itself, women's 'apologies' or self-justifications were often self-defeating. This was especially true for Catholic women. Being Catholic and female could doubly discredit an author attempting to compel belief. Both women and Catholics were assumed to be illiterate and deceitful. If Cellier had two strikes against her when she tried to raise an authoritative, persuasive public voice, the content of her message, quickly labelled libellous, provided her with an almost insurmountable challenge.

Given the climate, her topic, and her already well-established public persona, Cellier's emergence into print is inevitably a highly political, and therefore conspicuous and risky, act. Cellier picks up her pen/lance during one of several late seventeenth-century political crises which, Rachel Weil claims, 'opened up the public airwaves to people outside the formal political nation, while at the same time making the credibility of those people an object of political struggle'.[17] She also totters on the threshold of the period from 1684 to 1740 which Ros Ballaster argues 'provided significant and distinctive conditions of access for the woman writer into explicitly political discourse'.[18]

Cellier's story might be approached either through a success narrative, in which a specifically female kind of authority becomes available in the public sphere, or a failure narrative, in which Catholics steadily lose both authority and symbolic resonance in the public sphere and recede from engagement in the political process. That these two narratives work at cross-purposes – one step forward, two steps back – suggests their inadequacy to explaining the phenomenon of Elizabeth Cellier. Cellier does not represent either group, Catholics or women; the history of either group, taken alone, does not prepare one to understand her. However demonized and criminalized, most Catholics did not wind up in court, even in these volatile years; conversely, those who did were rarely acquitted. Accounts of both Cellier's trials attribute to her the claim that she stood 'singly and alone' before the court, that she lacked Catholic support;[19] yet on both charges she was tried as 'the Female Champion of the Cause'.[20] It was possible for both to be true. A controversial figure, especially a woman, might bear the blame for Catholic affiliation without getting any of the benefits.

Cellier also does not 'represent' other women, even Catholic ones. Although Cellier was married (to a French merchant), she is identified much more frequently as a midwife than as a wife.[21] As an adult convert to Catholicism, Cellier defies the assumption that most women clung to Catholicism because they resisted change; for her, Catholicism was a choice and an innovation. As a midwife and a gentlewoman, Cellier also occupies a class position between the two groups of women who appear most frequently in Popish Plot trials: working-class women (nurses, servants and housekeepers) who were introduced as witnesses, yet often ridiculed, and aristocratic and royal women, who were suspected but, for the most part, protected. Even Cellier's hoods, in which she appears in the three woodcuts reproduced here, serve as a kind of habit, distinguishing her from other women (see Figs. 9.1–9.3). Finally, Cellier was a spatially as well as a socially mobile figure, circulating through London's prisons and aristocratic households, gathering and disseminating intelligence. Even when at home she seems to have run her household as a base of political operations: she lodged, and perhaps coached, the thirty Catholic boys from St Omer's seminary who came over to be witnesses on behalf of six men accused by Titus Oates and tried in 1679; she sold her self-justifying texts; she employed scribes and secretaries; according to her accusers, she plotted treason and hid incriminating documents in her flour tub. In sum, despite her motto ('I never change'), Elizabeth Cellier can be difficult to locate in relation to the categories that often organize historical study. Yet it is also impossible to understand her apart from these categories or outside of history. To understand the Cellier phenomenon, it is necessary to keep multiple categories of analysis in play and to hold multiple histories in tension.

Figure 9.1 Cellier as author. Queen of Spades, from playing cards depicting 'The Meal Tub Plot'.

Figure 9.3 Cellier 'disgracing' the pillory. Queen of Diamonds, from playing cards depicting 'The Meal Tub Plot'. Note that Cellier appears to be wearing breeches.

Figure 9.2   Cellier as the pillory. From *The Popish Damnable Plot Against Our Religion and Liberties* (1681).

The biggest problem with approaching Cellier as a 'woman writer' is simultaneously the best reason for doing so: this status was conferred on her only conditionally and paradoxically in her own time. Although the fiction of the 'Meal Tub Plot' depended on a notion of Cellier as 'author', inventing a fictional sham plot and blaming it on Presbyterians, the extent of Cellier's responsibility for *Malice Defeated* was a point of contention in her libel trial and in the various polemics written around and in response to it. Cellier was tried for the 'virulency and Malice' of her pen,[22] yet most of the legal personnel at the trial and the polemicists who write about Cellier as author assume that she cannot have written the text alone; she must have been guided, for instance, by Jesuits, those 'Scribling Fathers'; or 'a priest got into her Belly, and so speaking through her, as the Devil through the Heathen Oracles' simultaneously impregnated and possessed her with the book (see Fig. 9.1, in which Cellier is depicted taking dictation from Jesuits).[23] In the context of this assumption that Cellier (at most) helped to deliver a text of which she was not the parent, any attempt to own the text can be viewed as self-defeating presumption. One account of the libel trial, for instance, ridicules Cellier for affirming her authorship: 'she loudly answered, – *My Lord, I wrote it every Line my self*. So Ambitious she was of being *Gossip* to the Spurious Libel, though 'tis well known to be *The whole Troops Child*.'[24] Cellier obviously had reasons for renouncing this bastard text, such as averting conviction; indeed, in another account of the trial she engages in some slippery maneuvering about what it means for the book to be 'hers': 'I said it was my Book, and so it was, because it was in my possession, but not that I writ it. This is my Fan, but it does not follow that I made it.'[25]

Taken together, the various accounts of the libel trial suggest that, at least at the discursive level, Cellier is held accountable for the book (and held in contempt for trying to avoid that accountability) while she is yet dismissed as an author (and held in contempt for claiming to be one). Insisting that 'the worthy Author, (whether *Lord*, or *Priest*, or *Monk*, or *Bawd*, or *all* together)' of *Malice Defeated* is irrelevant to the prosecution, the legal and polemical cases against Cellier manage to convict her of libel without ever conceding her competence as a writer or political analyst.[26] As Baron Weston explains in one account, 'I think it is not severe that you, who stand at the stake for all, must bear the blame of all.'[27] In short, a government outraged at the accusation that it tortured prisoners, and a legal system that needed someone to 'stand at the stake for all', required an author; that author was Elizabeth Cellier. Although various accounts of the libel trial evince interest in the processes of collaborative authorship – taking dictation, or hiring copyists, for instance – they make clear that, in Cellier's case, authorship is not a process but a position. That position is at the stake or, more literally, on the pillory. By whatever process *Malice Defeated* was composed, Cellier's name was on the title page, and she sat on the pillory and did the time. Thus, from the perspective of Cellier's accusers and attackers, authorship becomes a kind of martyrdom; she is a 'Joan of Arque handling her *Pen* for the Papistical Cause'.

Yet, as this same writer laments, Cellier did not share the 'glory' of Joan of Arc's martyrdom; that is, she did not die. As an autobiographical account of a treason trial, *Malice Defeated* is highly unusual because so few tried for treason survived and wrote, rather than died; certainly, no other women or Catholics did so. Unlike those women for whom the prospect of death, whether in childbed or on the scaffold, became the enabling condition of authorship or public speech, Cellier writes *rather than* dies (instead of writing on the condition that she die). Thus the existence of *Malice Defeated* is more interesting to me than its accuracy, which, in any case is difficult to determine.

In *Malice Defeated*, Cellier takes the inaccuracy of the charges and testimony against her as a gauge of the fictionality of the purported Meal Tub Plot: 'If there be no more Truth in the whole Story, than there is in what relates to me, every Play that is Acted has more Truth in it' (*MD* H2ᵛ). Yet *Malice Defeated* is itself another of the rival fictions that constitute this plot, rather than the truth against which they can be checked. Like any of the other texts, it uses conventions and form to interest and persuade. In struggling to contradict the 'whole Story' with another, equally interested story, Cellier in *Malice Defeated* faced a particularly difficult choice when it came to form, a choice complicated by both gender and religious affiliation. Of the available forms, familiar or emergent, none of the more obvious options quite fits the project, all exacted costs, and all could be turned against Cellier by her detractors.

Neither confession nor spiritual autobiography would work for Cellier because her story lacks an appropriate beginning. As Cellier tells it, it begins in adulthood and after marriage; it begins with conversion, a conversion more incriminating than justifying, rather than building towards it. Hardly a retreat into inwardness, Cellier presents her conversion as motivated by political struggle – her horror at the treatment of Charles I and Royalists 'for their being Papists and Idolaters' – and as, in turn, motivating further political struggle – her suspicion that the Popish Plot was merely 'pretended' and her determination 'to relieve the poor imprison'd Catholicks' (*MD* A2ᵛ). Her conversion initiates a story characterized by action not by inward reflection or private devotions; justifying herself more by works than by faith, Cellier presents herself as an agent, not as a vessel through whom the spirit works.

Criminal (auto)biography is the last form Cellier would want, because she does not concede guilt, therefore does not repent, and, at the time she writes, has miraculously 'delivered' herself from punishment. Similarly, Cellier does not present her text as a scandalous memoir, another genre available to notorious women. Instead, she insists that her sexual conduct or choices are not at issue, despite efforts in court and in print to shift the focus toward them. Furthermore, the tendency of both scandalous memoir and criminal biography to criminalize self-determination runs counter to the positive depiction in *Malice Defeated* of Cellier's ability to deliver herself.

Although the saint's life would appear to be the opposite of the criminal's biography, and an obvious choice for a Catholic woman's self-justification, it, too, downplays agency, in this case to emphasize virtuous suffering and divine interventions. Despite her religion, Cellier presents her story as one in which there are no miracles; she insists that she, herself, deserves the credit. Finally, Cellier's 'Brief Relation' is more suspenseful and provisional than any of these forms would allow because it does not head to the foregone conclusion of almost all of them – death. Even within Protestantism, as J. Paul Hunter points out, 'the person whose life was published was nearly always someone already dead'.[28] Vital and vocal, Cellier evades this conventional closure, yet in this evasion she also misses out on the authorization that dying well confers on a life.

Querulously in this world, rather than safely in the next, her narrative voice offers no assurances to readers. In refusing to wrap up the ends, Cellier insists that the future is uncertain not only for her but for England: 'But how long either my self, or any other Loyal Subjects, shall be secure from the like Conspiracy, God only knows,' Cellier concludes (*MD* L2ᵛ). It is that uncertainty, that sense that she might alter a course not already determined, that motivates action and speech.

Identified with a cause and with a community, Cellier also spills over the contours of the highly individualized narrator or protagonist, the speaking subject of autobiography, the suffering subject of hagiography and martyrology, the lawbreaking subject of criminal biography. While Cellier keeps her focus squarely on herself, her self-representations are discontinuous and contingent. She cycles through a variety of roles, which Weil catalogues as the royal jester, the martyr, the tragic heroine and the clever legal tactician, discarding each as she reaches the limit of its usefulness.[29] This sequence of different postures and voices suggests both self-consciousness about the options available for self-representation, and an awareness of the inadequacy of any one. As a vehicle for depicting this discontinuous subjectivity, *Malice Defeated* is not as much shapeless or formless as it is a compound of many voices, texts and forms. In the frequent transcripts of conversations which occur both inside and outside of court, *Malice Defeated* most resembles a play. At other moments, it resembles a published archive of Cellier's case; at the risk of obscuring a coherent narrative of events, Cellier provides the reader with most of the documents through which she built her case, and with the evidence against as well as for her.[30] As a consequence, *Malice Defeated* is noisy and visually chaotic.

Viewed as a whole, however, *Malice Defeated* is more than the sum of its parts; for Cellier does not simply move through forms and personae, revealing their inadequacy to the story she wants to tell and the self she wants to represent. Ultimately, she combines aspects of various forms and the subject-positions they confer on their protagonists to invent a new hybrid form (the trial account written from the defendant's perspective, the legal romance, the criminalized-politicized-spiritual autobiography) and a new position and voice (the midwife who delivers herself, the 'lady errant' who relieves her own distress). Cellier does not achieve the authority to set new terms or to invent new forms. Furthermore, her experimentation is certainly not unique; the climate of formal restlessness in the late seventeenth and early eighteenth centuries opened up the category of 'writer' to many it had excluded previously and promoted many uncategorizable texts. In 1680, every publication was politically inflected and necessarily partisan. But Cellier's double jeopardy as female and Catholic forces her to expose the very inadequacy of the available forms, and pushes her to the limits of the available options.

Even for those who wished to criminalize or dismiss Cellier's competence, genre posed a dilemma, forcing them to combine old forms in new ways to tell her story. Cellier's many detractors invariably respond to her own self-presentations, picking up the terms she uses, trying on the forms she rejects, attempting to fit her into roles she spurns. Their many such attempts reveal the inadequacy of those forms as much as her own text does. They also reveal that those who attacked her in the seventeenth-century read her more closely than those who defend her now.

Many of those who wrote vituperative accounts of Cellier's libel trial, and, especially, her visits to the pillory, thrust the role of martyr upon her, only to ridicule her unwilling and undignified performance. Although Cellier occasionally proclaims her willingness to die in defense of the truth, she focuses on the strategies by

which she avoids conviction, suffering and death. Many attacks on
Cellier condemn just this strategic avoidance of suffering, distinguishing her from martyrs and interpreting her survival as a defeat.
In the process, Cellier's detractors demonstrate more familiarity
with the conventions of martyrology than she does, writing what
amount to anti-martyrologies.

The pillory, a roughly cruciform 'wooden engine', served as
the focal point in parodic accounts of Cellier's 'martyrdom' (see
Figs. 9.2–9.3). Intended to display and humiliate, more than to
injure, the pillory was designed as a site of shame rather than an
instrument of torture. On the pillory, the offender's head and hands
were thrust through openings between two adjustable boards
placed atop a pillar. Thereby exposed, the offender could not move,
and could not dodge the objects and abuse that might be hurled at
him or her. According to Tim Harris, 'the use of the pillory as a form
of punishment effectively left execution of the sentence to the
crowd', which might be lenient – even protecting the offender – or
brutal, as they were to Cellier on her first appearance.[31] While the
concession that Cellier could wield a racket to shield herself on
subsequent occasions protected life and limb, it also provided even
more fodder for those who wished to mock her. Shielded physically, she was more exposed in print. Freed from viewing her as a
victim, her detractors, who were far more numerous and vociferous
than her defenders, ridicule her misplaced sense of importance, her
grandeur amidst '*rotten Eggs* and *Turnip-tops*,' her sense that she
was somehow above taking her lumps.[32]

Representations of Cellier on the pillory appropriated and parodied the rich Catholic iconography for representing the suffering
female body, inverting the conventions of martyrologies by belit-
tling her suffering – 'really she receiv'd no hurt from the Multitude,
yet she pretended herself *half-Martyr'd*' – or emphasizing how hard
she struggled to stay off the pillory.[33] The construction of Cellier as
martyr or 'she-saint' is invoked only in satires of her libel punishment. No Catholic texts constructing Cellier as a martyr survive,
although, in post-Reformation England, the production and consumption of saints' and martyrs' lives, in print and in manuscript,
was thriving, if clandestine. Catholic martyrologies contested Foxe's
aggressively Protestant version of the history of Christian martyrdom; where Foxe built up to the Marian martyrs, they culminated
in the Elizabethan and Jacobean executions of Jesuits, such as
Campion and Garnet, and in the Popish Plot casualties.[34] Like legal

prosecutions, Catholic martyrologies focused on priests, and there-fore tended to exclude women (except those few convicted of harboring priests); of 314 Catholic martyrs between 1535 and 1680, only four appear to have been women, none of whom died during the Stuart era (1604–80).[35] These female martyrs were revered, but accounts of their martyrdoms circulated orally and in manuscript, rather than in print. For example, Fr. John Mush's *Life* of Margaret Clitherow, who was pressed to death in York in 1587 because she refused to plead to the charge of harbouring priests, survives in multiple manuscript versions, but was not published in complete form until the nineteenth century.

Women figured more importantly, however, in the saint's life, which was a feminized genre; in the late sixteenth and early seven-teenth centuries, 'nearly half the printed lives were about women saints and the majority of dedications were addressed to women'.[36] Women also played important roles as translators (making texts written on the Continent more accessible to English readers, espe-cially other women with more limited language skills), copyists (aiding the manuscript transmission of saints' lives) and consumers, especially in convents abroad. Yet the role of martyr or saint is one Cellier's detractors mockingly thrust upon her, rather than one she assumes herself.

A look at one prototype of the genre suggests why Cellier would eschew it, as well as how it served the turn of her detractors. The most popular collection of saints' lives, John Heigham's translation of Alfonso Villegas's *Lives of Saints*, which went through many edi-tions, offers some sense of the conventions that Cellier's detractors parodied. In Villegas's chronicle, the majority of female saints are martyred; these saints are usually nobly born, beautiful virgins; they lose copious amounts of blood, and even body parts, without dying; they can withstand extraordinary torments; they transcend all efforts to shame or humiliate them; they long for death but are extremely difficult to kill. According to Villegas, saints 'were stead-fast and unapalled in daungers; never ama[z]ed nor changed with the force of fortune: never moved with hatred, nor pricked forth with anger, nor wonne by fondnesse of affection.'[37]

Various satires, which reveal an intimate familiarity with these conventions, depict Cellier as the opposite of a virgin martyr. The most sustained instance of the parodic anti-martyrology, the 'adventure of *The Bloody Bladder*: A Tragi-Comical Farce, Acted with Much Applause at Newgate by … Madam Cellier', presented by

Miles Prance, one of the prisoners whom Cellier claimed had been tortured, demonstrates how deftly satirists inverted the conventions of hagiography and martyrology. Although Antonia Fraser accepts Prance's scurrilous attack as an accurate description, I read it as evidence not necessarily of Cellier's conduct, but of how her gender and religion combined to make her a particularly vulnerable target of satire.[38]

While the gory detail in stories of martyred saints focuses on the ingenious torments they can survive without abjuring, the detail in Prance's 'tragi-comical farce' describes the shams Cellier supposedly employed to avoid standing in the pillory. First she took a purge, but a day too soon, as a result of which she 'feigned to be monstrous sick and discharged my whole Artillery at both ends, with such fury, that what for fume and noise, none durst approach me'.[39] Then she declared herself with child, which 'appear'd very improbable in a person of her *reverend years* [described later as '50-odd'], and one Midwife being sent to her retorn'd a *Non Inventus* on her Belly'. But the ruse does not end with this confrontation between a popish midwife and a credible one. When Cellier was about to be transported to the pillory she claimed to be in labor. Captain Richardson, her keeper in Newgate whom she had accused of torturing other prisoners, 'ordered 3 or 4 honest Women to go up and dress her, charging them to handle her with all *tenderness*, and let the Maid [Cellier's own attendant] be by, for he knew she would be ready enough to swear he had *Rackt and Tortur'd her*'.[40] Cellier's vociferous and seasoned performance of labor creates such a disturbance that it convinces those who were, according to Prance, already disposed to believe. 'By this time some of her female popish Gang were got about her, and all agreed, that she was *just on point of delivery*' (E2). 'She bellow'd out so hideously that one of the Popish Priests was over-heard to say *she over-acts it*, and some of the spectators thought her possest' (E2). When, at last, 'an able Physician and several discreet Women' search Cellier, they discover a blood-filled bladder. She 'had used her skill in creating the necessary *Symptomes*, and preparing certain *Clots* of it, and put them into her Body, (some of which sort design'd for a fresh supply, were also found elsewhere about her).' She '*mocks* God and *abuses* the World with counterfeiting Childbirth-pains, and this by such *immodest Practises* as are a *reproach* to *Nature*, and a *shame* to all her *Sex*' (E2ᵛ). In Prance's view, if midwifery has taught Cellier anything, it is only how to deceive not, as she had bragged in *Malice Defeated*, how to 'deliver' herself. Cellier has the skill to ape the symptoms of labor, but not so much skill that she cannot be found out and exposed by an 'able Physician' and 'discreet women'. In Prance's text, she is finally undone by the very association with the female body that she tries to use to escape the pillory.

Thus Prance's 'adventure of *The Bloody Bladder*' and other anti-martyrologies of Cellier depict her as the exact opposite of the virgin martyrs who populate saints' lives. She is common, old, homely and promiscuous; she is undesirable, but she makes claims to her own lust and her ability to provoke lust in others; the blood she loses is not even her own, but instead part of a ruse to avoid suffering; she complains bitterly about minor discomfort and scrambles to avoid her just punishment; she brings shame on herself through her disgusting and undignified attempts to avoid the pillory; she does not want to die. She is cowardly, inconstant and emotional. Her lack of bodily integrity – bleeding, bellowing, claiming to be pregnant – manifests her lack of spiritual integrity, just as the impenetrable virgin martyrs, whose bodies miraculously heal from attempts to rend them asunder, embody spiritual integrity. Far from resolutely silent, Cellier farts, belches and bellows.[41] In the various satires of Cellier's conduct on the pillory, she is criticized for making too much of her own suffering, for trying to avoid it, for not wanting to die and for not dying. Deflating her pretensions to either heroic endurance or heroic action, to use Mary Beth Rose's helpful terms, such attacks cast Cellier into a narrative she does not choose for herself, only to insist indignantly that she does not belong there.[42]

If martyrology, 'an intensely corporeal genre', as Elizabeth Hanson has argued, depicts spiritual agency which operates against or in spite of the suffering body, Prance's text suggests that Cellier's agency is wholly and degradingly corporeal.[43] On the one hand, Cellier's shameful performance of bodily uncontrol (vomiting, shitting and bleeding) associates her with the feminized body Gail Paster describes, whose emissions and porous boundaries are not under voluntary control.[44] This is the body that virgin martyrs transcend and whose meanings Catholic images (the sacred heart, the lactating virgin, the bleeding Christ) transform into positive icons of patient suffering and submission to forces beyond one's control. Yet Cellier's detractors censure her as much for her acts of will – taking the purge, devising the bloody bladder scheme – as for the resulting disorder and mess. It is that she tries to vomit, defecate, and bleed on cue that is so objectionable. She may be an immodest schemer, but she is a failed one, her disorderly body defeating her pretensions to skill. Her body – obviously past pregnancy, too quick to respond to the ill-timed purge – outwits her attempts at counterfeiting, restoring the order by which women's bodily disorders are involuntary and by which some fluids and some orifices are more redemptive or sacralizable than others. In thus marking her body as carnivalesque, rather than saintly or heroic, uncontrol diminishes the threat Cellier poses.

How this works will be clearer if we consider Cellier in the context of the available traditions for depicting the Catholic female body. Anti-Catholic polemic dwells on women's lack of bodily closure and control in order to discredit them. For example, Pope Joan and Joan of Arc are both exposed by their pregnancies; like Cellier, 'La Pucelle' is compromised by her attempt to use pregnancy to avoid martyrdom. Against this tradition, counter-Reformation hagiography and martyrology emphasize holy women's extraordinary control over their bodies, and fervent desire for death. Although saints' lives describe in gruesome detail the horrible mutilations and tortures inflicted on virgin saints, they observe a bodily decorum. The virgin martyrs' bodies are fountains of blood, yet they are not sexually penetrable and, apparently, excrete only from their wounds not from their orifices. In many ways, Margaret Clitherow seems more like Cellier than like the virgin martyrs; she is a married mother, who suffers imprisonment and execution in York in recent memory. However, by repeatedly telling readers that Clitherow refused to avoid or defer martyrdom by pleading her belly, *The Life of Margaret Clitherow* places her in the virgin martyr tradition, and preserves her from the implication that she belongs with the fecund Joans. By John Mush's account, Clitherow would have a good case: she is thirty, lending such a claim credibility, four women who search her pronounce her with child, and she herself confesses that she is inclined to believe that she is pregnant, although she cannot be sure, 'having been deceived heretofore in this'.[45] Since she is married, such a plea would not in any way incriminate her. Her friends and family, even her judges, beseech her. Yet she refuses. Martyrs, of course, always prefer death to the alternatives. But the gendered theological and narratological traditions shaping depictions of Pope Joan, Joan of Arc, virgin martyrs and Margaret Clitherow help to explain why Prance focuses his abusive satire on Cellier's attempt to avoid the pillory by pleading her belly. Seeking to avoid suffering and death, performing bodily uncontrol and confessing sexual activity (even if the confession is not believed) all exclude Cellier from that elite group of holy (and dead) Catholic women. These alleged activities thereby ally her with the discredited women who hold center stage in anti-Catholic discourses: the two Joans. Bodily uncontrol, then, does not really make Cellier a disorderly figure; instead, it puts her in her place.

The stones cast at Cellier in the pillory become crucial both to the purported attempts to construct her as a 'she-Saint' – attempts registered, as I have said, only as they are countered by her detractors – and to polemical efforts to discredit Cellier as a candidate for sainthood or martyrdom.[46] According to some witnesses, Cellier pocketed stones pitched at her on the pillory.[47] She is later accused of storing them up as potential relics: 'these hard Stones I carry home... / Which shallest soon be sent to *Rome*, / There to be Sanctify'd'; 'these Stones and Dirt ought to be Relicks high.'[48] In one satire presented as Cellier's own 'Lamentation', she describes her 'hopes of Saint *Celier* at last: Ile now begin to be in Love with a Pillory, and strive to merit it as oft as I can, and every Stone they throw I'le labour to preserve as Monuments of my Sufferings, and secure them for Rellicks to Posterity.'[49] The disdain both for the Catholic reverence for relics and for Cellier's claims to sanctity is also served by a crude sexual joke, since 'stones' is a slang term for testicles. Cellier cannot resist collecting these stones because she's always had a weakness for them: 'for stones I veneration had /... Those given by many a Lusty Lad.'[50] Whether as relics of her own martyrdom, or as souvenirs of her promiscuity, the stones are viewed as embarrassingly literal and corporeal. Miring Cellier in her body and anchoring her to the earth, the stones she puts in her pockets contradict any claims that she might make for her faith or purity.

Satires of the supposed sanctification of Cellier drew on a constellation of objections to Catholicism more generally, in which the theological cannot be disentangled from the political. First, the Catholic reverence for relics – otherwise ordinary, even distasteful objects (such as body parts), through which once-living persons continued to perform good works in the world – was widely disdained as a particularly superstitious, idolatrous practice. Up to death, Catholic and Protestant martyrs were much alike. After death, Catholic saints distinguished themselves from the merely holy or venerable through their ability to effect miracles and intercede in the world of the living, an ability focused in the concrete, yet wonder-working, relic. As Protestantism labored to achieve what Lyndal Roper has called a 'desomatization of the spiritual',[51] its difference from Catholicism was often described in terms of the latter's inability to distinguish the material from the spiritual, the corporeal, mortal and human from the divine. Just as the deft inversion of martyrology in attacks on Cellier reveals how complexly intertwined were the Catholic and Protestant imaginaries in this period, so, in a culture in which corpses' wounds opened to accuse murders, making a wax image was illegal, and iconoclasts found images so powerful that they had to destroy them, Protestants strenuously repudiated the belief in the efficacy of objects because it still shaped many of their own practices. The attribution of magical properties to dead bodies, especially the bodies of executed criminals, was not restricted to Catholics. Because the criminal and the saintly were never clearly distinguished in Christian tradition, many viewed a criminal's body as 'a collection of magical talismans, the pieces invested with supernatural power akin to the healing potential which relics contained'.[52] Protestantism could distance itself from its own reverence for the material by suggesting that Catholics were indiscrimate in their approach to objects, turning anything remotely associated with the Catholic cause into a relic. In the almost complete absence of material evidence of Catholic conspiracy at this time, polemicists had a hard time naming the evidence of crime and punishment that Catholics could transubstantiate into relics. The Meal Tub Plot was a more fruitful field than the Popish Plot: one satire claims that the pope has ordered the Franciscans to 'preserve the *Meal-Tub*, in which lay hid the Design of the holy Cause, among their chiefest Reliques'.[53] And, of course, there were those stones.

The anti-martyrologies of Cellier also drew on widespread contempt for Catholics' 'whole design of Canonizing those men for Saints, whom the Justice of the Nation hath Condemned for Traytors'.[54] In this process of transforming criminals into saints, Catholics published the last speeches of those condemned in relation to the Popish Plot, all of whom protested their innocence, and revalued objects associated with them.[55] Polemicists castigate this process as an affront to the English nation and to English law, as well as laughable proof that Catholics cannot tell a saint from a traitor, a nail paring or portrait from a man, a man from God. Yet the problem was that Catholics were not indiscriminate in electing saints or collecting relics, but rather revered as martyrs those very persons whom the state had marked and eliminated as traitors. They viewed a place of punishment as a site for pilgrimage. Reducing this complex cultural struggle to some nail parings, polemicts could minimize what was feared as dangerous. Similarly, in the case of Elizabeth Cellier – female, lay, alive – polemicists found a particularly fruitful occasion for ridiculing the whole project of transforming criminals into saints.

If the parodies of 'Saint Cellier' drew their terms from Catholic traditions, forcing Cellier into forms which ill-suited her, and simultaneously parodying both those narrative conventions and her failure to conform to them, then parodies of Cellier as a 'heroina' drew their terms from *Malice Defeated* itself. These attacks actually build on more observant readings of *Malice Defeated*, if equally great hostility and misogyny. For, while Cellier never depicts herself as a saint, she does borrow some elements from chivalric romance in telling her story.

The basic outlines of the romance, as found in the oft-told stories of English knights errant such as St George and Guy of Warwick, are simple: a knight slays dragons, conquers Giants, and frees 'tender Ladies from their harmes'.[56] As Guy of Warwick explains in Samuel Rowlands's version of the story, first published in 1609, but reprinted at least nine times by 1680, 'Men easily may revenge the deeds men doe, / But poore weak women have no strength thereto.'[57] In a dedication 'To the Honourable Ladies of England', Rowlands suggests that this is one of the ways that romances are rooted in the past: 'Ladies in elder times your sex did need / Knighthoods true valour to defend your rights.'[58] Through this association with a safely remote, fairytale past, the romance enables Cellier, like those women writers of romance whom Ballaster discusses, to justify her presence in the public sphere by 'dehistoricizing and mythologizing' it.[59]

Justifying her refusal to pay the jury that acquits her of treason the customary guinea per man, Cellier expresses her confidence that they 'will not forfeit your Spurs by oppressing the Distressed She, Your selves and the Laws have preserv'd from a raging Dragon' (*MD* N2ᵛ). While Cellier never explains exactly who plays the dragon in this scenario, she does insist that to pay the jury would be to disqualify them from knighthood ('forfeit [their] spurs'). Furthermore, if Cellier could pay them, she would not be as 'distressed' as she claims throughout the trial. But, conversely, she would also have to defer more to her champions than she seems to want to in *Malice Defeated*. Given her innocence, and her skill in demonstrating it, how could they have done otherwise than acquit her? Why should she pay them, when she did the work? As she concludes her text, she expresses her hope that 'the judicious Reader will pardon what is either forgot, or not well express'd, in consideration that I was forc'd to defend my life, both against the Knights and the Dragon, for in this unequal Combate there was no St. *George* to defend me against him' but rather an array of titled gentlemen in cahoots with the dragon. The 'knights' before whom she stood accused should 'blush at the weakness of their Combatant' (*MD* N2ᵛ). Cellier does not depict herself as a fierce female warrior, but nor does she depict herself as a martyr. She emphasizes her distress, dependency and gratitude to explain why she will not sacrifice her fragile finances to a custom; she simpers about her weakness as a combatant just after she has pointed out that she has acted as her own St George, stepping in for England's absentee patron saint, with whom Charles I had been associated, to save herself. At various points in *Malice Defeated*, Cellier appeals to the jury, the law and her readers (but never to God) to 'deliver' her, but she also points out that, in the end, she has had to rely on herself, combining the roles of the damsel in distress and rescuer. While her double jeopardy as a Catholic woman heightened Cellier's risk in various ways, at this moment the conjunction between two distinct roles creates a possibility for narrative agency. It's not just that Cellier regenders the knight errant feminine, creating the 'lady errant', as her detractors claim, but that she combines in one the sufferer and the rescuer. Only by monopolizing multiple narrative roles can the midwife tell the story of how she delivered herself. By combining the chivalric romance with the trial account, Cellier creates a hybrid role – the heroine/defendant/attorney – which enables the female protagonist to be simultaneously active and innocent, heroic and alive. This was as great a challenge in secular fictions as it was in sacred ones.

Several critics have discussed the centrality of the 'pathetic female protagonist' in late seventeenth- and early eighteenth-century genres, such as devotional tracts, prose fictions and she-tragedies. The suffering female protagonist had a long tradition; as I have shown, in representations of virgin saints, virtue equals suffering, and the more one suffers the more, paradoxically, one triumphs. Surprisingly, this narrative pattern in pre- and counter-Reformation texts was not doomed by its association with Catholicism, but, rather, became increasingly prominent and pervasive. According to Laura Brown, for instance, defenseless, victimized, masochistic figures in the drama and the novel are 'discursively passive' but also 'structurally threatening'.[60] Mary Beth Rose has demonstrated that texts as diverse as conduct books, sermons, epics, novels and plays in seventeenth-century England explore the 'heroism of endurance'.[61] While the value placed on the heroism of endurance made it possible to include women and a much broader range of men in the category 'hero', it did not open up a place for someone like Elizabeth Cellier. Describing how she ends her suffering, and building towards escape and survival rather than defeat and death, Elizabeth Cellier's *Malice Defeated* departs from these genres in which, according to John Richetti, 'utter helplessness' is 'required for heroic status', especially for women.[62] To depict her competent, energetic and successful strategies for avoiding the pyre, Cellier adapts the vocabulary and roles of chivalric romance to depict female agency positively.

Romance carried some risks, however, in that it was easy for Cellier's detractors to turn the form against her. By the mid-seventeenth century, in the wake of Cervantes' *Don Quixote*, it was hard to distinguish earnest representatives of the romance from parodies.[63] Before she was threatened with standing at the pillory herself, Cellier ridiculed her accuser and former employee, Thomas Dangerfield, for his stint 'mounted upon the Wooden Engine': he 'peep'd through it like *Don Quicksot* through his Helmet, when he was mounted upon *Rosinant*, and going to encounter with the *Windmil'* (*MD* D2).[64] There is something ludicrous, she suggests, in attempting to view one's self as a hero when immobilized and exposed on the pillory. Cellier describes the pillory as simultaneously Dangerfield's paralyzed steed and, like Don Quixote's windmill, a wooden and indefatigable enemy against whom opposition is fruitless and silly.

After she makes her own visits to the pillory, a satire presented as 'Maddam Celliers Answer to the Popes Letter' turns Cellier's wit against her, mounting her, like Dangerfield, on a stationary and humiliating steed, which is simultaneously her unconquerable opponent. Much is made of the fact that Cellier was allowed to face her final two encounters with the rowdy crowd wearing armor of sorts, a 'wooden Buckler and Fence of trusty Bull-hide'. 'This *She-Donna Quixot* encounters with many *Wind-mills*, and is armed

Cap-a-Pe with *Impudence* and *Lying* ... she is armed with a *Jesuits Launce* and a *Sword for the Cause*, which she furiously brandishes', especially at Dangerfield. The rest of this description simultaneously heroizes and ridicules Cellier, exaggerating her torments – she is battered with 1000 lb millstones and 100 lb iron globes – and her panache in resistance – she catches cannon balls 'like Sugar-plums ... between my Teeth'.[65] Rather than dwell on her stratagems for avoiding the pillory, this satire depicts Cellier as a fierce virago whose skills are entertainingly gladiatorial: 'strenuously (as *Romes* Championess) Like *Jezebel* I marched along to the War Charriot that they had prepared to transport me to the Theater wherein I was to Act my part, in view of all the gaping Hereticks.'[66] She is still 'standing at the stake for all' against her will, but now she is chained to it like a bear, raging against those who amuse themselves by baiting her. Like the 'adventure of the bloody bladder', this text confers power, skill and agency on Cellier, yet depicts a woman's defense of herself as inevitably grotesque. An active rather than passive female heroism can easily be caricatured; the slide from 'heroina' to Gargantua is a short one.

Romance was also a risky choice for Cellier's self-justifying narrative because the form, 'perceived as catering to a growing and commercially important female audience' was 'denigrated as a "women's genre".'[67] For the most part, men wrote romances, and reserved all the juiciest parts for themselves. As Anthony Fletcher points out, while works like *Guy of Warwick* offered guidelines for becoming a man, and espousing a masculine form of heroism, 'there was no comparable literature for girls who were learning to become women'.[68] Yet women did read romances, as frequent attacks on their doing so reveal. These attacks articulate the fear that female readers might learn a great deal about becoming women from *Guy of Warwick* and other romances, and that much of what they learned might work against their industriousness, chastity, and contentment at home. Furthermore, women might not just identify with the 'poor weak woman' the hero rescues, avenges, marries, abandons. They might, instead, identify with the wandering and adventurous hero; or they might resist, supplement, or adapt the narrative.[69] Certainly, *Malice Defeated* suggests that a female subject might insert herself into a romance narrative in highly creative and unpredictable ways.

Objections to women's relation to romance can be charted through dismissive or censorious references to the 'lady errant', a term which, as Hero Chalmers says, was often used 'for the parody of improper feminine pretensions'.[70] While romances were sometimes depicted as compensations for women's exclusion from public life (harmless, if indolent, distractions), these compensatory fantasies could also be depicted as encouraging women to leave their closets for a life of adventure, thereby making themselves even more ridiculous. For instance, in his widely quoted character sketch of a chambermaid, Overbury describes her as reading '*Greenes workes* over and over, but is so carried away with the *Myrrour of Knighthood*, she is many times resolv'd to run out of her selfe, and become a Ladie Errant'.[71] To identify with the lady errant is to long to 'run out of' one's self and one's life toward social mobility, sexual fulfilment, and adventure.

Numerous scholars have shown that the vocal, visible participation of women in public life during the religious and political upheavals of the mid-seventeenth century contributed to an increasing sense that the domestic should be kept separate from national, political life, and that women should stay out of the public sphere.[72] To cast scandal on women's public appearances, satires often construed them as signs of sexual disorder. This was hardly a new tactic. The well-codified caricature of the shrew, for instance, which pops up in countless jokes, stories, plays and ballads throughout the early modern period, depicted her not only as garrulous, but as aggressive and promiscuous. Her open mouth hinted at open genitals; both revealed that she was not under a man's governance.

Cellier's detractors invariably disparage her by claiming that she is motivated only by an unseemly and laughable sexual desire, despite the fact that Cellier's quest as described in *Malice Defeated* is not in the least amatory or erotic.[73] The most sustained send-up of Cellier as 'lady errant' is *Modesty Triumphing Over Impudence. Or, Some Notes Upon a Late Romance Published by Elizabeth Cellier, Midwife and Lady Errant.* The author claims that since 'our *Lady Errant* is resolved to keep up the Antick Mode of *Romances*', he will also, and proceeds to depict an encounter between 'our *Dido* and *Aeneas*' (that is, Cellier and Dangerfield) in which 'she huffs with many rants and resolutions, stollen out of Romances and Playes'.[74] In this 'romance', Cellier resembles Lady Wishfort, an older woman made ridiculous by desire. Obviously, the male knights in romances also counted sexual exploits among their adventures. Yet, unsurprisingly, women are more compromised by their sexual adventures than are men.

Thus, the lady errant was another manifestation of the unruly woman, distinguished by her engagement in public life. Like Cellier, women petitioners during the civil war were called 'brave Virago's' and 'Ladyes-errants' largely because they refused to stay home and stay out of the political process.[75] Like these other uses of the term 'lady errant', satires on Cellier censure her for trying to 'run out of' the self which is held accountable for libel, and depict female self-assertion as silly and racy. They also often suggest that a lady errant is not only one who wanders or travels, but one who strays, errs, makes mistakes, in part because, for a woman, to move out of acceptable roles and relationships, to leave home, is itself to transgress.[76]

Yet another risk in Cellier's borrowing from romance to tell a story she insists is true is that 'romance,' like 'fiction', was commonly used to mean a lie or an exaggeration. Cellier herself uses the word this way when she explains in *Malice Defeated* that: 'I durst not trust my self with such a Doughty Knight as Sir William [Waller] was, lest he shuld make Romances of me, as he had done of others' (*MD* G1). In its association with lying, the romance stands in the same double jeopardy that plagues Cellier, thus intensifying its riskiness for her. Fictionality and artful duplicity were often equated with femininity. In addition, Catholics were widely presumed to be adroit and shameless liars. *Mr. Prance's Answer To Mrs. Cellier's Libel* warns readers: '*Cellier* and her *Inspirers*, wanted not *Presidents* for their *Fiction*, their *Party* having so long *inur'd* themselves to Forging Untruths, that now they think they may lawfully *Lie* by *Prescription*.'[77] In the week of Cellier's sentencing, Henry Care claims that '"That's a Cellier Sir,"' was 'a modern and most proper Phrase to signifie *any Egregious Lye*.'[78] Because of the association of Catholicism and femininity with lying, even in the novel, the 'new', more capacious form that supposedly emerged from the generic dissatisfaction and searching in which texts like *Malice Defeated* participated, a female 'popish' narrator would have had a hard time asserting herself as a reliable one.

Thus, used in reference to Catholics, the word 'romance' took on all the resonances of 'Rome'. Owing their first allegiance to Rome, Catholics would 'make romances' rather than face the truth of Protestantism or of their own treason. In Defoe's *New Family Instructor* (1720), the Father provides what McKeon calls 'a false but suggestive' etymology for 'romance'. In the absence of real miracles, priests had to fabricate stories; ultimately, any lie came to be known as a *'Roman Legend'*. 'Hence, I derive the Word Romance, *(viz.)* from the Practice of the *Romanists,* in imposing Lyes and Fables upon the World; and I believe ... that Popery is a *Romantick Religion.'*[79] Strengthening the connection between romances and romanists, most chapbook romances were set in a pre-Reformation world, and are difficult to distinguish from saints' lives.[80] Like Catholics, often accused of 'backwardness in religion', the romance nostalgically imagined a lost world, even if it did not try to restore it. When Cellier, the 'Popish Romancer',[81] combines the pretensions to fact of the trial account with the presumed fantasy of the romance, when she tells the story of 'now' in the form and conventions of 'once upon a time', she compromises her already wounded credibility.[82]

Yet, if the Meal Tub Plot is a fantasy, whose fantasy is it? Since, by 1680, it had become clear that both Whigs and Tories could and did suborn witnesses, the 'Meal Tub Plot' provided particularly shaky ground for contesting Catholics' willingness to believe 'Roman Legends' and to tell lies, since it was itself dependent on improbable narratives and witnessings from the grave. What proof was there that Whigs could tell the difference between representation and reality? That there was such a difference? Many scholars have argued that the seventeenth century was a period in which the division between fact and fiction was uncertain, yet distinctions were starting to be made, especially in legal and narrative terms.[83] By combining the trial narrative, the romance and autobiography in the remarkable way that it does, *Malice Defeated* participates in the interrogation of standards of evidence which emerged from the Popish Plot trials. While Cellier's references to romance made it even easier to dismiss her and the veracity of her text, they also seem to have provoked anger and anxiety by forcing attention to the crucial roles of narratives as evidence and to the interconnection of politics and 'romance' at this moment.

As a result, many responses to *Malice Defeated* and to Cellier's public appearances more generally attempted to redraw a line between fact and fiction, and to fix Cellier in place (preferably on the pillory or in prison). In various satires, Newgate prison becomes an 'inchanted castle': 'the *distressed Damosel* was forced to take up her Lodging for that Night in the *Inchanted Castle* of *Newgate'*.[84] Since Cellier insists that Captain Richardson, the keeper of Newgate, tortures Catholic prisoners, she's warned not to venture 'within his *Inchanted Castle* again, lest you want an *Knight Errant* to release you, for he is a *Fell Gyant* as you have made him'.[85]

Extending the vocabulary of romance from the personnel to the location of Cellier's trials, these satirists depend on readers to recognize that crime and romance are incommensurate. Newgate is not an enchanted castle from which a knight can spring Cellier, but a prison into which she is committed because she has been indicted for libel. Captain Richardson is not a 'Fell Gyant', despite her outrageous and incredible charges; he is a responsible government official, and one to whom she may well be subject. These writers concede that Cellier is 'distressed', but even if she needs a knight errant, she will neither find one nor be able to become one. Written after Cellier's conviction for libel, and in response to her now criminalized text and qualified legal victory, such vituperations expose the limits of Cellier's legal and authorial competence, and the intransigence of the 'real', which is understood in terms of punishment and suffering. However imaginative she may be, she cannot turn Newgate into an enchanted castle, attract a knight's protection, or effect her own escape. If she wants to think she's in a romance, they will humor her. But her skills as a litigant and a storyteller cannot really transport her from the criminal biography in which her detractors think she belongs, with its grim and intractable conclusions, into a romance. She may think of herself as a lady errant, but the law will keep her in her place – at the pillory, in prison.

The many attacks on Cellier suggest that it is the aging, female body, with its 'fume and noise', which forms such as hagiography and romance cannot accommodate without collapsing into satire. They also express such obsessive interest in her body that they almost seem to lose track of their political project; misogyny so facilitates the attack that it almost pushes it out of control. Tory and Whig propaganda in this period were equally scurrilous, scatalogical, even pornographic; men's bodies and their sexual conduct might also become targets.[86] But the long-standing alliance between Catholicism and depictions of the female body, and between misogyny and anti-Catholicism, made a woman like Cellier an especially easy target of attack, and almost impossible to defend. The apparent hostility of the crowd who threw things at her suggests how difficult a figure Cellier was to champion. On the one hand, Catholic iconographic traditions provided her attackers with precedents for displaying the suffering female body in vivid terms, thereby turning her 'own' traditions against her; on the other hand, as Huston Diehl has argued, iconoclasm and anti-Catholicism both mobilized misogyny to justify and animate attacks on feminized images.[87] As a result, it was difficult for English Catholics to reclaim the depiction of the female body in this political context. Perhaps this is why there were virtually no published defenses of Cellier after her visits to the pillory, and why she apparently insisted in both her trials that she stood 'singly and alone'. As I have argued, this sense that she can depend only on herself infuses Cellier's depiction of herself as a romantic figure; through romance, Cellier can recast abandonment as independence. Cellier's claim that she stands 'singly and alone' can also be read as an admission that she is indefensible, that she has become, by the time of the libel trial, impossible to represent in positive terms. This was even more true after her visits to the pillory and in response to attacks such as Prance's 'adventure of the bloody bladder'. She was too female, too staunchly Catholic, too sloppily embodied. To engage in representing her was to wade into a mess, both literally (the bloody bladder, the stones, etc.) and generically. What middle ground might Catholic apologists have found between the hagiographic idealization of suffering and death and the ridicule which attends non-lethal punishments for women, such as the pillory, the cucking stool or bridling? Between the 'holy joy' martyrs experienced in the divine comedy of their executions and the ribald 'tragi-comic farce' of the bloody bladder?[88] Even if there had been forms available for defending someone like Cellier, it is not clear that there was a Catholic propaganda machine that could counter the Whig one at this moment. By this time, Tory propagandists 'had not only sought to disassociate themselves from the catholic cause, but had even defined their position in anti-catholic terms'.[89] What Catholic pamphlets there were 'attacked the details of the informers' evidence and pointed out the general implausibility of the Plot', but were not widely distributed and had little chance of convincing the unconverted.[90] As a result, the surviving defenses of Cellier are either retrospective or unpublished. In his *History of the English Persecution of Catholics and the Presbyterian Plot*, John Warner argues that Cellier 'deserved a happier fate, whether we consider her mental abilities, or her blameless morals, or the courage of mind with which she rose above every danger, or her zeal in defending the Royal Authority, which was the sole cause of her coming into danger and stirring up the hornets' nest, or finally her constancy in the Faith which she embraced as an adult.'[91] In his *Records of the English Province of the Society of Jesus*, Henry Foley discusses a manuscript entitled 'A true relation of some judgments of God against those who accused the priests and other Catholics after the pretended plot in England', which reported that

> nearly all those who had a hand in her accusation and unjust sentence were manifestly chastised by God. Two of them afterwards went mad. Many of those who cast stones at her in the pillory were wounded by their own companions. Another youth who was very active at this work, instantly fell sick, and, retiring to a stable close by, remained there for some days unknown, and then being carried to his parents' house, died there within three days, unable to pronounce any other words than '*Sellier, Sellier*'.[92]

The belief in such divine retribution, even if it did circulate among Catholics as a cheering rumor, has barely made it into the historical record. At one point in the treason trial in *Malice Defeated*, Cellier says to the Lord Chancellor: 'I know I am the talk of the Town; but what do the Judicious say of me, for it is that I value, and not the prate of the Rabble' (*MD* G^v). Unfortunately, those whom Cellier might have regarded as judicious do not seem to have published. Against the many attacks on Cellier, little was said in print in her defense. Nor does *Malice Defeated* set the record straight. In the case of a notorious woman with a missing past, what constitutes truth? Yet, by surviving the hangman's burning, this defense of Cellier does prevent her detractors from having the last word. Furthermore, it suggests that the town talk was more contentious than a Protestant-biased print record would lead us to believe.

The printing press perpetuates the conflicts over Cellier's innocence, extending beyond the courtroom and scaffold, even beyond the lifespans of the key players. In hindsight, the press also creates these conflicts; it first makes Cellier a 'wretched subject' of legal scrutiny and polemical attack; it then makes her available for historical study. The target of a barrage of sticks and stones, as well as of insulting names and scurrilous attacks, Cellier was hardly unscathed by her brushes with notoriety; in her case, representation seems to have had bruising material consequences. But any closure less decisive than death complicates the map of early modern options for representing women and of the conditions under which these representations were recorded, published, or read.

Cellier wisely feared the tyranny and intractability of literary forms and the unacceptable endings they might impose on her story and her life – 'for Tragedies whether real or fictious [*sic*], seldom end before the Women die' (*MD* H2ᵛ) – but her life does not seem to have bowed to any of the genres thrust upon her, in large part through accidents of history and dogged longevity. Unable to pay the huge fine which was levied against her, Cellier spent about two years in prison; Charles II may then have remitted her fine in response to her petition.[93] Confidence in Titus Oates and other key witnesses for the prosecution in the Popish Plot rapidly waned. With the accession of James II in 1685, Catholics briefly regained political favour; the key witnesses against the supposed Popish Plot conspirators were convicted of perjury and publicly punished. Like the infamous Titus Oates, Dangerfield, Cellier's nemesis, was tried and convicted of perjury, lashed and set on the pillory. In a broad-side published later, Dangerfield confesses to her that the Meal Tub Plot was his invention, and that she suffered unjustly for it. When he asks in amazement: 'Hast thou outliv'd my Fury? Withstood all the Volleys of Turnips and rotten Eggs, and lives yet to be my Tormenter?' she confirms: 'I have outlived the Pillory, to see thee recant at the gallows.' The broadside ends with Dangerfield led off to Newgate, the disenchanted castle.[94] Thus the changed political climate conferred innocence on Cellier, just as it had previously conferred guilt. During the brief, but doomed, resurgence of Catholicism during James's reign, the King's corroboration trans-formed Cellier's version of events into the official story, 'published by authority'. Cellier also served as fertility counselor and midwife to James's wife, Mary of Modena; under her guidance, Mary con-ceived an heir. Simultaneously the triumph and defeat of Catholic hopes, this Catholic male heir became the excuse for deposing James and ushering in William and Mary. With the 'Glorious' Revolution, and the securing of a Protestant succession in 1688, Cellier disappears from the historical record – as does any real hope of a Catholic succession. Unlike most other criminalized women, then, the sad ends of whose stories we know, Elizabeth Cellier dis-appears from the historical record with her writings in the late 1680s about midwifery. Perhaps she went into exile with James II's court in 1688.[95] But no one knows. The indeterminacy of Cellier's story – its ability to evade tragic closure – depends on gaps in our historical knowledge, failures of evidence, as well as political turmoil and change.

Many discussions of Cellier remove her from her lived present, in (unwitting) accord with the tragic or comic visions of her life and her cause which she herself defined as inadequate. Most political historians mention Cellier only briefly, depicting her cause as the doomed attempt to turn back the process of political change and restore a lost past. But they do not endow Cellier with any of the tragic grandeur this might suggest; instead, they dismiss her as 'clumsy' and officious, because, I think, they follow her contemporary detractors in deploring her engagement in political action and her prominence in public discourse as voluntary and, in themselves, unseemly. Why did she insist on being such a 'busie' body? Tim Harris twice refers to her 'clumsy' attempt to deflect blame from the Catholics to the Presbyterians; John Miller also dismisses 'the clumsy efforts of Elizabeth Cellier, the Popish midwife, and her little Catholic coterie to blame the Plot on to the Presbyterians'.[96] J.P. Kenyon reproves her for 'very bad judgement' and J.C.H. Aveling describes her as 'ardent and indiscreet'.[97] Considering Cellier in the context of 'female' rather than Catholic 'involvement in affairs of state', Elaine Hobby, too, argues that Cellier represents a regression, espousing a regrettable 'retreat … to virtue'. Hobby's claim that Cellier tries to dissociate 'social bravery' from 'sexual boldness' does not necessarily lead to the conclusion that Cellier, in defending her own modesty, 'exhorts women to quiescence and withdrawal from political action'.[98] To make this claim, Hobby must misread and dismiss Cellier's justification of women's involvement in public life. I read Cellier's assertion that 'it is more our [women's] business than mens to fear, and consequently to prevent the Tumults and Troubles Factions tend to, since we by nature are hindered from sharing any part but the Frights and Disturbances of them' as a call to action, not to retreat.

In contrast, Antonia Fraser closes *The Weaker Vessel* with a discussion of Cellier as a vivid representative of the trend towards women's self-determination, a feisty heroine who is, for 'those that came after … a more engaging, even perhaps a more admirable character than the submissive Queen [Mary]'. In Fraser's view, Cellier suffered because she was ahead of her time: 'her own society' was not yet able to appreciate her feistiness and so 'threw the stones'.[99] This assessment assumes that the difference between Queen Mary and Elizabeth Cellier was simply that between submissiveness and self-assertion, draining it of political and religious content. It also assumes that Cellier's 'society' was consensual; this assumption ignores the factionalism of London in the late 1670s and early 1680s, and seems inadequate to the picture of angry spectators throwing stones and Cellier parrying them with her wooden racket. Finally, Fraser's rousing finish promises that Cellier's day has come. All these narratives of change, whether they position Cellier as reactionary or as progressive, remove her from her moment and its political struggles. Because she cannot fit into either the narrative of progress (about women) or that of defeat (about Catholics, or, in Hobby's book, about women), Cellier's story falls through the cracks.

Most of these approaches accord Cellier a level of autonomy that it is hard to believe she had, given her double jeopardy as a Catholic woman. Historians otherwise attentive to the conjectural nature of purported Catholic plots seem to assume that there was a Meal Tub Plot; this enables them to confer more agency on Cellier than she may have had, but, like the Old Bailey, only in order to censure her for it. Harris and Miller, for instance, suggest that Cellier played into the hands of Whig propagandists, giving them just what they needed to sustain anti-Catholic sentiment in the wake of the Popish Plot.[100] In these interpretations, then, we find Cellier freely choosing, with good or bad judgment, to perform actions, skillfully or clumsily, for which she may now be praised or blamed. I don't want to claim that Cellier was simply a pawn, as some of her detractors did; nor do I want to celebrate her heroic agency, representing her 'as a lawyer represents a client'.[101] Instead, I have sought here to explore how Elizabeth Cellier's gender and religious affiliation shaped her representation as a 'wretched subject' and contributed to the particular conditions under which she entered into evidence and therefore into history.

ACKNOWLEDGEMENTS

Dympna Callaghan, Mary Jean Corbett, Arthur Marotti, Kate McCullough, Susan Morgan, Melissa Mowry, Scott Shershow, and Wendy Wall all read drafts of this essay, and offered valuable suggestions. Participants in the Seminar on Women in Early Modern Europe at the Center for Literary and Cultural Study, Cambridge, and audiences at the MLA and the Folger Library, also made helpful comments.

NOTES

1. See J. P. Kenyon, *The Popish Plot* (London: Heinemann, 1972); John Miller, *Popery and Politics in England 1660–1688* (Cambridge: Cambridge University Press, 1973); and Jonathan Scott, 'England's Troubles: Exhuming the Popish Plot', in *The Politics of Religion in Restoration England*, ed. Tim Harris, Paul Seward and Mark Goldie (Oxford: Basil Blackwell, 1990), 107–32, esp. pp. 108–9, 111.

2. *The Tryall of Richard Langhorn Esq., Counsellor at Law* (London, 1679), F1; John Dormer, *The New Plot of the Papists. To Transform Traitors into Martyrs* (London, 1679), 14. According to J. P. Kenyon, 'Not a jot of written evidence was given in, so everything hung on the oath of the witnesses' (203).

3. Rachel Weil, '"If I did say so, I lyed": Elizabeth Cellier and the Construction of Credibility in the Popish Plot Crisis', in *Political Culture and Cultural Politics in Early Modern England: Essays Presented to David Underdown*, ed. Susan D. Amussen and Mark A. Kishlansky (Manchester: Manchester University Press, 1995), 189–209. Weil focuses on how all the texts by and about Cellier address the issue of credibility, especially that credibility a woman might achieve when participating in political culture. I am grateful to Weil for sharing her work with me in manuscript.

4. Scott, 121.

5. *Mr. Tho. Dangerfeilds [sic] Particular Narrative* (London, 1679), R1^v; Thomas Dangerfield, *The Grand Impostor Defeated* (London, 1682), B2^v–C1.

6. Anne Barbeau Gardiner, 'Elizabeth Cellier in 1688 on Envious Doctors and Heroic Midwives Ancient and Modern', *Eighteenth Century Life* 14.1 (1990): 24–34, esp. p. 25.

7. Dangerfield also claims that he was first hired by Cellier because he was 'vers'd a little in the Law' and therefore could help her with her husband's debts (*The Grand Impostor Defeated*, C1); he suggests that she wanted to employ him sexually.

8. This text will subsequently be cited parenthetically as *MD*.

9. In *Malice Defeated*, Cellier claims that, while she was in Newgate, the jailor's wife and sister copied her letters and 'thrust in' incriminating words and phrases (*MD* G1^{r-v}), and that Sir William Waller ransacked her house after she had been arrested, 'filling his own and his Footmans Pockets and Breeches with Papers of Private concern, which he never carry'd before the Councel, nor as yet restor'd, though some of them be of *Considerable value*' (*MD* E2^v). Even in prison, Cellier is accused of acting as a publisher, or textual midwife. The *Calendar of State Papers, Domestic* claims that convicted priests in Newgate wrote texts arguing for a Presbyterian plot, which were then 'midwived into the world by the assistance of their fellow prisoner, the infamous Mrs. Cellier and her printer, Thompson' (*Calendar of State Papers, Domestic Series*, ed. F. H. Blackburne Daniell [PRO 1932], rpt. Kraus Reprint Limited [1968], vol. 22 [1680–1], 23 July 1681, 370.)

10. For notice of Cellier's trials, and her sentencing, see *The London Gazette*, nos. 1520 (10–14 June 1680), 1546 (9–13 September 1680), and 1547 (13–16 September 1680). During the months of Cellier's notoriety, June–October 1680, only this paper of record, 'published by authority', was in print. Neither of the rival papers that might well have discussed Cellier's case, Benjamin Harris's *Protestant (Domestic) Intelligence* and Nathaniel Thompson's *True Domestick Intelligence*, was published in these months. The only opposition newspaper to appear in these months was the 'Popish Courant', the brief commentary on the week's events Henry Care appended to his *Weekly Pacquet of Advice from Rome*.

11. *Calendar of State Papers, Domestic Series*, 14 September 1680, 16; see also p. 30 (20 September 1680, Newmarket).

12. Rachael Wriothesley, Lady Russell, letter to her husband dated 17 September,1680, in *Some Account of the Life of Rachael Wriothesley, Lady Russell*, 3d edn (London: Longman, 1820), 228.

13. O. W. Furley, 'The Pope-Burning Processions of the Late Seventeenth Century', *History* 44 (1959): 16–23, esp. p. 21.

14. *The Anti-Roman Pacquet: or, Memoirs of Popes and Popery* No. 12 (Friday, 24 September 1680), 95.

15. *The Midwife Unmask'd: or, The Popish Design of Mrs. Cellier's Mealtub Plainly Made Known* (London, 1680), 1.

16. John Warner, *The History of English Persecution of Catholics and the Presbyterian Plot*, ed. T. A. Birrell, 2 vols., Catholic Record Society xlvii–xlviii (London: Catholic Record Society, 1953), 2: 425.

17. Weil, '"If I did say so, I lyed"', 207.

18. Ros Ballaster, *Seductive Forms: Women's Amatory Fiction from 1684 to 1740* (Oxford: Clarendon Press, 1992), 11.

19. MD, I1ᵛ; *The Tryal and Sentence of Elizabeth Cellier; For Writing, Printing, and Publishing a Scandalous Libel, Called Malice Defeated* (London, 1680), 27.

20. *The Midwife Unmask'd*, 1.

21. In the early modern period, women were rarely identified, by themselves or others, by occupation. See Amy Louise Erickson, *Women and Property in Early Modern England* (London and New York: Routledge, 1993), 39.

22. *Tryal and Sentence of Elizabeth Cellier*, 14.

23. *The Complaint of Mrs. Celliers, and the Jesuits in Newgate* (London, 1680); *The Scarlet Beast Stripped Naked* (London, 1680), 4.

24. *The Tryal of Elizabeth Cellier, the Popish Midwife, at the Old Baily, Septemb. 11 1680. For Printing and Publishing the Late Notorious Libel, Intituled, Malice Defeated, &c. Where She Was Found Guilty. Together With Her Sentence* (London, 1680), 2.

25. *The Tryal and Sentence of Elizabeth Cellier*, 17.

26. *Mr. Prance's Answer To Mrs. Cellier's Libel* (London, 1680), B1ᵛ.

27. *The Tryal and Sentence of Elizabeth Cellier*, 30.

28. J. Paul Hunter, *Before Novels: The Cultural Contexts of Eighteenth-Century English Fiction* (New York: W. W. Norton, 1990), 314.

29. Weil, '"If I did say so, I lyed"', 201.

30. Michael McKeon argues that such collections of documents suggest that a real shift from oral to print culture has occurred, and that proof and authority are increasingly vested in the written (*The Origins of the English Novel, 1600–1740* [Baltimore: Johns Hopkins University Press, 1987], 127).

31. Tim Harris, *London Crowds in the Reign of Charles II: Propaganda and Politics from the Restoration until the Exclusion Crisis* (Cambridge: Cambridge University Press, 1987), 20, 130, 187.

32. Henry Care, *The Anti-Roman Pacquet: or, Memoirs of Popes and Popery*, No. 11 (Friday, 17 September 1680), 87.

33. *Mr. Prance's Answer To Mrs. Cellier's Libel*, E2^v.

34. A. G. Petti, 'Richard Verstegan and Catholic Martyrologies of the Later Elizabethan Period', *Recusant History* 5.1 (1959): 64–90; Elizabeth Hanson, 'Torture and Truth in Renaissance England', *Representations* (1991): 53–84; and John R. Knott, *Discourses of Martyrdom in English Literature, 1563–1694* (Cambridge: Cambridge University Press, 1993), esp. ch. 2, 'Heroic Suffering'.

35. Geoffrey F. Nuttall, 'The English Martyrs 1535–1680: A Statistical Review', *Journal of Ecclesiastical History* XXII.3 (July 1971): 191–7, esp. 194. On the women martyrs, see also Patricia Crawford, *Women and Religion in England, 1500–1720* (London and New York: Routledge, 1993), 62–8; and Retha M. Warnicke, *Women of the English Renaissance and Reformation* (Westport, CT: Greenwood, 1983), 172–3. Catholic martyrologies include: John Wilson, *The English Martyrologie* (St Omer, 1608 and 1640); G. K. [George Keynes], *The Roman Martyrologe* [a translation] (St Omer, 1627); and *Calendarium Catholicum Or, An Almanack for the Year of Our Lord, 1689* (London, 1689).

36. J. T. Rhodes, 'English Books of Martyrs and Saints of the Late Sixteenth and Early Seventeenth Centuries', *Recusant History* 22.1 (1994): 7–25, esp. p. 18. See also Helen White, *Tudor Books of Saints and Martyrs* (Madison: University of Wisconsin Press, 1963). Saints' lives were available in calendars of saints' days, collections of saints' lives, and lives of individual saints.

37. Alfonso Villegas, *The Lives of Saints*, 2nd edn (London, 1621), *2^v, *3.

38. See Antonia Fraser, *The Weaker Vessel* (New York: Knopf, 1984), 459.

39. 'Maddam Celliers Answer to the Popes Letter' (London, 1680), 2.

40. *Mr. Prance's Answer To Mrs. Cellier's Libel*, E2. Subsequent references in this paragraph are to this pamphlet. This incident is also mentioned in the broadside 'Commentation On the Late Wonderful Discovery of the New Popish Plot' (London 1680): 'she who midwifes Trade well understood / Miscarried with her bladders Cram'd with blood'. This text describes those who would defend Cellier as willing to 'stoop to wipe clean madam Celliers Tail'.

41. For instance, one pamphlet claims that the groans Cellier attributed to tortured prisoners in Newgate were actually her female drinking buddies' belches and farts (*Modesty Triumphing Over Impudence. Or, Some Notes Upon a Late Romance Published by Elizabeth Cellier, Midwife and Lady Errant* [London, 1680], B1).

42. Mary Beth Rose, *The Expense of Spirit: Love and Sexuality in English Renaissance Drama* (Ithaca: Cornell University Press, 1989), ch. 3.

43. Hanson, 68.

44. Gail Paster, *The Body Embarrassed: Drama and the Disciplines of Shame in Early Modern England* (Ithaca: Cornell University Press, 1993).

45. *Mr. John Mush's Life of Margaret Clitherow*, in *The Troubles of Our Catholic Forefathers Related by Themselves*, ed. John Morris, vol. 3 (London: Burns and Oates, 1877), 421.

46. *The Scarlet Beast Stripped Naked*, 2.

47. Lady Russell reports this, for instance. See Rachael Wriothesley, Lady Russell, Letter to her husband dated 17 September 1680, in *Some Account of the Life of Rachael Wriothesley, Lady Russell*, 228.

48. 'The Popes Letter, to Maddam Cellier in Relation to Her Great Sufferings for the Catholick Cause, and Likewise Maddam Celliers Lamentation Standing on the Pillory' (London, 1680), 4; 'The Devil Pursued: Or, The Right Saddle Laid Upon the Right Mare. A Satyr Upon Maddam Celliers Standing in the Pillory' (London, 1680).

49. 'Mistress Celiers Lamentation for the Loss of her Liberty' (London 1681), A1^v.

50. 'The Popes Letter to Maddam Cellier', 4.

51. Lyndal Roper, *Oedipus and the Devil: Witchcraft, Sexuality, and Religion in Early Modern Europe* (London and New York: Routledge, 1994), 177.

52. Ibid., 189. On the magical attributes of criminal bodies, see also Peter Linebaugh, *The London Hanged: Crime and Civil Society in the Eighteenth Century* (Cambridge: Cambridge University Press, 1992); and Katharine Park, 'The Criminal and the Saintly Body: Autopsy and Dissection in Renaissance Italy', *Renaissance Quarterly* 47.1 (1994): 1–33. Discussing the indistinct boundary between the criminal and the saintly body, Park identifies the martyr as the 'middle term' between the two (23).

53. 'The Pope's Letter to Maddam Cellier', 2–3.

54. John Dormer, *The New Plot of the Papists. To Transform Traitors into Martyrs*, 5.

55. Kenyon, 181–2. In an Appendix, Kenyon summarizes the slow process by which many of those executed for involvement in the Popish Plot were granted the status 'Venerabile' by Pope Leo XIII in 1886, then beatified by Pope Pius XI in 1929. A lucky few (6) were finally canonized by Pope Paul VI in 1970.

56. Samuel Rowlands, *The Famous History of Guy Earle of Warwick* (London, 1649), A3.

57. Rowlands, *Guy Earle of Warwick*, N1.

58. Ibid., A4. Along with endless versions of popular stories of 'knighthoods true valour', however anachronistic, some stories of female warriors, usually dressed as men, also circulated in the seventeenth century.

59. Ballaster, 35.

60. Laura Brown, *Ends of Empire: Women and Ideology in Early Eighteenth-Century English Literature* (Ithaca: Cornell University Press, 1993), 67, 74.

61. Mary Beth Rose, '"Vigorous Most / When Most Unactive Deem'd": Gender and the Heroics of Endurance in Milton's *Samson Agonistes*, Aphra Behn's *Oroonoko*, and Mary Astell's *Some Reflections Upon Marriage*', *Milton Studies* 33 (1997): 83–109.

62. John Richetti, *Popular Fiction Before Richardson: Narrative Patterns 1700–1739* (Oxford: Clarendon Press, 1969), 18, 208, 21.

63. *Don Quixote* was translated into English in 1612 and 1620. By that time, romance and anti-romance were intermingled in England. See Paul Salzman, *English Prose Fiction, 1558–1700* (Oxford: Clarendon Press, 1985), ch. 15; and McKeon, 52–64.

64. Dangerfield wrote a picaresque account of his youth, *Don Tomazo: or, the Juvenile Rambles of Thomas Dangerfield* (1680); Cellier parodied it as *The Matchless Rogue; or, A Brief Account of the Life of Don Tomazo, The Unfortunate Son* (London: Printed for Elizabeth Cellier and sold at her house, 1680).

65. 'Maddam Celliers Answer to the Popes Letter', 4.

66. Ibid., 3, 4.

67. Helen Hackett, '"Yet Tell Me Some Such Fiction": Lady Mary Wroth's *Urania* and the "Femininity" of Romance', in *Women, Texts, and Histories, 1575–1760*, ed. Clare Brant and Diane Purkiss (London and New York: Routledge, 1992), 39–68, esp. pp. 40, 46. See also, Ballaster, chs. 1 and 2.

68. Anthony Fletcher, *Gender, Sex, and Subordination in England, 1500–1800* (New Haven and London: Yale University Press, 1995), 89.

69. Caroline Lucas, *Writing for Women: The Example of Woman as Reader in Elizabethan Romance* (Milton Keynes, PA: Open University Press, 1989).

70. Hero Chalmers, '"The Person I Am, Or What They Made Me To Be": The Construction of the Feminine Subject in the Autobiographies of Mary Carleton', in *Women, Texts, and Histories, 1575–1760*, ed. Clare Brant and Diane Purkiss (London and New York: Routledge, 1992), 164–94, esp. p. 186.

71. Thomas Overbury, *New and Choise Characters* (London, 1615), J4^v–J5.

72. See, for instance, Sharon Achinstein, 'Women on Top in the Pamphlet Literature of the English Revolution', *Women's Studies* 24 (1994): 131–63; and Phyllis Mack, *Visionary Women: Ecstatic Prophecy in Seventeenth-Century England* (Berkeley: University of California Press, 1992).

73. See Weil on the aggressive eroticization of Cellier in the various attacks on her ('"If I did say so, I lyed"', 202–6). Contemporaries routinely assumed Cellier to be guilty of sexual misconduct. Gilbert Burnet, for instance, describes her as 'a popish midwife, who had a great share of wit, and was abandoned to lewdness' (*Burnet's History of My Own Time; Part I: The Reign of Charles the Second*, ed. Osmund Airy, 2 vols. [Oxford: Clarendon Press, 1900], 2: 244–5).

74. *Modesty Triumphing Over Impudence*, B1^v, C2^v, and D2^v.

75. Phrases are quoted from Patricia Higgins, 'The Reactions of Women, with Special Reference to Petitioners', in *Politics, Religion, and the*

English Civil War, ed. Brian Manning (London: Edward Arnold, 1973), 179–222, esp. p. 205.

76. According to the *OED*, the meanings of two originally distinct words – one meaning to journey or to travel, and the other meaning to stray or to wander – became confused. As a consequence to be a knight or lady errant might mean either being itinerant or being wayward (that is, straying from the proper course or place), or both.

77. *Mr. Prance's Answer To Mrs. Cellier's Libel*, C1ʳ⁻ᵛ.

78. Henry Care, *The Anti-Roman Pacquet: or, Memoirs of Popes and Popery*, No. 10 (Friday, 10 September 1680), 79.

79. McKeon, 89, quoting from Defoe.

80. In *Guy of Warwick*, for instance, Guy enjoins his wife to celibacy, goes on Pilgrimage to the Holy Land, then ends his life as a hermit. Thomas Deloney's *The History of the Gentle-Craft* (first published in 1627, and reprinted at least six times by 1672) begins with a martyrology – the story of Saint Hugh and his beloved, the fair virgin Winifred, both of whom are martyred for their belief in Christianity. See also Hunter, 87; Margaret Spufford, *Small Books and Pleasant Histories: Popular Fiction and Its Readership in Seventeenth-Century England* (Athens, GA: University of Georgia Press, 1981); and White, ch. 2, *passim*.

81. *The Scarlet Beast Stripped Naked*, 3.

82. Romance was also associated with royalists, who used the form to represent their experience of the Civil War. See Salzman, ch. 11; Susan Staves, *Players' Scepters: Fictions of Authority in the Restoration* (Lincoln and London: University of Nebraska Press, 1979), 51–73; and Annabel Patterson, *Censorship and Interpretation: The Conditions of Writing and Reading in Early Modern England* (Madison: University of Wisconsin Press, 1984), ch. 4.

83. See Lorraine Daston, 'Marvelous Facts and Miraculous Evidence in Early Modern Europe', *Critical Inquiry* 18.1 (1991): 93–124; Lennard J. Davis, *Factual Fictions: The Origins of the English Novel* (New York: Columbia University Press, 1983); and Barbara Shapiro, *Probability and Certainty in Seventeenth-Century England* (Princeton, NJ: Princeton University Press, 1983).

84. *Tryal of Elizabeth Cellier*, 2.

85. 'A Letter from the Lady Cresswell to the Madam C. the Midwife' (London, 1680), 4.

86. Harris, *London Crowds in the Reign of Charles II*, 146–48; Rachel Weil, 'Sometimes a Scepter is Only a Scepter: Pornography and Politics in Restoration England', in *The Invention of Pornography: Obscenity and the Origins of Modernity*, ed. Lynn Hunt (New York: Zone Books, 1993), 125–53; and Steven N. Zwicker, *Lines of Authority: Politics and English Literary Culture, 1648–1689* (Ithaca: Cornell University Press, 1993), ch. 4.

87. Huston Diehl, *Staging Reform, Reforming the Stage: Protestantism and Popular Theater in Early Modern England* (Ithaca: Cornell University Press, 1997), ch. 6.

88. On 'holy joy', see Knott, 78–83. On how the cucking stool and bridle encouraged the ridicule of afflicted women, see Lynda E. Boose, 'Scolding Brides and Bridling Scolds: Taming the Woman's Unruly Member', *Shakespeare Quarterly* 42.2 (1991): 179–213.

89. Harris, 169; cf. ch. 6, *passim*.

90. Miller, 177.

91. Warner, 425.

92. Henry Foley, *Records of the English Province of the Society of Jesus*, vol. 5 (London: Burns and Oates, 1879), 74.

93. For the petition, see *Calendar of State Papers, Domestic Series*, vol. 23 (1682), 613.

94. *Duke Dangerfield Declaring How He Represented the Duke of Mon* ——— (London: 1685), 2. See also *A True Narrative of the Arraignment, Tryal, and Conviction of Thomas Dangerfield for High-Misdemeanors Against His Present Majesty James the Second* (London, 1685).

95. Mary Hopkirk claims that, upon James's accession, Cellier 'was freed and given £90 from the secret-service money'. She also claims that Cellier was briefly in residence with the exiled Stuarts: 'Even Elizabeth Cellier, the Popish midwife, reached Saint Germain somehow, though she does not appear to have remained there for long.' The evidence for either assertion is unclear. See Mary Hopkirk, *Queen over the Water: Mary Beatrice of Modena, Queen of James II* (London: John Murray, 1953), 86, 171.

96. Harris, 108, 119; Miller, 175.

97. Kenyon, 189; J. C. H. Aveling, *The Handle and the Ax: The Catholic Recusants in England from Reformation to Emancipation* (London: Blond and Briggs, 1976), 213.

98. Elaine Hobby, *Virtue of Necessity: English Women's Writing 1649–88* (Ann Arbor: University of Michigan Press, 1988), 21–3.

99. Fraser, 454–61, and 469–70, esp. p. 470.

100. Harris, 108; Miller, 175.

101. I take this characterization of one kind of feminist criticism from Elaine Showalter, 'Representing Ophelia: Women, Madness, and the Responsibilities of Feminist Criticism', in *Shakespeare and the Question of Theory*, ed. Patricia Parker and Geoffrey Hartman (New York and London: Methuen, 1985), 77–94, esp. p. 78.

Index